END-OF-LIFE STORIES

Crossing Disciplinary Boundaries

Donald E. Gelfand, PhD, is a professor of sociology at Wayne State University, Detroit, Michigan, and Coordinator of the Wayne State University End-of-Life Interdisciplinary Project (WSU-EOLIP). He has conducted and published research on attitudes of Mexican Americans toward end-of-life care. He has also conducted extensive research on issues of aging among a variety of other ethnic groups including African Americans, Latinos, Native Americans, and individuals from a variety of European backgrounds. The second edition of his book *Aging and Ethnicity* was published by Springer Publishing Company in 2003.

Richard Raspa, PhD, is a professor and graduate chair in the Department of Interdisciplinary Studies at Wayne State University, Detroit, Michigan. In addition to his three other books, he has co-authored *Italian Folktales in America: The Verbal Art of an Immigrant Woman,* which was awarded the International Botkin Prize by the American Folklore Society for best first book. Raspa had had a Fulbright to Italy, was an Ellsworth Fellow, and regularly presents his research at conferences around the world. His current interests include literature and medicine and organizational folklore.

Sherylyn H. Briller, PhD, is an assistant professor of Anthropology and faculty associate in the Institute of Gerontology at Wayne State University, Detroit, Michigan. A medical anthropologist who specializes in aging, Dr. Briller has a long standing interest in cross-cultural gerontology and has conducted research in Asia and the United States. Her research program focuses on old-age support mechanisms, long-term care, innovative dementia care, and end-of-life issues. She is one of the authors of the four-volume series *Creating Successful Dementia Care Settings.*

Stephanie Myers Schim, PhD, RN, APRN, CNAA, BC, is an assistant professor in the Wayne State University College of Nursing, Detroit, Michigan. Her practice experience is primarily in home care, public health nursing, and nursing administration. She teaches community health nursing and is a certified End-of-Life Nursing Education Consortium trainer as well as maintaining board certification in community health nursing and advanced nursing administration. Her research program focuses on cultural competence among health care providers and culturally competent end-of-life care.

END-OF-LIFE STORIES

Crossing Disciplinary Boundaries

EDITORS

Donald E. Gelfand

Richard Raspa

Sherylyn H. Briller

Stephanie Myers Schim

 Springer Publishing Company

 Death and Suicide Series

Springer Publishing Company, Inc.
11 West 42nd Street
New York, NY 10036

Acquisitions Editor: Helvi Gold
Production Editor: Betsy Day
Cover design by Mimi Flow

05 06 07 08 09 / 5 4 3 2 1

Library of Congress Cataloging-in-Publication Data

End-of-life stories : crossing disciplinary boundaries / edited by Donald E. Gelfand . . . [et al.].
    p. cm. — (Springer series on death and suicide)
    Includes bibliographical references.
    ISBN 0-8261-2675-8
    1. Death—Psychology. 2. Terminally ill—Psychology.
   3. Terminally ill—Anecdotes. 4. Storytelling—Psychological aspects. I. Gelfand, Donald E. II. Series.
BF789.D4E53 2005
155.9'37—dc22   2005005647

Printed in the United States of America by Sheridan Books, Inc.

Contents

Contributors

Lynda M. Baker, PhD, is an associate professor in Library and Information Science at Wayne State University, Detroit, Michigan. Her research focuses on consumer health information needs and information-seeking behavior. She has published articles on the use of theory in consumer health research, information needs at the end of life, and the readability of consumer health material. She also co-authored the book, *Consumer Health Information for Public Librarians*.

Alexa Canady, MD, is Director of Neurosurgery at Children's Hospital of Michigan and a clinical associate professor at Wayne State University, Detroit, Michigan. Among her areas of expertise are craniofacial abnormalities, epilepsy, hydrocephalus, and tumors of the spinal cord and brain in children. Dr. Canady has made extensive contributions to research projects and to technological developments in the field of neurosurgery. She has also been recognized as one of 12 international "Women of Hope" who exemplify the aspirations and achievements of minority women.

Elizabeth E. Chapleski, PhD, MSW, is an associate professor of research in the Institute of Gerontology and coordinator of the Nonprofit Sector Studies program in the Department of Interdisciplinary Studies at Wayne State University, Detroit, Michigan. Her research program focuses on minority aging, long-term care, spirituality, and end-of-life issues. Her study of long-term care in American Indian elders of the Great Lakes region was funded by the National Institute on Aging, and she has numerous publications related to that body of work.

George A. Cooney, Jr., JD, practices law in Bloomfield Hills, Michigan, and is adjunct faculty of the Wayne State University Law School, Detroit. His practice and teaching concentrate in estate planning and elder law, as well as probate, trust administration, and litigation. A founding chair of the Elder Law and Advocacy Section, he is widely published on elder law and estate planning issues. He is a Fellow of The American College of Trust and Estate Counsel and a member of the National Academy of Elder Law Attorneys.

Dorothy E. "Dottie" Deremo, MS, MHSA, RN, CHE, is the President and Chief Executive Officer of Hospice of Michigan (HOM), Detroit, Michigan. She served as the Vice President of Patient Care Services and Chief Nursing Officer for the Henry Ford Health System prior to her appointment at HOM. Ms. Deremo has served on numerous state and national committees, is extensively published, and is in demand as a speaker and consultant on health care delivery and hospice care.

Ardith Z. Doorenbos, RN, PhD, is a post-doctoral Fellow in the College of Nursing at Michigan State University, Lansing, Michigan. Her research is centered on end-of-life issues including advanced care planning among ethnically diverse cancer patients and their family caregivers. On the basis of her extensive nursing experience abroad, she also has strong interest in international nursing education. She is currently principal investigator on a Department of Defense funded research project examining advance care planning among breast cancer patients.

John W. Finn, MD, FAAHPM, serves as Chief Medical Director of the Maggie Allesee Center for Quality of Life, the education and research arm of Hospice of Michigan, in Detroit. He is a Clinical Assistant Professor, Wayne State University School of Medicine, Detroit, Michigan, and is a past President and Fellow of the American Academy of Hospice and Palliative Medicine. Dr. Finn is certified by the American Board of Internal Medicine and the American Board of Hospice and Palliative Medicine.

Allen C. Goodman, PhD, is a professor of economics at Wayne State University, Detroit, Michigan. He specializes in both health economics (focusing on substance abuse treatment utilization and costs) and housing (focusing on housing prices and housing demand). His current research looks at the measurement and correlates of health care treatment episodes and at the determinants of housing supply. Widely published, Dr. Goodman is co-author of the leading textbook, *The Economics of Health and Healthcare.*

Megan Gunnell, MT-BC, is the board-certified music therapist for Bon Secours Cottage Health Services in Grosse Pointe, Michigan. While living in Munich, Germany, she performed with the Abaco Symphony Orchestra and developed cross-cultural music programs for international schools. She is proficient on five musical instruments and produced and recorded a CD titled *Doorway to Relaxation.*

LaDon Harris is the mother and primary caregiver of Malika Harris, whose story she graciously agreed to share for this project. Ms. Harris was born and raised in Detroit, Michigan, where she graduated from Mumford High School. She is a member of the greater Southern Missionary Baptist Church, where she participates in the Sisterhood Intercessory Prayer Group and the Woman at the Well Ministry, which helps support women and their spiritual needs. Ms. Harris is employed in the Detroit Public Schools Food Services Department and also works with Christ Child House Society Boys' Home. Ms. Harris requested that Malika's name be used to tell her story and agreed to share her personal perspective in tribute to her daughter's memory.

Allison M. Kabel is a PhD candidate in anthropology at Wayne State University, Detroit, Michigan. Her research is focused on hospice care, personhood, and end-of-life issues. She has conducted research in both the United Kingdom and the United States and recently co-authored an article regarding professional perceptions of maintaining personhood in hospice care.

Terri Kovach, AMLS, is a professor and reference librarian at Monroe County Community College, Monroe, Michigan, and a PhD candidate in sociology at Wayne State University, Detroit, Michigan. She has over 10 years of experience as a hospice volunteer and trainer. She is currently co-investigator on a study of suffering in late and terminal illness in a joint project at the John D. Dingell Veterans Administration Medical Center, Detroit, and Wayne State University Medical School.

Kathleen L. Meert, MD, is a professor of pediatrics at Wayne State University School of Medicine, Detroit, Michigan. She is a board-certified pediatric critical care medicine specialist who practices at Children's Hospital of Michigan, Detroit. She is a clinical researcher with special interests in end-of-life care and decision making for children as well as parent and family bereavement support. Her current teaching responsibilities include instructing medical students, pediatric residents, and critical care medicine fellows in the pathophysiology of disease, evidenced-based medicine, and family-centered care.

Steven M. Popkin, MA, MSW, ACSW, is a faculty advisor at the Wayne State University (WSU) School of Social Work, Detroit, Michigan, who mentors groups of graduate and undergraduate students placed at area hospice organizations for clinical experience. He is also a supervising geriatric social worker at Jewish Apartments and Services, as well as a medical social worker for St. John/Providence Hospice, Detroit, Michigan. A member of the geriatric research team in the WSU Institute of Gerontology, he has published articles based on his extensive field experience in geriatrics.

Kathleen Stever, APRN, BC, is a clinical nurse specialist with Bon Secours Cottage Health Services, Grosse Pointe, Michigan. She is a nurse practitioner who specializes in palliative care and pain management. She has an extensive background in hospice nursing and end-of-life care. She is a certified End-of-Life Nursing Education Consortium trainer and a frequent lecturer on end-of-life care issues.

Robi Thomas, RN, MSN, is an assistant professor of nursing and Chair of the West Michigan campuses for the McAuley School of Nursing for University of Detroit Mercy. She is completing her doctorate in nursing at Wayne State University, Detroit, Michigan. Ms. Thomas holds certification as an advanced oncology nurse and as a hospice and palliative care nurse. Her area of research is caregiving for terminally ill patients.

Celia S. Thurston, DMin, is manager of an interdisciplinary department of child and family services at Children's Hospital of Michigan, Detroit. She is an ordained Unitarian Universalist minister who specializes in crisis management, pastoral care, and bereavement care. Her research has focused on the needs of parents at the time of the death of a child.

Peter Wolf, MSW, MDiv, is a clinical pediatric social worker in private practice, specializing in children's issues of loss, abuse, and trauma. He also works with the Hospice of Michigan pediatric team. Reverend Wolf is a licensed independent social worker and a certified social worker and is active in a number of professional associations such as the National Association of Social Workers, Association of Oncology Social Workers, and the Academy of Certified Social Workers.

Robert Zalenski, MD, MA, is a professor of emergency medicine and internal medicine at Wayne State University (WSU), Detroit, Michigan. Board certified by both the American Board of Emergency Medicine and the American Board of Hospice and Palliative Medicine, he maintains an active practice as a physician in both urgent care and palliative care at the John D. Dingell Veterans Administration Hospital in Detroit. He is directing the development of a Center for Palliative Care Excellence in Research and Education with collaboration from WSU and the Detroit Medical Center as well as pursuing a program of research and publication in end-of-life care and palliative medicine.

Foreword

Kathryn L. Braun, PhD
Director, Center on Aging
University of Hawaii, Manoa

When I consider that the seminal work by Elisabeth Kubler-Ross was published in the 1970s, I realize that I am a relative newcomer to research and service focused on death and dying. Yet in the past decade, I have been surprised and pleased by the further evolution of thanatology, the study of death and dying. This book, written by my colleagues at Wayne State University in Detroit, Michigan, represents another forward step in the field because it explores aspects of death and dying within the frameworks of narrative, culture, and multidisciplinary care.

"Narrative" is a fancy word for story, and stories help us organize and make meaning of events. This book attempts to enhance end-of-life understandings by sharing stories of people encountering death. The stories are compelling, and the emotions and connections we feel toward a story help draw us in. In reading the varying perspectives around each death we see that there is no single way to know a story. In fact, as the editors point out, the power of narrative illustrates that there is no truth, only different ways of seeing. This is an important concept for helping professionals to grasp as they strive to reduce suffering and increase opportunities to find meaning at the end of life.

The health care field today depends on the work of different professionals, paraprofessionals, and volunteers. This interdependence is especially true for the dying, who likely will have medical, psychological, social, legal, economic, spiritual, and other needs. Each helping professional is trained to assess and prescribe within the perspective of his or her chosen discipline. But more emphasis is needed on how these disciplines can work together. In this book, the multiple disciplines bring their theoretical frameworks to bear on a death, and we are enriched by seeing the dying person from different disciplinary perspectives. In opening doors to new ways of thinking, students can gain respect for and curiosity about other disciplinary approaches. This book illustrates how care can be improved when representatives of this array of disciplines collaborate to build a multidimensional picture of the dying person.

The exploration of culture and diversity is imperative if a book is to be useful in today's training academies. The world is becoming more diverse with respect to age, ethnicity, religious beliefs, abilities, sexual orientation, and social status. This is especially true in the United States, where we expect growth in our older population (from 12% in 2000 to 20% in 2030) and reduction in the percentage of non-Hispanic whites (from 76% in 1990 to 53% in 2050). This book addresses the growing diversity of the U.S. by including cases about death in men, women, and children and different ethnic groups, including Native Americans and African Americans. Death stories of veterans and the homeless are included as well.

As a teacher, I know how much easier it is to hold a class's attention with case studies than with dry facts and figures. Research on adult learning has shown that the use of case studies can be more effective because they are presented within a context that elicits caring among the students. Their use makes this book an excellent teaching tool and will motivate students to find out more about the personal, disciplinary, and cultural perspectives of the persons profiled in the stories.

The authors include a number of recommendations, including one that is often made: that we learn more about each others' cultures and disciplinary perspectives. Doing this requires improving one's personal skills at asking, listening, remembering, and responding in respectful and nonjudgmental ways, and appreciating the stories we hear. This is called "narrative competence," and the book illustrates how developing narrative competence can help increase cultural competence.

As a health professional and a teacher, I see this book as an invaluable tool in our efforts to improve care at the end of life. Its readability and multidisciplinary perspective make it ideal for the classroom and for training programs. The case studies are poignant, and the varied responses are rich. This approach will help students see beyond either/or conceptualizations and help them develop an appreciation of the rich tapestry of multicultural America and multidisciplinary care. As summed up by the authors, stories can help us enhance end-of-life understandings in an increasingly diverse society.

Acknowledgments

There are many people who made this book possible. First, we thank all of the people who told their stories. Without them there is nothing more to say. A thank-you is also due to the members of the Wayne State University End-of-Life Interdisciplinary Project for their contributions and support and to the Wayne State University Humanities Center for providing grant support for many of the activities of the project. The editors also thank the following family members for their patience, love, and support: Katharine Messenger, Franziska and Nikki Raspa, James and Michael Hanggi, and Michael Myers Schim.

Introduction

In this book we set out to provide an understanding that people experience dying as they experience living—through stories. Human beings are story-making creatures. We make sense of experience through storytelling. We feel loss, anger, frustration, joy, and compassion through the tales we tell about what is happening all around us and inside us, and we justify our actions through the stories we construct about why we do what we do.

In short, we know the world and act in it through culturally and personally constructed narratives. These narratives provide the maps to guide us through the territories of life. Reality is not "out there," separate from our talking about it. Rather, reality is, to paraphrase the words of one theorist (Geertz, 1973), a story about a story about a story about a story, ad infinitum. Each of us carries a repertoire of tales about the way things are. Each of us has stories about our relationships, our work, our organizations, our families, and our friends. We have stories about time, wealth, sex, happiness, pain, past, future, and present. We love, hope, yearn, and fear through the narratives we tell and those we hear. In the end, we also experience death and dying as a story.

In this book the authors examine issues at the end of life as stories about individuals, families, communities, and broader society. We look at types of stories that are told within various domains, such as the physical, spiritual, legal, economic, political, and ethical. The stories are also explored from different and often contesting perspectives of health professionals, health systems, families, and relationships. Death is investigated as a life-course phenomenon situated in particular cultural contexts and environments. Our goal is to look at dying as a storied phenomenon and analyze it from multidisciplinary perspectives.

Many colleagues were involved in the Wayne State University End-of-Life Interdisciplinary Project (WSU-EOLIP) and in the development of this book. Dying raises complex issues that cross disciplinary boundaries. Only if we attempt to bring multiple viewpoints to light upon the issues of dying can we uncover the rich layers of meaning that attend the dying process. As the book proceeds chapter by chapter, the focus shifts here and there, back and forth, to hear and to respond to a variety of voices.

The Wayne State University End-of-Life Interdisciplinary Project

In Greek mythology, Athena sprang full-grown from the head of Zeus. Authors sometimes present their works as if there had been no period of gestation. Instead, the process from idea to completion appears to have been completely inevitable. This volume had a different genesis. It represents an evolution in thinking and discussion in a group of disparate faculty and practitioners interested in end-of-life issues.

Our group began with the interest of one faculty member and his initial effort, in 2000, to find other faculty colleagues who shared this interest. Over four years, the ad hoc group of faculty has expanded to include 34 individuals representing 14 different departments and colleges of the university. The WSU-EOLIP moved through a number of initial stages of development. These stages included early solicitations of interest across the university, development of rapport and working relationships, and setting of goals and objectives. These stages have been detailed elsewhere (Gelfand, Baker, & Cooney, 2003). Since our initial meetings in 2000, project membership has continued to expand in number and increase in diversity. Practitioners from a variety of local hospitals and hospice organizations have joined and become an enriching component of the membership.

This group has been remarkable and exciting. The ongoing interaction of academics from different units of a major research university and the incorporation of both academics and health care professionals working in clinical settings, provides a fertile environment for discussion among people who previously had little opportunity to engage in regular dialogue. Our expanding and diversifying group composition represents ways in which contemporary end-of-life education, research, and practice are evolving. The multifaceted nature of the WSU-EOLIP is well suited to provide forums for the increasingly complex discussions that must occur as end-of-life care moves forward. It is noteworthy that the

WSU-EOLIP has continued to come together on a regular basis, and we have planned and completed several significant activities.

During each year of the group's existence, we have chosen a specific focus that provides structure and goals for our monthly meetings. In the first year, the activity was to develop and pilot-test a graduate level interdisciplinary seminar on end-of-life issues. This course is now offered annually and is cross-listed by five departments and colleges within the university. In the second year, project members collaborated to write several articles to share our experiences about "best practices" for end-of-life education (Doorenbos, Briller, & Chapleski, 2003; Gelfand, Baker, & Cooney, 2003; Schim & Raspa, 2004). The third year was devoted to an exploration of the role of spirituality at the end of life, which included a conference featuring a nationally recognized authority on this topic. As year three progressed, the conversations among project members expanded and rapport deepened. Intrigued by the richness of the discussions, our group proposed the idea of creating a book to reflect our experiences.

The Genesis of the Book

When our group conceptualized this volume, we made a clear decision to avoid developing yet another "primer" on end-of-life issues. Instead, we wanted to both reflect the excitement within our group about the potential for crossing disciplinary boundaries and to make a contribution to the end-of-life literature that reflects the synergy produced when many voices engage in such discourse. Whereas many disciplines have produced significant bodies of work on death and dying, what has been largely missing is the dynamic sharing of ideas between disciplines and the opportunity to view end-of-life issues simultaneously through various lenses.

For the reader to understand this book, we believe that it is valuable to briefly explain our process in developing the stories and responses presented here. Initially, we asked project members to provide interesting cases from their experiences that would serve to stimulate multidisciplinary discussion. Cases submitted for consideration represented both unusual circumstances (e.g., the story of Jim, a homeless man who received hospice care) and more typical situations (e.g., the story of Ron, an older man who died surrounded by family in a hospital setting). Cases were reviewed by WSU-EOLIP members at monthly meetings, and we discussed possible organizing frameworks we might use. We drew upon the conceptual model that we had initially developed for the interdisciplinary course. We also considered a number of schemes to ensure that the cases presented would cover a wide range of end-of-life situations. We thought about several, including diversity of age, ethnicity, lifestyle, family structure, socioeconomic status, and trajectory to death as initially described by Glaser and Strauss (1965) and elaborated on by Lunney, Fynn, Foley, Lipson, and Guralnik (2003). The selection of cases was also premised on the idea that the book should have utility for students from a variety of disciplines, as well as for educators and health professionals. Most important, within the narrative orientation of our work, the cases selected needed to provide compelling stories for multidisciplinary analysis.

The story selection process was itself eye-opening. It provided a sense of the ways in which our different case authors and responders approached the topics, the information they chose to include or exclude in the narratives, and their areas of particular emphasis. Once we selected the stories for inclusion, we scheduled meetings for small groups to discuss each story with the author and to generate responses. Various workgroups tried different strategies. What proved most effective was to have each participant in the workgroup discussion write up a response based on both his or her own original interpretation of the story and the enriched interpretation following small-group discussion. These responses were themselves stories told from diverse personal, disciplinary, and cultural perspectives.

Our group designated the team of co-editors from within the WSU-EOLIP group to provide a smaller working unit to manage the substantial tasks of making a coherent whole from the various contributions. The editorial team comprised academics from the social sciences, health profession education, and the humanities. Editors brought their expertise and experience in academic scholarship, education, and practice to the tasks at hand. This lengthy and complex process inspired one member of the group to recall the quip that "a camel is a horse put together by a committee."

Multidisciplinarity

Given the increasing interest in collaboration within colleges and universities, we conceived this volume as a contribution to this trend. This book is a *multidisciplinary* collaboration. Toulmin (1982) has described *disciplinary* approaches:

> Every independent scientific discipline is marked by its own specialized modes of abstraction and the issues to be considered in each discipline are so defined that they can be investigated and discussed independently—in abstraction from—the issues belonging to other disciplines. (p. 229)

Multidisciplinarity occurs when a group representing different disciplines approaches a problem by bringing to bear its own distinct fields of endeavor. Each discipline remains within the confines of its own theoretical, methodological, and practice perspectives. In contrast, *interdisciplinarity* has been defined as "an intellectual conduct, coherent, rigorous and skeptical enquiry without necessary regard to the assumptions or procedures of, or claims to domain or phenomena by, any discipline" (Bates, 2002). Interdisciplinarity, according to Klein (1990), is the integration of theories, methods, and practices of separate disciplines.

The WSU-EOLIP has evolved into an exemplar of an effective multidisciplinary group. This volume provided an opportunity for our group to engage with others who presented perspectives not previously considered. This process enriched our analyses and understandings of end-of-life issues. There have been dynamic discussions, even arguments, challenging what we each took for granted previously about worldviews and ways to examine end-of-life processes. When a medical anthropologist, a nurse-scholar, a sociologist, and a folklorist came together over a computer to edit words submitted by a dozen academics and health professionals from other fields, we were each pushed to define and defend our disciplinary presuppositions. We were also challenged to let go of our particular positions. By the end of the editing process, we found that we were able to anticipate how each person might respond to particular issues. More important, we gained a greater appreciation for contesting points of view and for the value of bridging diverse perspectives. As we completed the editing process of this collection of stories and responses, we found ourselves at the threshold of a new level of interdependence in which we integrated our separate perspectives into a truly interdisciplinary view.

Suggested Use of This Book

The stories and the responses in this volume are varied, and the uses of this book can be equally varied. A few possible uses are suggested here.

1. *Help provide continuing education about end-of-life issues for professionals.* Concern about end-of-life issues continues to develop as do new initiatives in this field. During their professional education, many professionals have had only limited exposure to end-of-life concerns. There are current efforts by medical and nursing organizations to expand education about the end of life (End-of-Life Education Consortium [ELNEC, 2003]; Education on Palliative and End-of-Life Care [EPEC, 2003]). However, there remains a need for expansion of education for professionals. The stories in this volume offer a valuable resource for professional education programs. They may be used to arouse further interest in how death and dying is approached across many settings. Stories might be used alone or in combination with more traditional didactic approaches. It is hoped that the responses to each of the stories will help professionals gain a greater understanding of the need and potential for multidisciplinary approaches to the end of life.

2. *Help graduate students develop a multidisciplinary interest in end-of-life issues.* There is a need to develop greater numbers of individuals interested in active involvement in end-of-life efforts. These stories may spark an interest in the field among students in the health care professions, law, social sciences, humanities, and important ancillary fields, such as library and information science, or communication. The stories and the responses presented in this volume should also provide students with better understanding of the potential for multidisciplinary approaches to end-of-life issues.

3. *Help undergraduate students become more aware of issues related to death and dying.* Among college students, issues of death and dying may seem personally remote. This book may be particularly relevant to young first-time-in-college undergraduates. In our death-averse society, young adults are sometimes shielded from death experiences other than those portrayed in mass media. This book's stories can help undergraduates think about death and dying from a variety of perspectives.

4. *Help communities examine end-of-life programs and policies.* Many programs and policies explicitly mentioned in these stories have an impact on the experiences of dying individuals, their families, and other loved ones. Discussion of policy ramifications in these stories might stimulate community discussion about what is currently available for end-of-life care and what should be made available. Discussions of these stories and responses may guide recommendations for new and revised end-of-life programs and policies that meet the specific needs of communities.

5. *Help family members and small groups discuss end-of-life preferences.* It is often very difficult for people to discuss death and dying with family members and friends. The stories presented in this volume might be used as a starting point for such dialogue. Whether readers agree or disagree with the material, the book may be a good place to open channels of communication and clarify personal and family ideas.

6. *Help individuals think through end-of-life preferences.* It is certainly easier to contemplate someone else's death than our own. The dying experiences of the individuals in these stories are varied both in their nature and their quality. Readers of the stories and the responses will find positives and negatives in the experiences described. Reading and thinking critically about the stories of others, and observing the variety and complexity of some of the responses presented in this book, may help individuals uncover values, beliefs, and emotions about death and dying that they have not examined previously.

The End of the Beginning . . .

The stories in this volume are not presented as exemplars of "best practices" for particular disciplines, nor are they intended to provide answers to all of the myriad issues involved in securing high quality end-of-life care. Instead, our goal is to raise questions that lead to further exploration through interdisciplinary interaction and provide future directions for research, education, and practice.

REFERENCES

American Association of Colleges of Nursing & City of Hope. (2003). *End-of-life nursing education curriculum.* Washington, DC: Authors.

Bates, D. (2002). Muddling toward a functional definition of interdisciplinary. Retrieved April 3, 2004, from http://www.unix.oit.umass.edu/~hendra/Muddling.html

Doorenbos, A., Briller, S., & Chapleski, E. (2003). Weaving cultural context into interdisciplinary end-of-life curriculum. *Journal of Educational Gerontology, 29*, 405–416.

Emanuel, L. L., von Gunten, C. F., & Ferris, F. D. (Eds.). (2003). *The education for physicians in end-of-life care (EPEC) curriculum.* Chicago: The EPEC Project.

Glaser, B., & Strauss, A. (1965). *Awareness of dying.* Chicago: Aldine.

Geertz, C. (1973). *The interpretation of cultures.* New York: Basic Books.

Gelfand, D., Baker, L., & Cooney, J. (2003). Developing end-of-life interdisciplinary programs in university-wide settings. *American Journal of Hospice and Palliative Care, 20*, 201–204.

Klein, J. (1990). *Interdisciplinarity.* Detroit: Wayne State University Press.

Lunney, J., Fynn, J., Foley, D., Lipson, S., & Guralnik, M. (2003). Patterns of functional decline at end-of-life. *Journal of the American Medical Association, 289*, 2387–2392.

Schim, S. M., & Raspa, D. (in press). Stories of dying: Process, promises, and pitfalls of an interdisciplinary end-of-life course. In press, 2004 with *Journal of Hosopice and Palliative Medicine.*

Toulmin, S. (1982). *The return to cosmology: Postmodern science and the theology of nature.* Berkeley: University of California Press.

CHAPTER 1

The Model: Constructs, Story Domains, and Levels

In the Wayne State University End-of-Life Project's first year, one of the group's goals was to develop a conceptual model for an interdisciplinary course. The group developed the conceptual model displayed as Figure 1.1 for the course and subsequently revised it for use in this book. We made both graphic changes and refinements of central constructs and domains as we applied the model to the pedagogy of the course and to the preparation of this volume. The model is not comprehensive, but rather is intended to provide an orienting frame of reference for the stories presented. It remains a work in progress, and we anticipate that it will evolve as our discourse continues.

The model consists of three elements: constructs, story domains, and levels. In this chapter, we provide some brief analysis of what is meant by these terms and how the concepts work together to describe aspects of end of life. One important distinction in the model is that the elements are overlapping and intersecting in multiple, complex, and dynamic ways. Each element can also be considered from the perspectives of various academic and professional disciplines. We separate the elements in this chapter for clarity and ease of description while recognizing that the boundaries are constantly crossed. The dotted lines in the figure represent the idea that the borders between constructs, domains, and levels are all open and flexible.

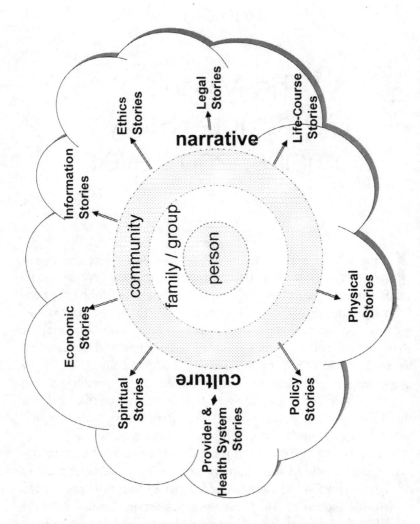

FIGURE 1.1 Interdisciplinary end-of-life model with constructs, story domains, and levels.

MAJOR CONSTRUCTS:
NARRATIVE AND CULTURE

Death is a human universal. However, death and the processes surrounding dying occur in widely varied contexts. To understand how narrative and culture shape all end-of-life experiences, it is useful to recognize the all-encompassing nature of these constructs. In the growing end-of-life literature, stories are presented both explicitly and implicitly. These stories represent the realities and hard choices that frequently accompany the dying process. They can poignantly illustrate how the dying process is often fraught with problems that make reaching desired goals, such as dying with dignity or a good death, difficult. In this book, narrative and culture are fundamental constructs used to understand end-of-life complexities.

Narrative Construct

Narrative is a way of thinking about experience. Narrative begins with a sudden reversal of circumstances (Bruner, 2002). When we are thrown out of the regularity of ordinary life the jolt provokes us to construct a story. "What does the change mean?", we ask. "How will it affect us? How will it interfere with our plans? And, perhaps, how will it help us?" When something happens that is out of the ordinary, we immediately, one could even argue instinctively, make up a story about it.

Narration, however, is more than storytelling. It implies the desire to know and to fix a meaning to experience. Even the root of the word *narrative*, from the Latin *noscere* (meaning to know) links cognition and language to this story-making impulse in people. The recitation of a sequence of experiences, real or imagined, is a way to understand and, therefore, organize life's experiences. We choose certain events and exclude others as we build our account. Our motives are complex. Had we chosen other events, we would have constructed a different story.

Narrative, in short, is a mode of knowing the world. It is traditionally understood as a literary genre, like lyric poetry or drama. Conventional categories of classification would regard narrative as fiction rather than fact, one which deals with imagined states of being rather than real-life situations (Mattingly & Garro,

2000). In recent years, particularly in the work of poststructural and postmodern philosophers and critics, the boundaries between literary and oral texts (i.e., belles-lettres) and ordinary genres of discourse have been blurred. Today the full spectrum of narrative texts is considered a legitimate subject of analysis. Novels and short fiction as well as oral genres, such as proverbs, jokes, superstitions, magic or tall tales, and personal experience stories are included in narrative analysis. Visual genres like film and TV drama are included as well. In addition, the entire universe of discourse has become interesting for what it can reveal about culture, society, and politics, as well as the identity of the writers or speakers of the texts. Popular culture is also mined for the range of narrative forms it provides. Advertising, electronic systems of communication, and radio and TV entertainment have become rich sources for narrative examination. Often in these contexts, the analysis is on a narrative of "facts" rather than imaginary experiences. In work-life, memos, contracts, and other organizational documents may be considered narrative constructions and become subjects of analysis. Such forms reveal much about organizational culture and the management of problems. Today, a vast constellation of narratives is considered legitimate for scholarly research and analysis.

Narrative gives us the power to make sense of life. It is the central instantiation of the human mind, as Jameson (1991) observes. In other words, story-making is the characteristic way humans use their mental powers. This process is a way to make meaning and give coherence to the random flow of events. When something happens that reverses the circumstances of our lives, we talk about it silently in our minds or in dialogue with others. We invent a story. Narrative connects one event to another in patterns of temporality and causality. It localizes human beings in a specific time and place and unfolds a pattern of order in the movement from past to present and into possible futures. Experience is given shape and normalized through narrative.

These are good reasons to insist that humanity is best described as *Homo Narrans*, the narrating being. The story-teller model contrasts with a grand narrative of the West that extends back into antiquity through the Middle Ages into the dawn of modernity in the 17th century that installed reason as the defining characteristic of humanity. The idea of people as narrators is also set apart from other interesting perspectives such as *Homo Ludens*, the playful being (Callois, 1962; Huizinga, 1955; Moltmann, 1972; and, more recently, Csikszentmihalyi, 1996). This model has deconstructed ordinary social arrangements to expose their play element and argues that human beings do their best work and are most fully alive when they can engage their worlds as exquisite forms of play. The best argument for the narrative model is its pervasiveness. As Charon and Montello (2002) suggest, there is nothing that is not narrative. Stories are the way people most often think about life and assign meaning to experience. Novelists have known about this process for thousands of years, even as far back into antiquity as the first written narrative—*Epic of Gilgamesh*—about 4,000 BCE. In that text, the existential question "Is there a way to avoid death?" is explored, not in dialectical form as a treatise but in narrative form as a story.

Our whole lives can be seen as story-telling enterprises. We live in and through stories from the time we are conceived. Even prenatal development is a narrative. At the basic level of cellular and organ formation, a sequence of events is unfolding—a story—authored in the DNA in every cell of the embryo. Birth, too, is a narrative. When we are born, we enter the world of story-making, as natural for us as breathing. We are born into a story that our parents and families have already begun inventing about us: where we fit into their lives, where we will live, who will take care of us, what dreams parents and families have about our future. We are endowed with an identity through the power of language when we are given a name, often in honor of someone else's story. We inhabit a world that is constructed through language. Narrative is the uniquely human performance of life in story formats.

From our early childhood onwards, we add various story constructions woven from the expectations of friends, teachers, and the social institutions in which we participate. These are stories that answer the questions of survival and meaning. Who are we? Where are we going? How will we fit in? We discover very early that the ordinary formulations of social exchange—Hi, how are you? Fine, thank you. Have a nice day! Take care now! and so on—stabilize our social connections and serve to lull us into believing that life is predictable. Even these banal expressions, when the formulas are changed, can be an occasion of story-telling.

One example of the way in which everyday discourse turns into narrative is found in the classic end-of-life tale, Shakespeare's

King Lear (c. 1608). The play turns on the unexpected response of the king's youngest daughter, Cordelia, to her father's playful question: "How much do you love me?" Lear plotted his entire future based upon an assumption of his daughter's unconditional love. He had planned to resign from active life and pass on his inheritance to his children. Imagining a retirement when he could "unburdened crawl toward death" (Act 1.1.41), Lear yearns for a life where he would be spoiled by his children. Lear, however, is chagrined and enraged by Cordelia's response, "I love your majesty according to my bond—nor more nor less" (Act 1.1.92-3). Lear denounces his daughter, cuts off her inheritance, and exiles her. This reversal of expectation sets the tragedy in motion.

Lear's story really begins at this moment. The reversal challenges his epistemology, his way of knowing the world. What he thought he knew is disrupted. He believed his youngest daughter loved him the most and would care for him at the end of life; but after Cordelia's cold response, he fears that she does not love him at all. What Lear took for granted—his plans for a secure future—now seems beyond his grasp. He dreads a future without the certitude of the family system he thought was in place to protect him in his old age. After Cordelia's response, Lear's world begins a downward spiral.

What is the relationship between stories and experience? One way of addressing the question is to frame it more generally as the question of the relationship between language and reality. Is language like a pane of glass through which we look at the world? Or is it more like a tapestry in which reality is woven into the very fabric of the piece? In other words, reality is constituted in language and our stories become our reality. What we recount about other people and the circumstances of life are expressions of what we believe about reality and become the basis for our thought and action. We know and act in the world through the stories we invent about experience. When we confront the reversals in our lives our stories subjunctivize experience.

Narrative Subjunctivizes Experience

Subjunctivizing is the consideration of prospects and scenarios other than what has actually occurred (Bruner, 2002). This mode of discourse raises the question "What if . . . ?" and allows one to think about alternative, hypothetical possibilities. In other words, this process enables one to entertain possible worlds rather than engage the actual one. Lear's subjunctivizing could be expressed in this line of reflection: What if I give away all of my land and property to my children, then who will take care of me in my old age? Will I be abandoned at the end of my life?

Although Lear's imaginings are highly personal, subjunctivizing has other uses in professional realms as well. For example, some contributors to this text (e.g., an attorney, physician, social worker, nurse, and music therapist) used this technique to reflect upon how their provision of end-of-life care might have been different in many stories presented here. As well, subjunctivizing allows people to reconfigure the meaning of the end of life, to see it as a possibility for completing relationships, and expressing forgiveness, apologies, and gratitude. Subjunctivizing can be useful to expand thinking about complex stories related to death and dying.

For many of the contributors to this volume, subjunctivizing was a novel and useful exercise that complemented their usual ways of thinking about practice. This way of knowing contrasts with scientific or paradigmatic knowledge, which focuses upon verifying what is (Bruner, 2002). In the scientific model, reality is understood through predictable laws and axioms that are empirically verified through conventions of evidence and proof. What was revealed in the collaborative writing and editing of this book was that some of the contributors found it easier to subjunctivize than did others. These differences were based on varied professional backgrounds and personal experiences. For some, it was not difficult to see that narrative knowledge evokes the world as a set of possibilities. However, for others, paradigmatic or scientific knowledge that examines the world as a set of verifiable actualities was much more comfortable.

When things do not turn out as we had planned or hoped, we instantly subjunctivize. We construct imaginary scenarios that embody alternative possibilities. This often sets off a chain-reaction of stories. King Lear's announcement of his retirement is a subjunctivization. Before the entire assembly of the court and guests, he begins to imagine the shape of the future kingdom as he divides his property among his daughters. In turn, his children begin to subjunctivize: What if my father divides his land in this way, then

will I get as much as my sister? And what if my father is doing
something very stupid? Is it possible that he is becoming senile?
And if my father treats my sister Cordelia so brutally, then how
will he treat me when he is unhappy?

In the final act of the play, Lear and Cordelia are defeated
in battle by armies led by the other daughters, Goneril and Regan.
They are about to be taken prisoner. At the low point of his
life, when he has lost everything—his power, his authority, his
kingdom, his fatherhood, and his reason—Lear says these words,
subjunctivizing his experience:

> Come, let's away to prison:
> We two alone will sing like birds in th' cage;
> When thou dost ask me blessing, I'll kneel down
> And ask thee forgiveness. So we'll live
> And pray, and sing, and tell old tales, and laugh
> At gilded butterflies, and hear poor rogues
> Talk of court news (Act 5.3.8–18).

Lear is going to prison, and yet he imagines it will be a house of
beauty where he and his daughter will sing like birds. He has been
transformed by his suffering. The arrogant, even tyrannical, old
king has become a compassionate human being who asks his daughter for forgiveness and understands the power of blessing to call
forth life. Although he has experienced a painful reversal of circumstances, Lear comes to this tragic insight: "The ripeness is all"
(Act 5.2.11). Circumstances do not matter. What matters in life is
the capacity to be ready to engage whatever circumstances present
themselves—those that were hoped for and planned, as well as
those that were dreaded and unanticipated. In the harrowing narrative of his suffering, Lear experiences connectedness to a broader humanity.

Narrative Creates Community

It is the stories that we share with other human beings, stories
that embed the history of our social life, traditions, and systems
of power that incorporate us as human beings into our cultures.
Human beings are narratively constituted in communities where
we live our lives as stories that locate us in the world. Who we
are and what our connections are to other people and situations

is expressed in the stories we tell and those to which we listen. When we participate as listeners in the narrative of others, we recognize the plight of others in all the plots and counterplots of life stories (Bruner, 2002). We behold the moments of reversal in the lives of other people. That recognition can inspire the breaking open of our hearts in compassion. It is in narrative that we become human. It is in narrative that we call forth the humanity of the other as well. Human life shows up as a story.

Culture Construct

Culture is one of two basic underpinnings of the conceptual model (see Figure 1.1). A classic definition of *culture* is that "complex whole which includes knowledge, belief, art, law, morals, custom, and any other capabilities and habits acquired by man as a member of society" (Tylor, 1871/1956, as cited in Erickson & Murphy, p. 26). Studying culture involves examining the shared values and beliefs held by members of a society and also how these views influence and shape behavior. Culture thus provides an orienting framework for considering how dying and death can be studied within and across a range of societies.

Aspects of the life-course including experiences of health, illness, disability, dying and death are integral to the human condition. However, there is great diversity in human behavior and how people respond to the end of life within various cultural contexts. It is necessary, therefore, to focus on what is different about the dying experience in diverse cultural contexts, and what is similar in the dying experience across cultures. For example, some physical symptoms of dying such as labored breathing will occur everywhere, but how this symptom is culturally interpreted and managed may vary tremendously between settings. Thus, taking a holistic and comparative approach to studying dying and death enables one to recognize death as a fundamental human experience while developing sensitivity to the extent of cultural variation in end-of-life practices around the world.

It is very important to understand how various human characteristics such as culture, biology, social organization, and language all interact and influence end-of-life processes. One's understanding more about several key characteristics of culture will shed further light on how to think about culture in an analytic way and provide insight about the role of culture in shaping how the end of life is perceived and how it occurs in various settings.

Culture Is Learned

In studying end-of-life issues, one must consider how cultural traditions and practices are transmitted between generations. Specifically, learning about these cultural customs helps members of societies know how to act in a socially appropriate manner and to make sense of their world during the potentially complex end-of-life period. Being familiar with the end-of-life care practices, dying processes, and mourning rituals of their society can often be quite comforting during a traumatic time in many people's lives. Knowing these social conventions also helps people to interact and receive social support from others. In some cases, these social structures enable the dying and/or the survivors to articulate to others what would be most helpful and meaningful and form the basis for the start of a healing dialogue. Of course, it is too idealistic to say that just because cultural practices are learned and transmitted that end-of-life experiences will always go smoothly. Indeed, the broad multidisciplinary literature on death and dying as well as some stories presented in this book reflect the myriad problems that often arise.

Although understanding how cultural traditions regarding the end of life are often transmitted is a good starting point, it is important to recognize that tremendous intragroup as well as intergroup variation exists in end-of-life experiences. Although culture is learned, this tenet does not mean that individuals rigidly adhere to whatever cultural knowledge and practices are transmitted to them. Rather, culture is flexible, dynamic, and can change over time. There is thus great possibility for both individual variation in how people act and for cultural practices to change over time. As Kottak (2002) states,

> Although cultural rules tell us what to do and how to do it, people don't always do what the rules say should be done. People use their culture actively and creatively, rather than blindly following its dictates. We are not passive beings who are doomed to follow our cultural traditions like programmed robots. Instead, people can learn, interpret, and manipulate the same rule in different ways. (p. 273)

The heterogeneity of dying experiences presented in this book well illustrate this point.

Culture Is Shared

Culture is a group-level phenomenon, and individuals learn about their culture and share their experiences as members of groups. In a culture, individuals will often share beliefs, expectations, key experiences, and cultural values (Kottak, 2002). In American culture for example, individualism is a widely shared cultural value. Because individualism is so highly prized, it seems natural to many Americans to stress individual autonomy, personal control, and individual decision making in discussions about the end of life. For example, *advance directives* are legal documents by which individuals state their preferences for medical treatment if they are not able to participate later in decision making. These documents resonate with the Western ethical principles of respect for autonomy and individual choice and are widely accepted in U.S. health care settings. Even if an emphasis on individualism is a cultural attribute tied to majority American cultural norms, it is not the way all Americans conceptualize end-of-life issues. Thus, the applicability of advance directives in a society such as this one where people have diverse backgrounds and ethical stances is not a given. For example, Blackhall, Murphy, Frank, Michel, and Azen (1995) found major differences among four ethnic groups (European Americans, African Americans, Korean Americans, and Mexican Americans) in their attitudes toward advance directives and end-of-life decision making. The results reflected variations in attitudes toward autonomy among these Americans.

Culture Is Symbolic

The use of symbols is a fundamental human attribute and one that is involved in every aspect of human life. A symbol can be verbal or nonverbal. Symbols involve using one thing to represent another. For example, language is a critical symbolic part of human culture in which words come to represent specific objects. Therefore, it is not surprising that one cannot study the end of life without examining all of the symbolic meanings associated with particular end-of-life communications, actions, and processes. One example is the Roman Catholic tradition of administering the

"Sacrament of the Sick" to persons nearing death. Verbal symbols include recitation of a specific litany of prayers that represent a change in the social and spiritual status of the dying person. Nonverbal symbolism includes application of holy oil to anoint specific parts of the body to represent purification and preparation for the afterlife.

Multidisciplinary Education

Multidisciplinary education about death and dying has increased over the past several decades. Only recently have cultural variations in the dying experience been incorporated as a significant component of this education (Braun, Pietsch, & Blanchette, 2000; Doorenbos, Briller, & Chapleski, 2003; Parkes, Laungani, & Young, 1997). Yet, one can see from the earlier discussion why it is critical to consider how culture operates and its role in shaping all end-of-life experiences. Despite the more frequent inclusion of cultural issues in end-of-life education today, the organization of end-of-life curricula remains highly problematic. Culture needs to be viewed as the context in which end-of-life communication and care provision occurs. Instead, culture is often included as a single self-contained module in which an understanding of important cultural processes, such as the negotiation of decision making, is not stressed.

A further limitation in many current end-of-life curricula is that the greatest focus has been simply to help practitioners gain a better understanding of the beliefs and practices of specific ethnic and religious groups. Increased understanding of cultural traditions and practices regarding the end of life is very important in U.S. health care in which increasingly diverse communities are being served. Caution, however, needs to be applied to guard against merely using an "ethnic cookbook" approach; the variations in perspectives among members of a particular cultural group must always be considered (Braun, Pietsch, & Blanchette, 2000; Doorenbos, Briller, & Chapleski, 2003). Too often clinicians rely on the ethnic cookbook approach with confidence, yet at best it is only capable of producing limited understandings of patient values and preferences (Chrisman & Johnson, 1996).

Culture and organizational issues are also important areas requiring further exploration in the provision of end-of-life care.

First, it is critically important that end-of-life scholars explore the multiple layers of subcultures that coexist within U.S. health care as well as in other settings. These layers may include a number of elements: (a) the subcultures that patients and their families bring with them into a care setting, (b) the subculture that dying patients create for themselves (e.g., residents in an inpatient hospice), (c) the subculture of the care staff, (d) the subculture of organizations, and (e) the subculture of biomedicine. More research is needed to explore all of these dimensions.

Another area that must be considered further is the way in which the organization of the U.S. health care system interacts with the provision of palliative care for the dying. For example, our culture stresses the importance of productivity. In contemporary American biomedicine, productivity is often related to providing necessary services to individuals in the shortest amount of time. This approach typically maximizes the numbers of individuals who are served, as well as payments to hospitals, clinics, or medical practices. Numbers of patients served per day per provider is often the quantifiable measure of success in health care organizations. The needs of terminally ill patients, however, do not usually fall neatly within these constraints. Zucker (2004) eloquently describes the problem:

> Hospitals are running on empty these days, empty pockets, that is. Admitting patients brings in cash. Caring for them does not. Hospital doctors know that the surest way to incur administrative wrath is to lavish not expensive tests on patients, but expensive time. The sooner patients are discharged, the better. . . . The pace of disease, though, remains its old slow, sad self. Disease will never change. It pleads for a place for a dying patient to rest and eat and get his strength back for a few days. . . . Bed rest and observation are the oldest, the simplest, and often the best possible kinds of health care. Are they too expensive for us now? (p. D5)

The pace of medical care has been pushed to the breaking point to accommodate this dictum, yet effective palliation often requires significant time to deal with alleviating social, emotional, and spiritual as well as physical pain. Better understanding of the cultural and organizational issues that arise from this disjuncture is critical.

In summary, culture plays a central role in the dying process. Cultural categories regarding health and illness, functional capacity, the definition and meaning of death, and what constitutes a good death may vary tremendously between and within cultures. Only upon recognizing these fundamental concepts can one begin to consider the heterogeneity in dying experiences in the United States, such as those reflected by the stories in this book. Such an understanding can help readers see the cultural complexities involved in end-of-life decision making and will hopefully result in a more humane and nuanced way of approaching death and dying.

STORY DOMAINS

The domains chosen for this volume represent important perspectives used to conduct rich multidisciplinary analyses of the stories. The domains are not exhaustive but they are critical components of dying processes that deserve intensive examination: economic, education and information, ethical, legal, life course, physical, policy, provider and health system, and spiritual. Using these story domains as the framework, we were able to cross disciplinary boundaries more easily and learned to respond to end-of-life stories from many perspectives. We recognize that each of these areas is the subject of extensive practice, and theoretical, and research literature. Full description of the important work in each area is beyond the scope of this volume. What is presented in this section is intended to provide an overview of the domains as they were conceptualized in this book. The domains are presented here in alphabetical order, rather than hierarchically.

Economic Stories

Economic stories at the end of life in the United States typically recount attempts to balance benefits and costs of decisions made by patients, families, and providers. These decisions, which may include doing nothing, often influence the length of time to death and the quality of life for dying persons. Choices are always made about how many resources to allocate at the end of life (Folland, Goodman, & Stano, 2004). Societies do not base decisions totally on costs versus benefits or on predictions of an individual's future productivity or dependency. If they did, then these societies would not dedicate scarce health treatment and care resources to those people who will not or cannot work, even if treated.

"Free" care provided by family members is not free. Time is a scarce resource and the family members must give up time that they could otherwise spend earning income or participating in other activities. Family members who would gladly provide 10 to 20 hours of care per month in the short term might find such time allocations increasingly difficult in the longer term. Although it has been argued that one "can't put a price on peoples' lives," decisions made by patients and providers suggest otherwise. The price, however, is not simply a reflection of treatment costs. What must also be taken into account are the costs to provide a high quality of life and the burden imposed on society and caregivers by prolonging life. The debate about the "duty to die" has been a focus of well-known controversial reports. Put another way, the crux of the economic question is, what value can be placed on what kind of existence, at what price, and by whom?

Education and Information Stories

Education and information empower people to make important decisions about the direction of their lives. The explosion of information about health in recent decades has been remarkable and has changed the patient/practitioner relationship in many ways. For example, numerous Internet sites are dedicated to health issues. One result of this concentration of information is the rapid dissemination of new knowledge about illness and treatments. Rather than only being known by health professionals, reports of important research results are quickly announced in newspapers and on radio and television where consumers have the same access as the providers.

Despite the rapid growth of health information resources, there remains a vast deficit in public knowledge about end-of-life issues. This lack of knowledge probably stems, in part, from the reluctance of Americans to come to grips with the emotionally fraught topic of death and dying in this death aversive culture. The lack of education and information about end of life is apparent in many of the stories and responses in this book. This deficit hampers health care providers in their efforts to provide quality care for their patients and hampers individuals in their ability to make informed decisions. For example, a lack of correct information about the effects of opiates to relieve pain may cause health care providers to avoid their use. Confusion regarding the legal standing of advance directives may result in treatment decisions for dying patients being made that do not reflect their wishes. Lack of awareness of the availability of palliative-care programs, including hospice, may result in families not using programs that could provide the type of supportive care they need during a difficult time. These failures can only be remedied by intensive efforts to provide the type and quantity of information about end of life needed by all segments of the American public.

Ethical Stories

Ethical stories deal with issues concerning what is considered good and bad, what constitutes moral duty and obligation, and the principles of conduct within a person, group, or culture. In Western biomedicine, for example, ethics is usually discussed in terms of the four principles of beneficence, nonmaleficence, autonomy, and justice (Beauchamp & Childress, 2001). As Western medicine has expanded its technological abilities, it has become possible to keep people alive despite conditions that in earlier eras would have resulted in death. However, the capacity to prolong life and delay death does not imply the necessity to do so. The stories of "what ought to be" from an ethics perspective involve complex and often contested interpretations of what is best for the person facing death, the family and community, the health care professionals, and society at large.

A simple example of an ethical decision is whether to fully inform a patient about prognosis. Western biomedical culture places highest value on patient autonomy, self-determination, and informed choice. On the basis of these values, patients in the United States are legally entitled to read all of their medical records and asked to sign complex consent forms. However, many individuals do not want direct negative news about their terminal condition. Others believe that it is the family's duty to manage bad news, to shield the ill person from stress, and to make significant care decisions for the individual. Given the individual, family, and cultural range of preferences for information, ethical issues commonly arise regarding whether a health care provider should formulate and present a prognosis. These and many other ethical issues will continue to confront individuals, families, and providers dealing with death and dying in the increasingly complex technological environment of 21st century health care.

Legal Stories

Legal stories involve application of specific laws to a variety of end-of-life issues. These include the seeking or avoiding of treatment, issues of autonomy, and legal questions that confront health professionals. Legal experts faced with the task of interpreting and applying the law to end-of-life situations must be concerned with the setting of precedents for future cases. Legal stories address what has been done in previous decision situations (precedents) and what must be done (mandates of law). Landmark end-of-life cases from different eras, such as *Quinlan*, *Cruzan*, and *Schiavo*, demonstrate how evolving ethical and moral understandings in U.S. society influence the development of laws (Goodnough, 2004; Webb, 1997).

The development of American law concerning end-of-life issues reflects ongoing public discussion, over the past 30 years or so, about how much and what kind of attention must be paid to the rights and desires of those nearing death. Today, patients, families, and health care providers play out legal stories shaped by the struggle for balance between various concerns. These concerns include such highly charged issues as preserving individual autonomy, maintaining professional integrity, honoring the rights of individuals with disabilities, and addressing physician-assisted suicide. In partial response to some of these areas, individual states have created laws, policies, and documentation procedures to enable people to articulate end-of-life preferences and appoint surrogate decision makers. Instruments such as medical power of attorney and living wills have become more widely available across the country. There remain, however, differences in availability, rates of participation, and legal recognition in these forms of advance directives. In this book's stories, confusion and conflict arise among family and caregivers when personal preferences have not been explicitly expressed. These stories call attention to the need for further discussion of the legal ramifications of end-of-life care.

Life-Course Stories

Life-course stories tell of the many patterned ways through which people continue to grow and change over time, both physically and socially. There are different classification systems that people in various societies use for categorizing phases of the life course. For example, not all societies consider adolescence as a distinct phase of the life cycle. In American society, however, this age category is considered very meaningful and is viewed as an important developmental stage on the path to adulthood. Many societies have social expectations concerning appropriate behavior at different ages and stages of life.

Important experiences at one stage of life influence interpretations and reactions at other times. Among significant life experiences are the onset, course, and treatment of illnesses. The experiences people have with death at various times in their lives and how meaning is created from these experiences is another important aspect of life-course research. Responses to death and dying are related to the processes of human development. Children react differently to death than do older adults. For instance, understanding the causes of death, the meaning of death, and the aftermath of death is not the same for young children as it is for mature adults. Concepts of death are influenced by the physical, social, emotional, and spiritual changes that occur as a person develops over his or her lifetime. The types and specific circumstances of losses experienced at particular times in life also influence a person's responses.

Families and communities also experience death as a developmental or life-course phenomenon. Because life-course expectations are culturally constructed, some deaths are considered timely, untimely, devastating or blessed, public or private loss. When losses occur out of the "normal" sequence within a family or community, the implications are often significant.

Physical Stories

The *physical stories* of death and dying involve the manifestation of pathology or disease in an individual person. Physical stories are complicated by uncertainties in diagnosis, prognosis, and treatment alternatives. These uncertainties often confound decisions made by patients and health professionals and can have a significant influence on the course of events.

The physical story can detail all of the changes that individuals undergo as their illnesses progress. These changes often include alterations in physical functioning and mental capacity. Physical stories at end of life also include discussion of the physiological processes that accompany dying, the various options for control of pain and other symptoms, and care for the human body at the time of death. End-of-life stories are often couched only as physical stories. These stories need to be expanded and examined through the lenses provided by the other domains. This approach helps to avoid the temptation to reduce a person's life to that of merely a physical body.

Policy Stories

Policy stories encompass guidelines and procedures that have an impact on end-of-life experiences at both micro and macro levels. Policy stories have major implications for individuals, organizations, and the wider society. End-of-life stories help to reveal diverse viewpoints that need to be addressed through public dialogue and the creation and adjustment of public policy.

There are many policy stories about end of life that are not clearly identified as such. Instead, the stories may be couched as bureaucratic problems or interpersonal conflicts. Policy is dynamic and there is a strong political component to policy formation that involves multiple voices and constituencies. A well-known end-of-life example with policy implications was the politically charged decision about whether and when to prosecute Dr. Kervorkian for his physician-assisted suicide activities in Michigan. Another example is the personal involvement of the governor of Florida in the *Schiavo* case, which concerns a woman in a 13-year-long persistent vegetative state (Goodnough, 2004). A case such as this highlights the complexities of negotiating and implementing policies in the climate of contested claims from various advocacy groups including religious and disability communities.

There are always unanticipated consequences that arise from changes in policy. These consequences, which provoke new questions, are embedded in many end-of-life stories. The continued collection and discussion of stories like those in this book will help shed light on one way to keep policy issues in the forefront of thinking about the end of life.

Provider and Health System Stories

Provider stories address the educational preparation, practice patterns, and cultural perspectives of a wide variety of people who engage in professions that provide care to others. In most cases, the provider stories are told within the broader context of health system stories that include the various settings, organizations, agencies, and communities in which care occurs. Both provider and health system stories reflect both differences and commonalities. Diversity among providers can spring from many sources, including particular ethnic, religious, and family backgrounds, as well as the values common among a particular age cohort. The diversity can also have its roots in the philosophy and orientation of the institution where the individual was trained. There are also important differences in the professional cultures of different providers as evidenced by variation in the focus of services (e.g., care vs. cure), symbols of authority (e.g., white coat, stethoscope, black bag, and so forth), and language use (e.g., medical diagnosis vs. nursing diagnosis). Common elements in the Western biomedical traditions that permeate practice disciplines include such values as timeliness, speed, efficiency, maximum use of technology, and the primacy of patient autonomy.

Health care providers, including a variety of therapists, nurses, physicians, and social workers, often do not share common views regarding the roles of the traditional health care provider, family members, and patients in decision making. Health care providers may also have disparate views about the value of various forms of treatment, including palliative care. Such variation between providers and the patients, families, and communities they serve can complicate end-of-life care. Each health care provider approaches patient and family stories with his or her own personal attitudes, values, and professional interpretations. A common theme in the stories told by those who work in end-of-life care relates to the ways in which interactions with dying people brought them closer to discovering meaning and purpose in their own lives.

Spiritual Stories

Spiritual stories are those that focus on the human search for meaning in life and death. Dying persons, families, and communities tell spiritual stories from different perspectives. For some, the journey to find meaning includes participation in organized religious observances, formal rituals and rites, and guidance from designated religious leaders. For others, the spiritual journey for meaning occurs in individual, family, or community contexts not associated with specific religions. The distinctions between the concepts of spirituality and religion have been the subject of extensive discussion and research (Thomas & Eisenhandler, 1999). The relationship between spirituality and health is well documented (Daaleman & Vandecreek, 2000; Mueller, 2001; Puchalski, 2002).

Spirituality and religiosity, in whatever form observed, may hold particular importance at the end of life. Especially when the course of a terminal illness allows time for saying goodbye, mending relationships, and putting affairs in order, people often return to previous spiritual and religious roots or seek new connections. Families and communities faced with losses also often express the need to participate in spiritual or religious traditions as part of the communal grieving process. The need to engage in spiritually meaningful rituals at a time of community grief was reflected, for example, in the ad hoc memorials that appeared at the sites of the 9/11 tragedies and the public memorial services commemorating those killed in the terrorist attacks. Although the United States observes constitutional separation of church and state, the public ceremonies after these nationally significant deaths incorporated many symbols and rituals common to different spiritual traditions in the United States. Such elements included the playing of music, lighting of candles, tolling of bells, and the litany of naming the deceased. There is a powerful connection between spirituality, end of life, and the ongoing human search for meaning in the face of death.

LEVELS OF ANALYSIS

The conceptual model developed by the WSU-EOLIP group describes three levels of analysis that intersect all of the story domains within the constructs of narrative and culture. These levels are the individual, the family or group, and the community. Each level is briefly described in this section as it is applied within the model.

Individual Level

Death is constructed differently within various cultures and their narrative traditions. Although death has been termed *the great leveler* and is one of the most universal of human experiences, it is interpreted in some cultures as an individual passage and in others as a collective experience. In the West, with the emphasis on individuality and autonomy, death is regarded as a personally focused event. In other traditions, death is regarded as a group phenomenon. In both constructions, every person undergoes the physical demise of the body alone. As we witness the deaths of others around us, each individual personally experiences and constructs meaning with the loss. As depicted in the model (see Figure 1.1), the individual is at the center, as in our Western context. However, the boundary between the individual and the family or group is drawn as a dotted line to represent the awareness that death is both an individual and collective experience and that the importance placed by self and by family or group varies widely. Health care providers, bystanders, family members, and friends each have personal stories they tell themselves about the dying person and the process of dying. Each incorporates his or her losses into the overall narrative of his own life.

Family or Group

Although each death involves one physical body, people live and die in the context of families and social groups. Across varied cultures, different stories are told about who is included in *family*. For example, each group defines for itself what persons are included and excluded from family membership, the roles and responsibilities of family members, the social exchanges that can and cannot occur, and how family units relate to each other and to the larger community. Those definitions, in turn, determine how we live and to a large extent, how we die. Whenever a person dies, families and groups lose a member. The loss must be dealt with and the family must find a way to change in the absence of the deceased.

Therefore, each story of the end of life for individuals is also a story of families and groups.

Community

Much as each individual is a part of a larger family or group, each family is part of a larger community. The term *community* is widely used and carries various connotations. For the model used in this book, we use the term in an open and inclusive sense. The community for end-of-life stories can refer to a geographic community such as a neighborhood or city, a community of service such as a veterans' group, an ethnic community such as a Native American tribe, or a community of interest such as bikers or woodworkers. Most individuals are concurrently members of many communities of different types at any given point in time. Community takes its definition from the Latin word *communitas*, which implies a powerful bond among people which transcends social role and function (Turner, 1969). When one person dies, the communities in which the person participated also must deal with the loss and find ways to continue after the loss. In these cases, the various individual and family stories are profoundly affected by the collective stories being told. In turn, the collective story is affected by changes at the family and individual level. Once again, the model is drawn with dotted lines to suggest that the boundaries between the community, family or group, and individual levels are highly permeable and that interactions across levels are dynamic (see Figure 1.1).

INTERSECTIONS

The model used in this book suggests that there are multiple dynamic ways to tell end-of-life stories. The distinctions presented herein are made in an attempt to characterize some of the myriad domains that are commonly used as frameworks for constructing and understanding end-of-life stories. However, it is recognized that every story can reflect a complex combination of domains and levels of analysis within both narrative and cultural contexts. Any domain can overlap with any of the others at any level. For example, a story ostensibly about a legal issue can often also be told or interpreted from an ethical perspective, an educational or informational perspective, and a policy perspective. Narrators from different academic and practice disciplines may tend to emphasize particular domains in the end-of-life stories, but the model suggests that any of the domains and domain combinations can and should be subject to discourse analysis from many disciplines. For example, an economist may be most comfortable addressing the economic domain and a physician or nurse most familiar addressing the physical domain. However, the benefit in the model is the support for people to approach the broad spectrum of end-of-life story domains both within and outside of their professional expertise and to attempt dialogue across domains and levels. This is the heart of interdisciplinarity.

The stories told in this book are not all the stories that can or should be told. They were selected and developed to illustrate points and stimulate discussion. The stories told herein were initially brought forth by practitioners with personal and professional expertise in end-of-life care in a variety of programs, agencies, and settings. Most of the stories were first presented as case studies in a Western biomedical format. As the multidisciplinary team reviewed and discussed the case studies, we looked for ways to incorporate the breadth of domains and to reflect the various levels of analysis. Whereas the selected stories are not intended to be representative of the full scope of end-of-life experiences, they do feature a variety of cultural backgrounds, health care choices, genders, ages, religions, socioeconomic statuses, and illness-to-death clinical courses. In the process of working with the case studies submitted for consideration, we consciously moved away from a medicalized *case* format toward a more humanized and holistic *story* format. The goal of this endeavor was to create a rich text of end-of-life perspectives. We invite you, as the reader, to enter the dialogue and extend the conversation. But first, let us tell you some stories. . . .

REFERENCES

Beauchamp, T. L., & Childress, J. F. (2001). *Principles of biomedical ethics* (5th ed.). New York: Oxford University Press.

Blackhall, L., Murphy, S., Frank, G., Michel, V., & Azen, S. (1995). Ethnicity and attitudes towards patient autonomy. *Journal of the American Medical Association, 274*, 820–825.

Braun, K., Pietsch, J., & Blanchette, P. (Eds.). (2000). *Cultural issues in end of life decision-making*. Thousand Oaks, CA: Sage.

Bruner, J. S. (2002). *Making stories: Law, literature, life*. New York: Farrar Straus Giroux.

Callois, R. (1962). *Man, play, and games*. London: Thames and Hudson.

Charon, R., & Montello, M. (Eds.). (2002). *Stories matter: The role of narrative in medical ethics*. London: Routledge.

Chrisman, N., & Johnson, T. (1996). Clinically applied anthropology. In C. Sargent & T. Johnson (Eds.), *Medical anthropology: Contemporary theory and method* (2nd ed.). Westport, CT: Prager.

Csikszentmihalyi, M. (1996). *Creativity: Flow and psychology of discovery and invention*. New York: HarperCollins.

Daaleman, T. P., & Vandecreek, L. (2000). Placing religions and spirituality in end-of-life care. *Journal of the American Medical Association, 284*, 2514–2517.

Doorenbos, A., Briller, S., & Chapleski, E. (2003). Weaving cultural context into an interdisciplinary end-of-life curriculum. *Journal of Educational Gerontology, 29*, 405–416.

Erickson, P. A., & Murphy, L. D. (2001). *Readings for a history of anthropology theory*. Peterborough, ONT: Broadview Press. p. 26.

Folland, S., Goodman, A., & Stano, M. (2004). *The economics of health and health care*. Upper Saddle River, NJ: Prentice-Hall.

Goodnough, A. (2004, May 7). Florida judge authorizes removal of feeding tube. *New York Times*, p. A 20.

Huizinga, J. (1955). *Homo Ludens: A study of the play element in culture*. Boston: Beacon.

Jameson, F. (1991). *Postmodernism, or, the cultural logic of later capitalism*. Durham, NC: Duke University Press.

Kottak, C. P. (2002). *Anthropology: The exploration of human diversity* (9th ed.). Boston: McGraw-Hill.

Mattingly, C., & Garro, L. C. (Eds.). (2000). *Narrative and cultural constructions of illness and healing*. Berkeley: University of California Press.

Moltmann, J. (1972). *Theology of play*. New York: Harper & Row.

Mueller, H. (2001, May). *Spirituality and end-of-life care*. Paper presented at the University of Leeds, England.

Parkes, C., Laungani, P., & Young, B. (1997). *Death and bereavement across cultures*. London, Routledge.

Puchalski, C. (2002). Spirituality and end-of-life care: A time for listening and caring. *Journal of Palliative Medicine, 5*, 289–294.

Shakespeare, W. (1608). *King Lear*. In *The riverside Shakespeare* (2nd ed., 1997). (G. B. Evans, Ed.). Boston: Houghtin Mifflin.

Thomas, L. E., & Eisenhandler, S. (Eds.). (1999). *Religion, belief and spirituality in late life*. New York: Springer.

Turner, V. (1969) *The ritual process: Structure and anti-structure*. Ithaca, NY: Cornell University Press.

Webb, M. (1997). *The good death*. New York: Bantam.

Zucker, A. (2004, April 27). Time heals, but it's a luxury physicians and patient rarely get. *New York Times*, p. D5.

CHAPTER 2

Stories of Ron:
Music to His Ears

If music be the food of love, play on . . .

—Shakespeare, *Twelfth Night* (Act I.i.1)

Ron's Story
Megan Gunnell

Today was the first day I witnessed death. I saw a man's last breath leave him like a whisper and was in awe at the fragility of life. Almost instantaneously his last breath left him, his heart stopped beating, his chest stopped the rise and fall that was happening moments before, and his color changed. It looked as if the rush of blood—that driving force that circulates and pumps through us every second we are alive—suddenly fell to stillness. There was a pause of disbelief and wonder in the room from family and friends who were gathered all around his bed.

I remember that my pager went off almost immediately after I turned it on that morning. The Intensive Care Unit (ICU) Clinical Nurse Specialist had made the referral for Music Therapy services to assist in the terminal wean process and to provide comfort to the dying patient as the respirator was removed. As it turned out, the work that I provided was much more a family process than an exclusive intervention for the benefit of the patient. When I received the notification about this referral, I felt anxiety surrounding the unknowns. To prepare for the session, I spent a few minutes in the small hospital prayer chapel centering myself and opening to trust the process. In those moments, I visualized that my hands were like gloves playing the harp easily without judgment or inhibition.

As I walked with my harp to the ICU on Monday morning not knowing what to expect, I looked out the window at the budding trees and flowers. Seven months before, I had given birth to my first child. I realized in that moment that if I could accept new life, birth, and the coming of spring, then I could also accept death and dying as part of the life cycle; for there can not be renewal each spring without the death in the fall and a time to harbor grief in the winter. In some cases, death makes life possible. As you will see, the music therapy intervention was the bridge between one man's passing and a family's renewed will to live.

The following is what I read on his chart and learned from conversations with my colleagues on duty. Ron was a 64-year-old Caucasian male who was admitted to the hospital because of cardiac arrest. He had received chemotherapy earlier that day and was reported to have taken his last breath before emergency medical services (EMS) arrived at his home and resuscitated him using cardiopulmonary resuscitation (CPR). Ron had a history of lung cancer, colon cancer, chronic obstructive pulmonary disease, diabetes mellitus, hypertension, and a deep venous thrombosis of his right upper extremity. He was also a longtime smoker and a former alcoholic. Ron presented to the emergency department without a pulse and with apnea. The Emergency Medical Technician (EMT) team was still doing CPR. The patient was placed on mechanical respirator for ventilation (vent), an endotracheal tube was inserted, and an arterial catheterization was done. Ron was then transferred to the ICU and was unresponsive on the vent. The physician noted that his prognosis was poor.

Four days after his admission, the staff recommended that they wean the patient from the vent. The family agreed. I was notified and went to meet the family and explain my services. Ron's wife was alone in the room stroking his head and speaking softly to him. I explained that because our auditory sense is so strong, we can still receive the benefit of music even when we are not able to communicate in other ways. Music therapy can not only help a patient relax during a medical procedure, but also can provide solace for the family.

Ron and his wife had been married for 42 years. Together they had a large family—four children and several grandchildren—almost all of whom were present for the terminal wean procedure. There were about 20 family members around the patient's bed. I immediately sensed the uncomfortable energy in the room and the feeling that no one knew exactly what to expect or what to do or say. I explained my services to the family and that I had been contacted to provide live music for the patient before and during his procedure to help reduce his anxiety and to comfort him. I also indicated that the music was for the family members, as well. I encouraged them to allow the music to lead them wherever they needed to go and to feel free to communicate whatever they wanted to the patient while I was playing.

One of the sons-in-law was a professional musician and started telling me about their musical family. The patient had played piano. Some relatives sang. Some played other instruments. They all loved music. The patient had previously requested his favorite Irish lullaby to be played when he died, and the son-in-law had recorded it on the patient's out-of-tune piano the night before. He brought it in on a tape to play in the room. It was the most beautiful out-of-tune piano I had ever heard, and it set the tone for an open and loving experience.

The family was all gathered silently around the bed listening to the tape and after it was done, no one said a word. I lifted my hands to the strings and continued the Irish theme with another Celtic lullaby on the harp. Looking back on this experience now, it is my belief that the music provided the family with a cushion to express themselves. Music held the space for them to emotionally open and share their deepest feelings with Ron just before he died.

I stopped for a moment between pieces. Without the sound of the music, the room seemed too empty for anyone to utter a word. Just moments after I started to play again, I heard Ron's son's voice.

> Dad, I want to tell you how much I love you. I never thanked you for everything you've given me. You were the one who accepted me and my partner coming to our family Thanksgiving dinner. You said to me on the phone, "any friend of yours is a friend of ours—and we love you."

The son broke down and by doing so, paved the way for each family member to say whatever he or she wanted to say.

There were pauses in the music—time for silence and breaks in the soundscape. The interludes provided a chance for family members to regroup and gain strength. But each time the music started, more members shared their feelings:

> Grandpa, you always used to say "Hi, Beautiful!" and I loved that. You stopped telling me that a while back and I asked you why and you told me "because you don't need it anymore!" But I did and so you started saying it again. The patients' wife said, "Roll on, Ron. Roll on by to Heaven. We don't want to let you go, but we don't want to see you suffer anymore. We'll see you again someday."

The family shared many stories and laughed and cried together at his bedside. Clearly, this man was the pillar and patriarch of his family. Whether he was sifting through the sand on a beach for a lost wedding ring or calling a cab for his out-of-town daughter when her car was in the shop and she needed to take her baby to the doctor, he was always there for everyone. Ron led the way with everything from the acceptance of his son's homosexuality to helping out a neighbor in need.

I heard them talk about the song *A Bicycle Built for Two* (aka *Daisy Bell*, Dacre, 1892) as being one of his favorites. Ron and his wife used to sing it to each other. I invited the family to join me by saying, "If you can, let's sing it together for him." Their voices filled the room with song. It seemed as if the music was providing the direction and guidance they craved. Ron's wife continued on the second verse alone. She sang directly to him: "Ronnie, Ronnie, here is your answer true; I'm not crazy over the likes of you; it won't be a stylish marriage, if you can't afford a carriage; so I'll be damned, if I'll be crammed on a bicycle built for two!" She was crying and laughing all at once and ended with "It was a great ride on our bicycle built for two for 42 years!"

The family was not sure how to make the transition from this moment to the terminal wean procedure. Again, I could feel their need for guidance. I quietly suggested that if they felt comfortable in doing so, they could lay a gentle hand on him or on his bed and silently in their hearts and minds offer him a blessing before they left the room. I started playing a very full harp piece—very safe and warm. One by one, each family member came over to

Ron's side and expressed love for him and touched him. Each in turn kissed him goodbye, then left the room.

It was everything I could do to stay in the music and hold the space for them to have this experience. Ultimately, this intimate and sacred experience belonged to the family. The music was merely a vessel that helped them express what they needed to say. And it was this powerful session that reminded me that sometimes a single intervention makes a significant impact.

A few family members stayed behind for the procedure. The daughter was an RN and held his hand as the ventilator was removed. I offered music throughout the procedure. The respirator was stopped and tubes removed with apparent ease and grace. Ron continued breathing on his own. The family re-entered the room and gathered around his bed. The priest came in and offered a prayer for Ron, and it was during the prayer that Ron died. Perhaps his death was so peaceful because he was surrounded by family who loved him and, more important, were able to tell him so.

Had I, as a professional, missed this chance to connect with Ron's family, their opportunity to openly celebrate the honor and meaning of his life might have been lost. Our lives are validated through remembrance and sharing. The lesson I learned from this special encounter was how a special kind of listening and musical response could validate a human life in a new way. I developed a deeper understanding of the relationship between the universal need for acknowledgment and the power of music. Hearing the synopsis of Ron's life story through his family's voices and songs showed how the creation of permanent memories can be enhanced through the sacred spaces that music can provide.

That powerful experience left me with the intimation that despite Ron's physical death, his life and memory would live on. It was one brief moment between this earthly life and heaven. It was one moment between 64 years of this man's life full of stories and laughter, tears and joy, to becoming a memory. It was one moment's reminder that we should never take love and living for granted.

Narrative Response
Richard Raspa

This case demonstrates how stories can inspire powerful therapeutic interventions for patients, families, and health professionals.

The sensitive listening of the therapist and her playing of the harp envelop the family in uncommon grace. At the same time, the respectful listening of the family to the therapist and the offering of their own musical gifts expand the therapeutic event into a celebration of the life of a man and his family. Everyone is swept into the rhythm of the stories and songs, including the therapist. The result is collaborative healing. In this model of care giving, all those connected to the patient can find in death an opportunity to complete relationships and heal the wounds of living. Collaborative healing replaces the linear model of a professional doing something to a passive patient. In this story, caring is exchanged rather than administered.

Synergism occurs in the narrative—the whole effect is greater than the sum of its parts. Although the focus is ostensibly upon the dying patient, Ron, all participants are touched. The expectations of what is possible in a terminal wean, are extended through the power of stories. The narrator connects this, her first experience with a dying patient, with her first experience of giving birth. She accepts the cycle of life in nature and in humanity: Without winter, there is no spring. Without death, there is no life.

The gay son says goodbye as he reaffirms his father's love, which welcomed him and his partner as members of the family; the granddaughter confirms the importance of Ron's praise as she was growing up; and the wife expresses the humor and enduring love in their 42-year marriage.

The pain of loss is tempered by a gentle letting-go of the dying patient. In this narrative context, healing is not the clinical recovery of the patient; it is rather the expression of gratefulness for the joys of being alive with Ron as a spouse and as a parent. This hospital meeting could have surfaced as a clash of bitter feelings about past failures and mistakes. Ron was an alcoholic and a smoker, and the chronic diseases from which he suffered may have been associated with these addictions. Instead, what arises is the family's spontaneous celebration of Ron's humanity. When people are capable of gratitude, life is experienced as complete, no longer lacking something.

Such healing begins with listening. The music therapist listens to all the stories around her. She attends to the clinical narratives recounted by professional staff and anecdotes told by family. She tells the medical details of the story in a dispassionate way. The patient is treated as a cluster of symptoms—"Ron presented to the emergency department without a pulse and with apnea"—and is passively acted upon using biotechnology—"the patient was put on mechanical respirator for ventilation (vent), an endotracheal tube was inserted, and an arterial catheterization was done." Although there is modern medicine in the room, it quickly fades. In the foreground something more compelling takes place—the stories and songs affirming life in the face of death. Such expressive genres marking life transitions extend back to humanity's most ancient rite of passage from the visible domain to the invisible. Death is confronted, and while people experience the sadness of loss, they express gratefulness for the life that was given. To respond to life's ending in this way is to appreciate life as a gift. It is to experience life not as an inevitable given, an inalienable right, or something that is owed to us as inhabitants of this planet. But rather, gratefulness is an expression of wonder at the ordinary things that are most often taken for granted—like being alive. To be grateful is to revel in that which exists wherever and whenever it manifests itself.

The sterility of the hospital and biomedical discourse give way to the warmth and cheer generated by the narrative and musical texts. The expression of tenderness first occurs as she writes, "Ron's wife was alone in the room stroking his head and speaking softly to him." As the therapist explains, Ron can hear even if he is in a coma "because the sense of hearing is so strong." The therapist encourages the family to communicate with Ron. She functions as a grand maestro who conducts the family in an end-of-life symphony: All have a part to play, all are invited to give voice to their feelings. Together the whole ensemble expresses something meaningful, allowing "the music to lead them wherever they needed to go and to feel free to communicate whatever they wanted to the patient. . . . " This is a daring step. It brings the professional to the edge of her discipline, where training and skill meet raw emotion and intuition.

It is a chance worth taking, for this is a collaborative enterprise. The music therapist and the family together construct narratives in words and songs based upon memories of the tender ways the family have engaged each other. Throughout, the therapist remains vulnerable. She does not know beforehand what things she will do for the patient. Before she acts, however, she listens. It is a listening from the heart, as Steindl-Rast (1990) would say, from intuition and feeling rather than from strategic maneuvers. Such listening breaks through walls of embarrassment and fear and invites human rather than formulaic responses.

Music and stories intersect to produce a life history that will live on in the memory of the participants. The son-in-law, a professional musician, tells the remarkable story of the musical family. In this moment, the patient's favorite Irish lullaby is played. The therapist gauges the response of the family, watching for the moment when she can make her intervention. The room becomes silent. The therapist continues with a Celtic lullaby. Intimacy deepens. The wife sings *A Bicycle Built for Two*, (aka *Daisy Bell*) (Dacre, 1892) and, laughing and crying, she completes the relationship with "It was a great ride on our bicycle built for two for 42 years." Love is made public and binding, affirmed and reaffirmed in acts of storytelling and singing, in expressions of compassion and praise. Ron's death is accepted and spoken out loud before the whole group: "Roll on, Ron. Roll on by to Heaven. We don't want to let you go, but we don't want to see you suffer anymore. We'll see you again someday."

As the final weaning process draws near, the therapist listens, and senses the uncertainty of the family. She suggests they gently touch Ron before they leave the room. Each member of the family gives a final expression of love.

Because of this elegant synergy between therapist and family, everyone underwent a healing: What was incomplete was finished, what was unspoken was said. Unexpected connections were made, even between traditional health care providers and receivers in a conventional medical setting like an ICU. And gratitude was the fundamental human response to the conditions of living and dying. In this hospital room, a narrative was spun that changed a public place of intervention into a ritual space of transformation as old life received its final blessing and the new life was called forth.

Informational Response
Lynda M. Baker

The concept of information is difficult to define because information can mean different things to different people at different times. In the classic narrow definition, information is a set of symbols that have potential meaning for the receiver (Faibisoff & Ely, 1976). From a broader perspective, information can be anything a person finds informing (Dervin, 1977). In this sense, the thing that informs could be a book or a conversation (an external thing) or past experience, intuition, nonverbal communication, or emotions (an internal thing). Whether something can inform depends on a person's interpretation. According to Dervin, Harlock, Atwood, and Garzona (1980), "Information does not inform unless the individual can make personal sense of it and personal sense can only be made when information can be processed in the frame of personal understandings" (p. 592). In the story of Ron, both external and internal things inform the health professionals, the family, and the music therapist.

For the health professionals in this story, information that played a role in the decision-making process emanated from both internal and external sources. For example, when the EMTs arrived at Ron's house, they found him dead. Most probably, they ascertained the time of his last breath from the family, thus obtaining basic information on how to proceed from an external source. Their knowledge, training, and past experience (internal sources) with cardiac arrests informed their decision to begin resuscitation procedures. Similarly, the emergency room (ER) staff received information about Ron verbally from the EMTs, as well as nonverbally through their visual and physical examinations of him. When Ron was hooked up to a cardiac monitor, the staff also had continuous, real-time information about his cardiac activity. Thus, their immediate treatment decisions were based on the information they received from external sources (EMTs and the cardiac monitor), as well as internal ones (intuition, education, past experiences). Other external sources that would have affected further treatment decisions included Ron's family and his medical chart.

In the story, evidence exists about the nature of conversations between health professionals and the family. The physician informed the family about Ron's prognosis. To give their consent, they must have been told about the procedure to remove Ron from the respirator. It is plausible that the professional who unhooked the ventilator told the family what to expect. Nonverbal communication (the act of removing) is also a component of the procedure. The few family members who remained at the bedside to witness it could now make sense not only of the procedure, but also of the finality of Ron's impending death.

Family members used information in a variety of ways to gain an understanding of who Ron was in their lives and to make sense of his demise. They talked to Ron in the form of stories about life events that clearly demonstrated their love for him or his love for them. In doing so, each person (his son, grandchild, and wife) provided information to Ron and about Ron to other members of the family.

The family also shared stories with each other. From an information perspective, the stories are important because the listeners gain new information about Ron from each storyteller's viewpoint. Frank (1995) stated, "People tell stories not just to work out their own changing identities, but also to guide others who will follow them" (p. 17). Thus, the purpose of the stories is to allow each family member to reflect on, and to reaffirm, personal identity within the context of Ron's life. The stories also shed light on the nature and meaning of individuals' relationships with Ron. Without hearing their stories, it is not possible to determine if the stories contained any elements of who they will be after Ron's death. The reader can only assume that each storyteller might have hinted about life without Ron.

Information about Ron's relationship with his wife can be gleaned from her rendition of *Daisy Bell (A Bicycle Built for Two)* by Dacre (1892). She revealed her conditions for the marriage (i.e., she wanted more than what a bicycle represents) and yet also indicated her satisfaction with the "ride" they had had during their 42 years of marriage. In the song, it seems she was giving the family an intimate sense of their marriage, their ups and downs, her ultimatums, and their togetherness.

Nonverbal communication is also evident in this story. The family members communicated their affection for Ron by stroking his head, holding his hand, and kissing him goodbye. These gestures are important from an informational perspective. My interpretation is that through them, each person is informing the others about personal feelings, such as their love of Ron, demonstrating lack of fear in the presence of a dying person, sharing acceptance of Ron's imminent death, and displaying togetherness in this deeply emotional situation.

Finally, verbal communication about taking Ron off the venti-lator must have occurred between the health professionals and his wife. It is plausible to suggest that Ron's wife talked with other family members, because they all agreed to it. During these ex-changes, each individual would gather the information he or she personally needed. Such information may have included details about the procedure, pros and cons of a decision to allow Ron to die, and factors influencing personal decisions whether to be pres-ent during the procedure.

The presence of the daughter who is a nurse, at the bedside when the respirator was disconnected, suggests several things. Her informational need as a nurse may have created a need to know that the wean was being done properly. She may also have wanted to know how her father responded to the procedure, whether he gasped for air, breathed quietly, or did not breathe at all. Her family may have requested that she be at the bedside because, as the health expert in the family, this daughter could provide them with authoritative information about Ron's last moments.

The music therapist initially receives information about Ron and his family through verbal communication from the intensive care staff. Following this, she meets with the wife and then the rest of the family to provide information about her services. These exchanges give her some indication about her specific role as a music therapist with this family's needs. What is so powerful in this story is the information the music therapist derives from the tension she encounters when returning to the bedside with her harp. Her intuition, emotions, and sense of the environment pro-vided her with the necessary information to enable her to quickly determine how she must respond to the situation.

The importance of music in the cold environment of an ICU room cannot be overstated. The ICU environment is often disori-enting with its clamor of unnatural mechanical sounds. The music provided informational cues to memories of past experiences with Ron. The memories allowed the family to understand and make personal sense of Ron's death within the context of his life and theirs.

Although the music therapist-narrator gives information about spiritual issues, the priest also plays a role in this story. Although his role is minor, it is implied that the priest delivered significant religious-based information. Depending on the prayers he said, the priest might have provided information on the state of Ron's soul, comfort about absolution from his sins, and reassurance of God's love. The family may find solace in this information. It can reaffirm their beliefs and give them hope that they will meet Ron in the afterlife.

Spiritual Response
Donald E. Gelfand

This case study provides an excellent example of how a music therapy intervention can meet the needs of the dying individual, family members, and health care providers. In the words of Puchalski (2002) this intervention helped the family and perhaps Ron find "hope in the midst of despair" (p. 290). Although the case description does not provide detailed information about the relationships among the family members, it is easy to infer that the intervention facilitated the healing process for the family members who were present at Ron's bedside.

The case study indicates that Ron's family was large and devoted. A substantial number of family members assembled for this final time with him. Although the large group had come together, it seems as though no one individual was prepared to take a leadership role in the proceedings. The music therapist was faced with the challenge of setting the spiritual tone for Ron and the family. She also suggested to family members that there is spiritual meaning in the auditory events even though Ron was not conscious.

The spiritual tone of this bedside session does not mean that the actual impending nature of death is easier for the family to see. Deep feelings are revealed in the sharing that takes place, but it remains intensely difficult to bear witness at the deathbed. Few of the family members are able to actually cope with staying in the room for the removal of the ventilator.

This case study indicates that spiritual involvement can be multidimensional. It may include formal religious practice and the presence of a priest. Spiritual meaning also can be communicated through forms that do not necessarily involve formal religious practice. In this case, the spiritual nature of the intervention is initially developed through the process of the singing of songs and the telling of stories at Ron's bedside. When the ventilator is removed, the narrator tells us that a priest arrives. Although the involvement of the priest is not unexpected, the stage at which his involvement takes place may be significant in this narrative. We do not know what the prior relationship might have been between Ron, his family, and his church. We do observe that the priest arrives just prior to the moment of death. The combination of the priestly rites and the musical background may have provided a richer spiritual context for the family than either alone would have done.

There is little information in the case story about the spiritual needs of the health care providers attending to Ron's terminal wean and subsequent death. The spiritual needs of health professionals who work with dying patients are often overlooked. This case does not represent a formal effort to provide an intervention that will meet the spiritual needs of the professional, but the narrative communicates a strong sense that this intervention had a significant spiritual impact on the therapist as well as the family, and hopefully, Ron. From her first contact with the family when she informs them that there is no correct way to structure the experience to her comments about the beauty of the out-of-tune piano, the writing communicates a feeling of growth and spiritual meaning. The therapist's involvement is beautifully expressed in her comment: "It was everything I could do to stay in the music and hold the space for them to have this experience."

Discussions about spirituality and the end of life often center on the needs of dying individuals (Koenig, 2000). The question of what is needed by loved ones of the dying individual is less often asked. Even less commonly asked is the question: What are the spiritual needs of the health care providers assisting the dying person during the final stages of life? Tulsky, Fischer, Rose, and Arnold (1998) and others have explored the inadequate communication process that often takes place between physicians and their patients, but we are still at the beginning of a process of learning about the spiritual needs of formal caregivers. These spiritual needs may be complicated by conflicts between current professional norms about treatment and care of dying patients and personal views about death and dying.

In an involving narrative, Saranaik (2000) provides a poignant example of conflicts about how to handle the desire of parents to have their four-year-old child die at home. The conflict was not between the parents but between a medical student, the student's professor, and a nun who was providing counseling for the family. Terkel's (2001) collection of narratives about end of life provide examples of the strains faced by physicians, EMTs, and nurses who are involved with dying individuals, and how these individuals face the strains of often witnessing deaths of patients and individuals they are called upon to assist. In that same storytelling tradition, Ron's narrative illustrates the problems, the potential, and the power of end-of-life interventions.

REFERENCES

Dacre, H. (1892). *Daisy Bell (A Bicycle Built for Two)* (1892). TB Harms, Inc. (Warner Chappell Music, Los Angeles.) Public domain.

Dervin, B. (1977). Useful theory for librarianship: Communication not information. *Drexel Library Quarterly, 13,* 16–32.

Dervin, B., Harlock, S., Atwood, R., & Garzona, C. (1980). The human side of information: An exploration in a health communication context. In D. Nimmo (Ed.), *Communication yearbook 4* (pp. 591–608). New Brunswick, NJ: Transaction Books.

Faibisoff, S. G., & Ely, D. P. (1976). Information and information needs. *Information Reports and Bibliographies, 5,* 2–16.

Frank, A. W. (1995). *The wounded storyteller: Body, illness, and ethics.* Chicago: University of Chicago Press.

Koenig, H. (2000). The role of religion and spirituality at the end of life. *Gerontologist, 42,* 20–23.

Puchalski, C. (2002). Spirituality and end-of-life care: A time for listening and caring. *Journal of Palliative Medicine, 5,* 289–294.

Saranaik, A. (2000). A student, a nun and a professor. *Pediatric Critical Care Medicine, 1,* 176–178.

Steindl-Rast, D. (1990). *Gratefulness, the heart of prayer.* New York: Paulist Press.

Terkel, S. (2001). *Will the circle be unbroken: Reflections on death, rebirth, and hunger for a faith.* New York: New Press.

Tulsky, J. A., Fischer, L. S., Rose, M. A., & Arnold, R. M. (1998). Opening the black box: How do physicians communicate about advance directives? *Annals of Internal Medicine, 122,* 441–449.

CHAPTER 3

Stories of Ryan:
Too Little Time

Each second we live is a new and unique moment of the universe,
a moment that never was before and never will be again.

—Pablo Casals, *Salute to Life*

Ryan's Story
Kathleen L. Meert

Ryan was a typical 14-year-old, 9th-grade boy. The day before was much like any other. Ryan had gone to school, had run track in gym, and had relaxed shooting hoops in the driveway that afternoon. However, by evening, he had a headache. The next morning, he awoke feeling warm and nauseated. He showed his mother a bruise on his shin that appeared to be spreading. Ryan and his mother drove to the local ER in the family car. They arrived at the triage desk at 11:15 a.m. and were directed to an exam room. Ryan walked to the exam room but felt dizzy and decided to lie down. His condition deteriorated rapidly. His medical chart contained the following documentation:

11:20 a.m.: An IV was placed, blood tests were taken, and fluid and medications were given.

11:35 a.m.: A bladder catheter was inserted and bloody urine was obtained.

11:48 a.m.: Ryan's breathing was fast and labored.

11:55 a.m.: A breathing tube was inserted in Ryan's throat to help him breathe. More fluids and medications were given.

12:00 p.m.: A decision was made to transport Ryan to a children's hospital. A transport team and ambulance were called.

12:08 p.m.: Ryan's blood pressure was falling. The bruising had spread over his chest and forearms. He was difficult to arouse.

12:15 p.m.: A large IV was inserted in his groin.

12:22 p.m.: Ryan involuntarily emitted bloody stool.

12:45 p.m.: The team arrived to transport Ryan to the children's hospital.

1:15 p.m.: Ryan and the team were en route.

1:25 p.m.: In the ambulance, Ryan's heart stopped. The team began chest compressions that were continued for the rest of the trip—about one half-hour.

1:55 p.m.: Ryan arrives at the children's hospital. Resuscitative efforts continue in the trauma bay.

2:05 p.m.: Ryan's parents arrive at the children's hospital.

2:25 p.m.: Resuscitation was unsuccessful. Ryan was pronounced dead. Diagnosis—meningococcemia, a virulent blood infection.

Before the end, Ryan's parents waited in the Quiet Room to hear results of the efforts to save their son. They were raw and terrified. Physicians suited in accordance with Occupational Health and Safety Administration (OSHA) standards pulsed in and out asking a plethora of medical questions. Ryan's mother's face was red and tear-streaked as she answered question after question about her son's life and medical history. Ryan's father's face was taut with anguish; wide red rings surrounded his pale blue eyes. He anxiously tried to contact family members from the phone in the Quiet Room.

The doctor came into the Quiet Room, heavy with the grave news. She took off her face gear and gloves, embraced the eyes of Ryan's parents, and gently told them that Ryan was dead. Ryan's parents, throbbing, taut, on the precipice of knowing, heard her news. The surface tension of the room overflowed. Ryan's parents poured themselves into each other and spilled into every inch of the room. They were sobbing and holding, knowing and disbelieving.

A nurse prepared Ryan for viewing. Because of the infectious nature of his disease, all staff and family donned OSHA suits before going in to say goodbye. Ryan lay on the gurney, a tall, budding, gangly adolescent. He was his mother's child. He had blonde rumpled hair and large feet at the bottom of growing limbs. His knees were still scuffed from active play. He wore orthodontic braces. His teeth were almost in alignment.

Ryan was a promising, beautiful, basketball-playing, track-running teenager just starting to sprout a beard and to look for a girlfriend. He was the son, the hope, and the promise of his parents. Suddenly, he was dead.

The ER chaplain proceeded with prayers and ritual, arrangements, and information. At 4:40 p.m., Ryan's parents gathered the shattered fragments of their lives and went home. Their lives were changed forever.

Postscript

One year later, I spoke with the family. Ryan's parents have turned the tragedy of loss into a commitment to increase awareness of meningococcemia. They work with public policy groups to educate people about the disease and ways of coping with it.

Physical Response
John W. Finn

This story tells of the death of a child and the shock of sudden death in a medicalized context. The case has implications as widening ripples reach beyond immediate family members to close school contacts, the wider community, professional caregivers, and other families with similar losses.

Neisseria meningitidis is a bacterium that is often implicated in childhood *meningitis*, an infection of the lining tissues of the spinal cord and spinal fluid. Bacteria lodged in the nasal passages seed the bloodstream and quickly invade the meninges, joints, heart muscle, and elsewhere. Fulminant infections in the blood can be fatal within 24–48 hours, even before signs and symptoms of meningitis appear. The endotoxin of these bacteria in the bloodstream may damage blood vessels and alter the clotting system, causing bruising and bleeding, and may lead to circulatory collapse and sudden death in about 20% of patients. Fatal infections may be related to an inherited or acquired disorder of the clotting system.

Two-thirds of cases occur in the winter and spring months, often following an outbreak of Influenza A. The reason for an increased incidence among teenagers is unknown. Those who succumb quickly usually exhibit infection in the bloodstream without signs or symptoms of meningitis, circulatory collapse or coma, extensive bruising, bleeding, low white-blood-cell and platelet counts, or evidence of inflammation of the heart muscle.

A high index of suspicion for this infection leads to initial medical treatment before confirmation of the diagnosis is established by blood tests. Intravenous antibiotics are administered immediately, ideally upon transport, prior to arrival in the emergency department. Vital signs and respirations are supported with intravenous fluids, chemical agents to maintain blood pressure, transfusion blood products, oxygen, and ventilator machine, if necessary. Isolation masks, gowns, and procedures are a safeguard against infection spreading to health care workers and others. Patients who survive the infection may be left with temporary or permanent complications such as deafness, nerve palsies, mental retardation, and chronic inflammation of the joints, blood vessels, and heart.

From what is described, no fault can be assigned to Ryan's parents or medical providers. There are, however, serious questions remaining. Of concern is the experience of the parents subsequent to their child's death in the children's hospital emergency department. Details are provided regarding giving the bad news, dealing with their reactions, viewing the adolescent body, saying goodbye, and making final arrangements.

The reader is not provided with details of the manner in which Ryan's parents were informed as to his condition while yet in transport, upon arrival in the ER, or in the short time following. One can imagine the phone conversations, the waiting area outside the ER, the nearby conference room, and perhaps a hospital chapel. The parents would have repeatedly inquired about Ryan's condition of the receptionist, triage nurse, medical intern, resident, or the ER physician coming in and out of the waiting area. They certainly would have witnessed the frantic resuscitation efforts with supplies, a crash cart, anesthesia personnel, various technicians rushing in, and stat specimens being sent out. They would have heard shouted medical orders. They would have experienced compassionate presence and human touch—or the absence of it.

The very real possibility of their son's death was beginning to become apparent before their arrival at the hospital. They most likely hoped for the best, but prepared for the worst as they supported each other. By the time the physician spoke to them, their relationship was able to sustain the shock of the bad news. The described emotional response is understandable and appropriate. The reader is not informed of what exactly was said or how it was said and by whom. It is hoped that the chaplain was with them throughout the ordeal, and that the staff provided privacy.

What is missing is whether a postmortem examination was offered or performed. Were immediate family, as well as close school and neighborhood friends, counseled to take prophylactic antibiotics? Was community education provided regarding signs and symptoms of *N. meningitidis* infection? Did the family avail themselves of grief counseling? Was counseling offered to Ryan's schoolmates?

The postscript to the story indicates that Ryan's parents found meaning in his death through their mission to increase awareness of *N. meningitidis* infections. Still, they clearly lost part of their future. Physicians and other health care providers are experts in the physical diagnosis and treatment of emergency conditions such as Ryan's. However, the sudden death of a child presents challenges that exceed the knowledge and experience of many providers. It is often not clear in a case such as this who is or should be available to provide solace in the loss of a child, the loss of a significant part of themselves.

Although the long-term social and psychological implications of such a tremendous loss are not emphasized in medical education, physicians must be aware that grief may be intensified on certain dates such as birthdays, holidays, or when the child's friends graduate from high school or get married. Even though the initial shock of his death may have lessened, coping with events such as these would clearly be difficult for Ryan's parents and would require courage and fortitude.

Spiritual Response
Elizabeth E. Chapleski

A death is not a death is not a death. For the most part, attention and practice in end of life are focused on those with terminal, life-threatening diseases and the very old. Considering the small percentage of sudden deaths, people expect there to be stages of death and a prepared readiness for that ultimate journey (Lunney, Fynn, Foley, Lipson, & Gurainik, 2003).

This is not so for Ryan and his family. His death is unexpected, abrupt, shocking, off-time. He is shooting baskets one day and laid in one the next. Ryan's parents had no warning, no opportunity to prepare. Among children aged 5 to 14, only 0.2 deaths occur per 1,000 (Stillion & Papadatou, 2002), and perhaps half of those occur with no warning. In violent or unexpected death, health care professionals' concern is with the *secondary victims*—the siblings, the parents, the extended family and friends, and the surrounding community. The ER chaplain appears to be the first person, aside from the doctors, to provide support. We don't know if the parents wanted the chaplain to pray and perform rituals but good practice says the chaplin asked first. The family may have wished to be counseled by their own minister or priest, but it is not clear here whether they even have one.

It is also not evident what kinds of social support were available to them. The chaplain, similar to a social worker, might conduct an informal, simple social and spiritual assessment to assist with grief counseling. This family may have follow-up counseling, but it is not evident whether it was available through the hospital, because of the short time they were involved with the hospital services. The situation would be different if Ryan had been a patient at a hospice, where follow-up counseling is part of hospice services. It is critical that these families who have undergone such trauma receive similar help and do not fall through the cracks of the medical system.

It is hoped that Ryan's family was informed of peer support groups for parents who have lost children to sudden deaths. Often the most helpful comfort and guidance comes from those who have experienced similar losses. For many who are facing or have faced end of life themselves or with a loved one, faith and spirituality offer some sense of peace and inner calm and can deepen the meaning of life. However, no timetable can be placed on the length or nature of grief. This family has experienced a sudden, traumatic death and will need to grieve in their own way, in their own time.

There is no hint of what followed. How did this family cope? Lessons from grief therapy suggest that there are universal tasks that must be performed in grief work: accepting the reality of the death, experiencing the pain of the loss, adapting to a world in which the deceased no longer lives, and redistributing emotional energy to new relationships (Neimeyer, 2003; Worden, 1983). The inflexibility of the term *tasks* implies that each is necessary to healing and the growth of meaning.

This family may find it difficult to find meaning in their suffering. As Viktor Frankl (1984) reflected on his Holocaust experience, "If there is a purpose in life at all, there must be a purpose in suffering and in dying . . . each must find that purpose for himself. If he succeeds he will continue to grow in spite of all indignities" (preface, p. 9). This search for meaning is the essence of spirituality. For many, being part of a religious community provides spiritual sustenance through cultural (religious) rituals of a mass, shivah, or memorial service that "affirms shared bonds while recognizing changed statuses for those most intimately affected by the loss" (Neimeyer, Prigerson, & Davies, 2002). Grief is both a natural and a constructed event and survivors struggle to integrate their loss into their existing self-narratives. "Deaths that violate the natural order (as in this case) pose additional challenges to the survivor's adaptation" (Neimeyer et al.).

Ultimately, the framing of grief and the development of meaning is the families' prerogative and challenge. Kubler-Ross and Kessler (2000) advise that "grief is always individualized and as long as we are moving through life and have not become stuck, we are healing" (p. 5). Therefore, in whatever way this family was able to cope with their loss, we are glad that they have been able to find some meaning in their suffering.

Narrative Response
Richard Raspa

This story reveals what narrative can do more potently than any other idiom of communication: render in language what Jerome

Bruner (2002) calls "peripeteia," or the reversal of expectation. The three-part structure of this story moves with the inexorable cadence of fate. The narrative owes its crushing impact to the tension between banal expectation and incomprehensible result. Part 1 represents the ordinary, taken-for-granted flow of everyday life. Part 2 chronicles the high pitch of an emergency medical intervention. Part 3 dramatizes the horror of reversal, the pain of helplessness, the death of a child, and the encounter with an inscrutable terror beyond the range of human control. In these contrasting structures, the narrative allows the reader to consider the range of possible responses to unexpected death. It is a process that Bruner calls "subjunctivizing experience" (p. 93). The subjunctive mode of discourse is contrary to fact, one in which alternative possibilities of thinking and acting can be tried. It permits people to address the question: "What if . . . ?"

In Part 1, Ryan did the things that are regarded as normal and healthy by American society: went to school, ran track in the gym, and shot hoops after school. Even the grammatical structure is normal: subject predicate, subject predicate, and so on, in a series of assertions in the indicative mode, as if the world were knowable and predictable. Nothing unusual occurs, not even Ryan's headache that develops. It would be reasonable for Ryan's parents to expect that the headache would be gone in the morning. Perhaps Ryan picked up a little flu bug, but he would get over it. In the past, he always had. This case has the aura of a Flannery O'Connor short story. The innocuous clichés by which people interpret and routinize the world such as in *A Good Man Is Hard to Find* (1955), transmute into the grotesque. In O'Connor's title story, killers invade the life of an ordinary rural family caught up in the routine of everyday life, a routine that suppresses the dreadful, the deviant, and the chaotic. In O'Connor's fictive universe, the repetitive qualities of social life are lulling disguises that are shown to be illusory. Ordinary situations become lethal and good country people are mutilated. There are no longer safe zones for people to inhabit.

The fiction of Flannery O'Connor evokes an unfathomable world by dramatizing the connection between the ordinary and the grotesque. Both the story and the case of Ryan are structured by the quality of peripeteia. Both narratives stun the reader with the twists and turns of the common flow of experience into the tragic idiom. That which is hidden and horrifying is exposed as constitutive of everyday life. Unpredictable and unsafe, life is not controllable. In Part 1 of the case, for instance, an ordinary headache sends Ryan to bed early. The next morning anxiety shows up in the obscure bruise on his shin that appears to be spreading. Then, quickly, as the disease progresses, Part 2 begins. The narrator shifts into the clinical mode, anatomizing the disease with the countdown. The clock moves in increments of roughly 10 or 15 minutes, and with every interval, a major organ begins to break down: Labored breathing at 11:48 is followed by falling blood pressure and the advance of bruising over chest and forearms at 12:08; the heart stops at 1:25. Despite the intervention of sophisticated technology—breathing tube, bladder catheter, and medications—nothing stops the blood disease's relentless pursuit of the boy's life.

In the 21st century, the trajectory of Ryan's sickness is incomprehensible. It is as if the boy is gripped by a force from an earlier epoch, one that did not have the benefits of miracle drugs and biomedicine. Terror stalks this medical chronicle, like the personifications of death in medieval frescoes throughout Europe. The speed of the disease has the quality of the bubonic plague that killed one-third of Europe—20 million people—during the 14th century. So virulent was the epidemic that it came to be called *The Black Death* and became a metaphor for mortality. In the 21st century, seven centuries later, it is still known as The Black Death. In the 14th century, no one knew the plague's cause or its treatment. Only later did research reveal that the disease was carried by rat fleas and infected bodily fluids. Today in small Alpine villages, one can see frescoes from the late Middle Ages depicting people during the bubonic plague using a scythe to drag the body of a child across a field to a common burial site. Here ordinary categories of human experience are reversed. Touching—an expression of affection—becomes the kiss of death.

Just as medieval peasants used the scythe as a shield, the OSHA suits that the parents must don to shelter themselves from contamination by their dead son extends the aura of tragedy. Parents look like space travelers coming from another planet to observe their son laid out on a gurney. Even in this moment of loss, parents cannot embrace their child.

Ryan's story is a tragedy. It discloses the fundamental existential terror that lingers beneath the surface of rationality: namely, that human beings are small, helpless creatures who live in an absurd universe, without divine intelligence, where we can be swallowed up capriciously by natural forces that will resist our most efficacious drugs and our most technically sophisticated interventions. Humanity's original dread is that we live in a world without meaning.

The disease takes its toll. The beginning and ending prose narratives, which frame the clinical document, evoke the impotence of medical technology in the face of a scathing disease that overwhelms doctors, parents, and, ultimately, the adolescent boy. This disease has ruptured life categories and coherent social arrangements. Ryan's family is crushed by the death of their child.

"What if," the narrator invites us to ponder, this happened to you? What are the possibilities for surviving this? Would you be able to resume your life? The narrative is distressing. The grief that fills the hospital room, the lives of parents and health care workers is so profound and encompassing, as they "poured themselves into each other and spilled into every inch of the room." The pain feels as though it will last forever. Everyone is devastated. What the narrator leaves the reader with are lost possibilities: "Ryan was a promising, beautiful, basketball-playing, track-running teenager just starting to sprout a beard and to look for a girlfriend. He was the son, the hope, and the promise of his parents." There are no words to lighten the pain. Even the ER chaplain seems to go through the motions of funereal prayer and ritual. No human action appears adequate in such a universe, with so profound a loss of potential, with the end of so young a life. Parents are left in fragments. Their lives will be altered forever.

REFERENCES

Bruner, J. (2002). *Making stories: Law, literature, life.* Cambridge, MA: Harvard University Press.

Frankl, V. (1984). *Man's search for meaning.* New York: Simon and Schuster.

Kubler-Ross, E., & Kessler, D. (2000). *Life lessons.* New York: Simon and Schuster.

Lunney, J., Fynn, J., Foley, D., Lipson, S., & Guralnic, M. (2003). Patterns of functional decline at end-of-life. *Journal of the American Medical Association, 289,* 2387–2392.

Neimeyer, R. A. (2003). *Conversations at end of life*. A pre-conference workshop presented at the Annual Meeting of the Gerontology Society of America, San Diego, November 21–25, 2003.

Neimeyer, R., Prigerson, H., & Davies, B. (2002). Mourning and meaning. *American Behavioral Scientist, 46,* 235–251.

O'Connor, F. (1955). *A good man is hard to find and other stories*. New York: Harcourt Brace.

Stillion, J. M., & Papadatou, D. (2002). Suffer the children. *American Behavioral Scientist, 46,* 299–315.

Worden, J. W. (1983). *Grief counseling and grief therapy*. London: Tavistock.

CHAPTER 4

Stories of Abby:
An Ojibwa Journey

Speak to the earth and it shall teach thee.

—Job 12:8

Abby's Story
Elizabeth E. Chapleski

This is the story of a death in a nursing home across the Canadian border, the death of a 76-year-old Ojibwa woman named Abby. The story was told to me by Abby's daughter Mary, a nurse who administers a Native American health clinic. I have known Mary for more than 15 years through my research with Native American elders and as a member of the governing board of the health clinic. I am honored that Mary entrusted me with this story so close to her heart and overflowing with Ojibwa traditions.

Abby gave birth to 18 children, and 13 were still living at the time of their mother's death. Although Abby had been living independently for many years following her diagnosis of Alzheimer's disease 5 years earlier, essentially, Mary had cared for Abby. As her disease progressed, Abby became increasingly in need of 24-hour care and was eventually placed in a skilled nursing facility located near this daughter. Mary visited her daily and brought her home on weekends and holidays. Mary explained her mother's dementia as "being in another place," perhaps "another dimension that we can't understand." She talked about how the family visited frequently and often "argued about Mama's care—even in Mama's presence."

During her last two weeks, Abby had refused most of her food and become increasingly unresponsive. The family wanted her to receive IV feeding and oxygen, believing it would relieve her suffering. Mary, on the other hand, believed that her mother, the dying person, knew what she needed and what was best for her. Mary noted that "our efforts to relieve pain and suffering are based on our needs, not the patients' wishes." Also, Mary wanted to help her mother pass on in the "Indian" way: naturally, "taking cues from the universe, the earth," as well as from the dying person, and really listening, often to nonverbal, subtle communications.

As Abby's condition worsened, the family arguments increased, especially around issues of advance directives. Although no one in the family wanted Mother to suffer unnecessarily, Mary's perspective lay in opposition to the rest of the family's. Mary believed that the "universe was telling them" of their mother's imminent death. She was convinced that although her mother appeared to be comatose, or at best semiconscious, her ability to hear or understand at a deeper level should be respected. "I was the tool, spiritually," Mary reported.

> I was submerged in the process of her passage in a way the others weren't. The subtleness of the earth and its constellation tuned me in to the timing of when her passage was going to be. I was listening to many layers of understanding—I watched the flowers change, the constellations visible in the night sky, and the full moon was coming. I knew then the time was close.

She was alone in her views, however; her family believed in the modern medical system whereas she wanted her mother to die an "Indian." This desire stemmed in part from Mary's knowledge that so much had been taken from her mother during her life, especially at "Indian Boarding School." These residential schools, often under the auspice of the Catholic Church, were the Canadian government's solution to the "Indian problem." These schools were assimilation efforts designed to remove all vestiges of the indigenous culture: language, religious and spiritual beliefs, dress, ceremonies, and even ties to family and clan.

Mary's comment about the physicians' and nurses' willingness to allow the traditional treatment was that "it didn't really matter to them—in Canada it was just another Indian dying . . . but that was okay, it made my work easier."

The day came when Mary, after observing the earth and sky and her mother, informed the family that Mama had only a few days to live. Mary requested that Mama-nan be placed in a private room so that the family could prepare her for her final journey. The move was approved, and the family spent those last few days preparing. The room was cleansed with sweet grass and sage. Abby was washed down with cedar and tobacco was offered. Mary cradled her mother in her arms as her culture had taught, singing and speaking to her in the native language. She explained that her family was disturbed by the agitation and stress the physical body often exhibits as organs fail and life wanes. Mary said, "The family thought Mama was in pain and wanted to sedate her—they were 98% against me." But Mary was firm and persevered.

As time went on, Mary's physical and spiritual presence seemed to permeate the room, calming her mother and finally her family. This process of *moving into another's reality* seemed to make Abby's passing as joyful as the passage into life at birth. Not without stress, as in the birth passage, yet meaningful. Mama-nan had given life to Mary and the others many years before this day, and now Mary "accompanied" her mother to the brink of this final journey. Abby was not alone. Everyone there at the time of crossing-over experienced a deeply spiritual phenomenon. The nurses were allowed to observe the process and remarked on how peaceful Abby looked after she breathed her last breath.

Mary continued,

> biidaabin—a time in the morning when night shifts to day—is a very powerful, meaningful time for passage. That is when my mother passed. I left the room to observe my mother's spirit travel on her journey. . . . The sky was remarkably clear, the Milky Way brilliant beyond belief. I never saw the Milky Way like that, not like that . . . that's how I know it was her choice to go then. Everything, all the physical signs equaled the rightness of it. I was just the facilitator—I removed the barriers, so things could happen naturally.

Mary had visions of the deer taking Mama-nan to the brink, and the white horse met her and rode with her to the "next place." Mary felt she had taken one step into that space and was allowed to feel its beauty and peace. She was honored:

All these things are a part of American Indian belief—the deer opening the garden path, the Milky Way as the path, the white horse or *thunder being* who accompanies the person to the spirit world. Mama's traveling box had been carved out of pine, with all her clan and her children symbolized on the box.

The family had studied Basil Johnston's (1976) work on Indian hieroglyphics, seeking to design this box in the old, old way, when Indians put ghost boxes over the graves. Abby was clothed in a new dress made by Mary, and laid on a quilt also made by Mary, with new moccasins for traveling, and a satchel bag over her heart filled with special symbols of Indian life.

Everything was researched and had deep spiritual meaning. I really prepared . . . [I] wanted her to have what she deserved as an Indian woman, so I researched the teachings of the Anishnabe, the Ojibwa.

I believe in my heart our mother couldn't have chosen a more profound time to pass over—it was an incredible gift for me. It was her choice, her timing, and she continued to teach us . . . it had nothing to do with me. It was all about my mom, the spirit world and the unveiling of those things. I was left with a feeling that I had stepped for a moment into 'that' world . . . it was so profound. I thank her for allowing me to experience that. . . . It has given me insight into the living and palliative care. It made me even more sensitive. My mother taught me more about nursing than I learned in nursing school.

Cultural Response
Ardith Z. Doorenbos

In its broadest sense, culture refers to the world view, values, norms, and behavioral guidelines shared by a group of individuals (Leininger, 1991). Culture is the framework that members of a society use to view, understand, behave, and pass on information to each succeeding generation. Traditionally, the word *culture* is associated with a specific ethnic group; however, it also can be applied to a specific religious group, and in many cases it encompasses both.

For Abby, being a member of the First Nations defined both her ethnicity and her spirituality. The region Abby and her family inhabited is the Upper Great Lakes area (in Wisconsin, Michigan, and Ontario, Canada), where the Anishnabe (the indigenous people of the Ojibwa, Ottawa, and Potawatomi tribes) live. State or national borders did not always recognize tribal boundaries. However, as Canada and the United States are nations in which people from a variety of countries and traditions coexist, their histories as related to this story are similar. Beginning in the 1800s and lasting well into the 1900s, both nations desired to create unified cultures. To promote these social policies, First Nations children such as Abby were sent to boarding schools to force assimilation. Such policies were later abandoned. Instead, there have been policy shifts toward a greater appreciation for the value of diversity within these nations. A devastating consequence of these prior policies was the loss of the widespread knowledge of many these groups' own traditional practices. As Jackson and Chapleski (2000) note, however,

> Some American Indians have managed to retain certain features of their traditional culture *in addition to* (rather than instead of) having adopted those of the American mainstream, and it is these people who might reasonably be considered more traditional, relatively speaking, than those who retain no such traits of Native American culture. (p. 233)

Even within individual families, there is variation in the amount of interest in reclaiming lost traditions. Mary, Abby's daughter, finds herself alone within her family in embracing their native Ojibwa practices.

A prominent feature of indigenous culture (Jackson & Chapleski, 2000) that Abby's family seems to share is respect for elders; disagreement grew out of how this respect might best be shown. Abby's children, whose ages span 30 years, may have experienced different acculturation pressures throughout their lives and represent it in varying degrees. Nevertheless, the family disagreements about Abby's treatment did not inhibit Mary from persisting in her research of the "old ways" and preparing so that Mamanan could pass naturally into the spirit world. In Mary's view, her mother had suffered great indignities as a First Nations woman in an alien culture, and her passing should restore the respect that she had always deserved but never received. Abby's story exemplifies Williams' and Ellison's (1996) claim that American

Indians have historically believed that the loss of freedom to express themselves in traditional ways is an undeserved oppression.

The story illustrates how Abby's final days began in an environment of competing agendas—of Mary, of her family, and of the nursing home staff. In Abby's story, there were varying levels of interest in her having a traditional Ojibwa death. For Mary, preparing Mama-nan for her final journey in the "old-old way" was critically important. After initial resistance, the rest of the family came together and participated in this ritual. At first, the nursing home staff responded passively when the request was made to perform these rituals. They did not put up barriers because holding the rituals did not interfere with their daily routines. Yet, when the nursing staff experienced the power and beauty of Abby's death, they were profoundly moved. One could hope that positive experiences of this kind would encourage health providers to be more open to a diversity of approaches to dying.

Narrative Response
Richard Raspa

Narrative shapes human life. The stories people tell, the tales they believe in, become their reality. The story of Abby is a web of narratives that catches in its strands the contesting realities of First Nations naturalistic medicine and Western biomedical practices.

The narrator is Abby's daughter Mary, a nurse who manages a Native American health clinic. Mary is an educated specialist in Western medicine. At the same time, she reveres her own native Ojibwa traditions. Her story documents not only her mother Abby's transition from life to death, but also Mary's own transition from a Western nurse to a First Nations healer. These opposing models of health care are dramatically woven through the tapestry of the story.

At the beginning, Mary refers to her mother's dementia as "being in another place," an Ojibwa concept that contrasts with the biomedical labeling of Abby's condition as pathological. Mary's category of *place* neutralizes the negative assessment of the word *Alzheimer's*. It is simply another psychic space to which human beings can go, although neither inferior nor privileged in relation to other places. The place metaphor reveals the limits of our understanding rather than measuring the deviance of Abby's condition. Here, the deeper implication that health involves a relationship to sickness, rather than a dichotomous separation, is drawn. For Mary, everything in the universe is connected: sickness and health, past and present, life and death, humanity and nature, self and other. Mary chooses to appropriate her Ojibwa traditional knowledge to assist her mother in making the transition from life into death. The experience is primarily spiritual rather than biomedical. Someone is, indeed, dying; but something continues as well, beyond death and into the spirit world.

Mary researched the traditions of the Ojibwa. She learned these traditions not the native way through oral transmission but through the modern technology of books, which reconfigured original tribal knowledge into the Western idiom of literacy. Mary's mother Abby may have forgotten, or more likely had never known, the sacred traditions of her people through her training at residential schools and could not pass them on to her children. The Canadian government regarded Abby as part of the problem— the "Indian problem"—that could be fixed through indigenous cultural erasure. In this story, Mary becomes the postmodern tradition bearer, straddling the chasm between opposing systems of meaning, teaching the family, and administering palliative care to the mother.

Mary reads the universe as text, a system of signs to be deciphered. She "watched the flowers change, the constellations visible in the night, and the full moon," and endows these natural phenomena with meaning. Nature speaks to Mary's shamanistic listening; it tells her Abby is about to die. In the old ways of the Ojibwa, nature talks. Everything in the universe pulsates with life and responds to everything else. In contrast to the IV feeding and drug interventions the family wanted for Abby, Mary takes "cues from the universe, the earth," and the dying person. Mary "was listening to many layers of understanding," and she knows when her mother is about to die. Like a healer performing a divination rite, she informs the family of Abby's pending death. In the end, the family concedes to Mary's acting as traditional healer. They clean the room with "sweet grass and sage" and wash Abby with cedar. As healer, Mary becomes the mother figure, cradling her "child" in her arms, singing and speaking to her in her native language, comforting her on the journey to the spirit world. Mary is swept into the enactment of the tradition so completely that she has "visions of the deer taking Mama-nan to the brink, and the white horse met her and rode with her to the next place."

Abby's transition becomes an event of singular beauty. Everyone is moved, the narrator says. Even the health care professionals are observers of the transition. Mary says her mother's death was a gift that lent insight into the nature of living: "My mother taught me more about nursing than I learned in nursing school." Death was not a thief, sneaking in the middle of the night and robbing life from an unwilling victim. Death was a gift that provided insight into the nature of living. Mary learned that death and life make up the threads that continue through eternity. Mary's transition from biomedical caregiver to native healer has given her a glimpse into the world of her indigenous forebears.

The sacred texts of the past expanded Mary's world of health care and provided healing for the whole family. In returning to the old stories of dying, Mary is a catalyst for the healing of the family. Abby is restored to wholeness, returned to her native values now blessed by family and Western professionals as they watch the rituals of death. Abby's family is brought together as they participate in their traditional heritage, and Mary integrates the powerful Ojibwa story of how to die into her professional life as a health practitioner in North American society. The end of her life has transformed those whom Abby has left behind, as new beginnings are made and new futures awakened.

Provider Response
Robi Thomas

I am writing about Abby's story from my perspective as an oncology nurse. The story of Abby and her death is remarkable in many ways. Mary's devotion to her mother was wonderful, and her insight into the manner in which she wanted her mother's life to end was poignant. Because nurses are educated to care for the entire family, not just the patient, this is the story of Mary as well as Abby.

Alzheimer's disease is cruel, slowly robbing a person—and loved ones—of the mind and often spirit. Typically, it evolves over years, as in Abby's story. In the best-case scenario, after diagnosis the patient and family can discuss end-of-life issues and hope to avoid the conflict that Mary and her siblings experience. Abby was eventually placed in a skilled nursing care facility; physicians are typically on staff at these facilities, which makes one wonder what the role of the physician was in Abby's case. In my view, good care should have involved a health care provider-facilitated discussion about how Abby would die and allowed Abby to provide input about the end of her life while she was still able to make these decisions.

Mary, as the main caregiver for her mother, appears to have spent the most time with Abby, at least in the latter years of Abby's life. It is reasonable to assume that Mary and Abby talked about important issues during that time, but the communication patterns of the family prior to Abby's illness are not known to us. It seems that Mary came to understand Abby well during this time, suggesting that Mary is speaking and acting according to her mother's own wishes.

Mary's sensitivity to nature and her surroundings is important. Her awareness of the earth provided her not only with information she needed for her mother, but also with some peace and guidance in her own life; not only was Mary needing to prepare her mother for death, she was also needing to prepare herself for life without her mother. Allowing her mother to die in the manner that Mary felt Abby wanted can be seen as Mary's final gift to her mother.

The conflicts in situations such as those between Mary and her siblings, unfortunately, are not unusual. Often, family members experience conflict about end-of-life decisions, and, as in Abby's story, these conflicts can occur within sight or hearing of the patient. Many health care practitioners believe that the sense of hearing is the last sense to leave when someone is dying, and it is important for family and friends to be made aware of this. Ideally, it would have been much more pleasant for Abby's family to tell her how much they loved her in those last days, rather than arguing about how her life should end within her presence.

Mary's love for her mother and her physical closeness as her mother died were powerful factors in Abby's passing. There is nothing more comforting than to know that family will be with you when you die, and in that respect, we should be glad Abby did not die alone. The narrator recounts how Mary's calming presence filled the room and seemed to reduce the stress. The text, however, is silent about other family members. Did they feel comfortable in the room? Did they feel the spiritual power that

Mary did? Did they feel any connection with their mother's passing spirit?

The nurses who entered the room as Abby was dying were moved by the peacefulness that permeated the room. It is hoped that the nurses were offering their support not only to Abby, to make sure she was not uncomfortable, but to the family members as well, again, caring not only for the person who is in their immediate charge, but for the family members. The facility should be applauded for allowing the family to prepare for Abby's death in the manner they requested, rather than in the conventional, often sterile, manner associated with health care facilities.

There remains a concern regarding the role the nurses played during the family's conflict over whether to sedate Abby to try to manage her pain or to keep her sedative-free. Abby's nurse could have been available to the family to answer their questions and address their concerns, for the concerns that Mary's siblings had seem valid. It is difficult to know how a patient who is unresponsive is feeling, and this situation warrants attention and information intervention from health care professionals.

It is also important for the nurses, knowing that Mary was a nurse, to remain aware that in this particular situation Mary filled the role of the daughter of a dying woman, *not* that of a nurse. Often, it is assumed that health care professionals are able to act professionally at all times; yet when they are placed in a familial situation—particularly in stressful situations such as Mary's—they are not acting as health care workers, but as family members. Far from being Mary's role, it was the responsibility of the nurses and physicians to educate the family about what was happening to Abby. Because the dying experience is a powerful one for the narrator and the nurses, it would be useful to expand the educational curriculum of health professionals to include learning about how death and dying are experienced culturally.

Informational Response
Lynda M. Baker

As a former nurse, I have witnessed the deaths of many persons. In some cases, the family was present as their loved one took her or his final breath. Other deaths were stormy because the relatives displayed their annoyance at the inconvenience of death, were anxious for the person to die, or were fighting among themselves. I found one death particularly difficult because the patient was an elderly gentleman with whom I had become friends. Despite his very deformed, arthritic joints, he managed to write a poem for me. At his death, I was the only one in the room who mourned his passing. While the family struggled to pull the gold jewelry from his hands, I cried. The beauty of Abby's final journey brought back the contrasting memory of his difficult death.

The role of information in Abby's story is both dramatic and subtle. It is dramatic because the story emphasizes, or rather shouts about, the importance of culturally sensitive material. The information needed in this story relates to the First Nations way of dying. The role that information plays is subtle as it is revealed through brief comments about the family arguments and the health care professionals' attitudes toward "just another Indian dying."

The story of Abby's journey from her diagnosis of Alzheimer's disease to her passage to the other world is really Mary's story of how she ensured that Abby would die in the "traditional Indian way." The family's belief in the ways of the "modern medical system" begs the question of Abby's wishes and information needs. Did she want to follow her aboriginal tradition, or was tradition more important to Mary, who worked in an American Indian health clinic? The arguments with the family, who also visited frequently, suggest that they had different opinions about Abby's wishes. Mary does not address these issues, so the reader can only assume that she, as the predominant caretaker, was acting in accordance with her mother's wishes. Some evidence for this supposition is found in Mary's statement that she believed "that her mother, the dying person, knew what she needed and what was best for her."

The information needs of the family were quite varied. They talked about the use of oxygen and IV therapy in relieving suffering and about advance directives. Did they get this information from health professionals, from Mary (a nurse) or other relatives, or from print or electronic sources (e.g., the Internet)? The reader can assume that the family received more information about these options from the physicians and nursing staff than from Mary for two reasons. First, their mother was in a skilled nursing facility, so the family had access to health care professionals who may have talked about the need for oxygen and water to relieve pain and suffering. Mary, on the other hand, would not have offered these suggestions because of her belief that she "was submerged in the process of her [mother's] passage in a way the others weren't" and that "our efforts to relieve pain and suffering are based on our needs, not the patients' wishes." I wonder what information Mary *did* provide to her siblings to encourage them to change their views from the biomedical system to the aboriginal way of dying. According to Mary she was successful because the family came together when "Mama had only a few days to live" to prepare Abby for her final journey.

One other issue that relates to the family and Abby concerns the conversations or arguments the family enacted in Abby's presence, without their realizing that hearing is the last sense to go. As a nurse, Mary would know this information, but why did the family not know? Did the health care professionals mention this important information to the family? It appears that the family may not have obtained or internalized this information; otherwise, these caring individuals might not have argued with each other in their mother's presence.

The crux of this story lies in Mary's information needs and how she gathered and used information. One strong influence on Mary's decision to help her mother "die an Indian" must have been earlier communication between these two about the latter's treatment in boarding school. Knowing how the church and the government worked to divest aboriginal children of their Ojibwa culture, Mary worked hard to ensure that her mother's final journey would be in accordance with traditional cultural death rituals.

Mary took informational cues from her mother, nature, and the cultural materials that she researched. She explained that she listened to the "nonverbal, subtle communication" from the "the universe, the earth" and from "the dying person." Although she is an Ojibwa of the younger generation, Mary seems to have learned how to listen to and gather information from the flowers, the moon, the constellations, and the earth. Her training in information acquisition allowed her to surmise when her mother would die. This training also provided her and her siblings with the information they needed to request a private room and prepare it for Abby's final passage. By singing and speaking to Abby in her native language, Mary was able to help her mother relax. When

Abby died, her family "experiences a deeply moving phenomenon," which Mary describes to the reader as being able to accompany her mother "to the brink of this final journey."

Mary's description of her mother's passage is filled with information that may be relevant to the experiences of other First Nations people who are trying to learn more about cultural traditions that they were not allowed to practice during the boarding school era. Although people of other ethnic origins certainly can appreciate Mary's beautiful description of Abby's death, they may not be able to gain as much solace from it as Mary did. It was highly meaningful for Mary because she was able to regain some formerly suppressed cultural practices. Mary's ability to accompany her mother "for a moment into 'that' world" provided Mary with the comfort of knowing that her mother's journey was progressing naturally according to tradition. How fortunate Mary was to have that experience!

Mary, and ultimately her siblings, wanted Abby to leave the world in "an Indian way." Therefore, to design Abby's traveling box and prepare her according to the teachings of the Anishnabe, the Ojibwa, they consulted Basil Johnston's (1976) book, *Ojibwa Heritage*.

In this story, information came from a variety of sources, including past knowledge about their mother's life and their aboriginal culture, intuition, verbal and nonverbal communication, and books. It is a story truly rich in the value of information.

REFERENCES

Jackson, D. D., & Chapleski, E. E. (2000). Not traditional, not assimilated: Elderly American Indians and the notion of cohort. *Journal of Cross Cultural Gerontology, 15*, 229–259.

Johnston, B. (1976). *Ojibwa heritage*. Toronto, ONT: McClelland & Stewart.

Leininger, M. M. (1991). *Culture care diversity and universality: A theory of nursing*. New York: National League for Nursing Press.

Williams, E. E., & Ellison, F. (1996). Culturally informed social work practice with American Indian clients: Guidelines for non-Indian social workers. *Social Work, 41*, 147–151.

CHAPTER 5

Stories of Grace:
Gifts and Givers

The spirit in which a thing is given determines that in which
the debt is acknowledged; it's the intention, not the face-value
of the gift, that's weighed.

—Seneca, *Letters to Lucilius*

Grace's Story
Dorothy E. Deremo and Kathleen L. Meert

One of the joys I have in being the president and Chief Executive
Officer (CEO) of a large hospice organization is the opportunity
to visit our many satellite offices across the state. Although our
headquarters are located in a large city, many of our smaller offices
are located in suburban and rural areas. As CEO, flying at 30,000
feet above our organization, I spend much of my time worrying
about resources, about begging for bucks, and about trying to
position our organization for survival in the rapidly changing health
care environment.

As anyone in such a position will attest, it is easy to forget in
the frenetic day-to-day activities of running an organization why
you wanted to do this work in the first place. My visits to staff,
volunteers, and patients in our various offices always remind me
of our true mission. Many hospice workers speak eloquently of
the great privilege of being allowed into patient and family lives
at a most personal time. Whenever I can make visits with team
members I am privileged to witness the profound work that our

staff does every day. I always return to the executive office after such visits enriched and with renewed energy for the challenges of hospice administration for the nearly 1,000 patients and families we serve annually. It was on one outreach visit to a rural hospice team that I made a house call with a social worker and received the gift of Grace.

The way in which Grace and I crossed paths is one of those serendipitous gifts with which life surprises you. While driving to meet Grace, the social worker and I passed through the rural midwestern terrain dotted with inland lakes nestled between steep hills and flatlands covered in forest. Clearings of rugged rural farms were carved out of the forest, leaving splashes of gold scattered amongst a verdant palate of greens.

When I first met Grace, she was sitting at the top of a hill with her face tilted into the wind, catching the warm early summer sun and breathing the pine-fragrant air. Summer comes late to the upper midwest, making the warmth even more precious. She was sitting on a folding chair with a book resting in her lap. I was struck by how young and fragile she looked with the pirate-like black patch on her left eye creating a bitter gash across her angelic face.

Grace was 30 years old, and had an inoperable brain tumor. She had come home from California to be with her parents to die. Grace's parents, in their early 60s, came to the North Country to live their dream retirement. They had pulled together their modest pensions from a lifetime of hard work to buy this small farm cradled in the back woods. Grace's father, Joe, a great woodworker, had built the studio he had always imagined. Grace's mother, Sarah, an avid gardener, had planted large flower and vegetable gardens. Joe and Sarah's retirement dream never included the nightmare of caring for their dying daughter and her young children. When Grace returned home, she brought her 5-year-old daughter Amanda and 9-month-old son Todd. Grace had no medical insurance and was not eligible for Medicaid because she had not been a state resident.

As Grace, the social worker, and I walked down the hill toward the house, I thought of the overwhelming emotional trauma thrust on this young woman and her family. Even as we settled on the porch to enjoy the sun with Joe, Sarah, Amanda, and Todd, the conversation began to turn to somber matters. Joe soon excused himself to retreat to his woodworking studio with Todd bouncing on his back at each departing step. Amanda gave her mother a quick hug and kisses and ran to catch the school bus for afternoon kindergarten. Sarah and the social worker went inside to the living room to complete some paperwork. As her loved ones scattered like petals from a wilting flower on the wind, Grace looked at me, took my hand, and said, "It's a lot to leave behind."

My heart broke for her. I could do nothing but hold her hand and listen, bearing witness to her life and courage. Grace looked at me with a single tear from her unpatched eye coursing down that beautiful face and said, "I don't know what we would have done without you." Grace told me how hospice was helping her take care of unfinished business so that she would be able to leave this world with peace in her heart. Grace shared that the father of her children had been abusive, and she was fearful that he might gain custody after her death. Hospice was assisting her with free legal aid to ensure that custody of her children would go to her parents.

Grace expressed gratitude for the provision of medications to treat her swelling, seizures, and pain. Her goal was to stay alert for as long as possible so that she could take care of all of her unfinished business. Grace said that our staff was helping her to write letters to her children for important future milestones in their lives—the first boyfriend or girlfriend, prom, graduation, marriage, and the birth of their first children. She wanted them to know that she would love them always. The team was also helping Grace complete a videotape so that her children would have a visual treasure to hold onto far into the future.

Grace told me what a comfort it was to her to know that we would still be caring for her family during their time of mourning. She worried about her elderly parents taking on young children. She worried about how her children would adjust to their loss. The knowledge that our counselors would provide bereavement support gave her great solace.

Grace's gift was to re-anchor me to the profound mission of hospice. Her matter-of-fact courage to face her own mortality and take care of unfinished business reinforced my own will to face the challenges of our work. Grace taught me that much can be accomplished in a short time under seemingly impossible circumstances. Hospice workers address not only the physical suffering that comes with terminal illness but the emotional, social, and spiritual suffering that surrounds a dying patient and grieving family. Hospice work is a privilege. We enter lives at a difficult time with the intention to help. In return, we receive confirmation of the meaning and purpose of our own lives and work. This was Grace's gift to me.

Spiritual Response
Stephanie Myers Schim

Death is a universal human experience that is uniquely contextualized. Because of this universality, hospice and palliative care programs aim to offer services congruent with differences of culture and religious affiliation (National Hospice & Palliative Care Organization, 2004). Some hospice programs are church-sponsored; many more are secular institutions. Like the families they serve, hospice nurses, social workers, physicians, volunteers, and other staff members represent a wide variety of backgrounds and spiritual traditions. In the Jewish tradition, caring for others is a "mitzvah," or good deed. One of the five pillars of Islam is caring for others. In the Christian tradition, the central commandment is to "love one another." It is important to respect the diversity of religious, spiritual, and cultural traditions surrounding end of life. It is also instructive to examine end-of-life issues from within each unique tradition.

The story of Grace can be interpreted using a Christian spiritual perspective. The end-of-life encounter between the administrator of the hospice program and the dying young woman sparks dialogue about the nature of spiritual gifts and givers. There are many different gifts identified in Grace's story, including the idea that a good death itself can be a gift. Throughout the New Testament there are many different spiritual gifts identified; some are overlapping concepts that I have chosen to group together for this discussion. The gifts that this story reveals to me as a nurse educator and former nursing administrator include (a) leadership and administration, (b) mercy, (c) healing, helping, and service, and (d) knowledge, teaching, and wisdom.

The narrator of the story embodies both leadership and administration. *Leadership* is defined as standing before people to direct them with care to accomplish goals (Rom. 12:8). *Administration* is defined as the steering of others toward the accomplishment of God-given goals through planning, organizing, and supervising (1 Cor. 12:28). For this leader, going out into the field with staff restores her soul and reminds her of the reasons she chose hospice nursing work. Many nurses who are drawn to hospice care are motivated in part by a sense of calling to attend to the sick and dying. Even the language used to describe home visits as *going out into the field* resonates with New Testament images of the Good Shepard. The central metaphor in Christianity is the spiritual leader who guides, directs, and protects as a shepherd leads his flock. From hospice's early roots as medieval hostels where people could rest and find respite from the road, it has had a strong tradition of pursuing the achievement of both physical and spiritual goals. The early roots of Western professional nursing are also found in the church-sponsored hostels of medieval Europe (Donahue, 1996). Even as nursing education and practice became more secular, the concept of nursing as a spiritual calling has remained evident. In this era, when many choose nursing as a job more than as a vocational calling, there are still nurses who consider it their life work to care for the sick and the dying. The aspect of calling is particularly evident among those select few who choose to work in the specialties of hospice and palliative care.

Just as nurses often act as midwives assisting in the transitions of birth, they also have an important role to play as midwives at life's end. Those who practice in the end-of-life specialty often speak, as does the CEO in the case study, of the privilege of working with patients and families as this final significant life transition is made. Nurses give their personal and professional gifts to their clients, but they also speak of the many intangible gifts they receive in return. As the hospice administrator who shares this story so eloquently points out, the gifts received most often are not of the material world, but rather gifts of the spirit and of grace in their own lives.

In the Christian tradition it is said, "Unto whomsoever much is given, of him shall be much required" (Luke 12:48). As the hospice CEO points out, administrators often fly "at 30,000 feet above" their organizations. This altitude is both a blessing and a curse. Along with the organizational leadership tasks and the premium parking spot comes an often-overwhelming sense of responsibility. It is a privilege to lead a program that has a major impact on people's lives and deaths. However, along with the power to make positive changes comes an unending and often intensely challenging to-do list. It is easy to feel remote from the real world of direct patient care as one struggles with budgets, buildings, and benefit plans. A nursing administrator may well sit in management meetings trying to recall why it was she wanted this career and whether her efforts make any difference. As is demonstrated in the Grace narrative, taking the opportunity to interact directly with a patient and family recharges the nurse-CEO in her dedication to leadership and administration.

From my perspective as a nurse, the CEO demonstrated mercy in her presence with Grace on the porch on a lovely afternoon. *Mercy* is sensitivity towards those who are suffering physically, mentally, or emotionally so as to feel genuine sympathy. Mercy is demonstrated through both words of compassion and deeds of love and care that help to alleviate distress (Rom. 12:8). Words of compassion were probably spoken in the CEO's encounter with Grace, although they are not reported. The narrative reflects the sensitivity of a nurse who is able to sit quietly with a dying young woman and encourage her to tell her story without interruption or critique. This is a deed of love and care. Often, the most helpful thing a nurse can do with a dying person is to do nothing. Listening without comment allows Grace to express herself without imposition. Being present and silently bearing witness as another human being tells her story is often the most welcome and merciful gift the nurse can give. The opportunity to hear a patient in this way is also a precious gift for the listener.

The spiritual gifts of healing, help, and service are also demonstrated well in Grace's story. *Healing* is the means through which people are made whole either physically, emotionally, mentally, or spiritually (1 Cor. 12:9, 28, 30). *Help* is the ability to render support or assistance to others in bodily ways so as to free them to attend to spiritual growth. *Service* is the ability to identify tasks that need to be done, however menial, and to apply available resources to get the tasks done (Rom. 12:7). The gift of healing is often thought of as the ability to perform medical miracles to restore or prolong life or to cure illness. In the hospice program, the goal is not cure but care at the end of life. Healing and help are directed toward comfort care and the relief of physical, emotional, and spiritual suffering. Hospice service tasks are sometimes menial but they are never insignificant. Hospice staff helped Grace carry out the letter-writing for her children and with a videotape as her legacy of love. Although physical care could not restore Grace's health, hospice nurses helped her to come to terms with her impending death and make the most of the time remaining. When physical cure is not possible, the quest for ways to promote spiritual, emotional, and interpersonal well-being becomes the central focus of service.

In the Christian spiritual tradition and in hospice nursing practice, the gifts of knowledge, teaching, and wisdom are closely related. The gift of *knowledge* is the ability to seek information and analyze that information (1 Cor. 12:8). *Teaching* is the sharing of knowledge in a way that promotes true understanding and growth (Rom. 12:7; 1 Cor. 12:28; Eph. 4:11). *Wisdom* is the application of knowledge to life in such a way as to make spiritual truths relevant and practical in proper decision making and situations of daily life (1 Cor. 12:8). *Knowledge* is often acquired over time to those who are open to learning. *Spiritual knowledge* is revealed to those who are willing to share, teach, and lead others as guided by the divine.

The hospice administrator is both a teacher and a learner as demonstrated in this story. She is making a home visit with a staff member from a rural office in part to fulfill her responsibility to assure that the service being provided is appropriate. As a nurse administrator not only has she expert knowledge but she also can bring this to bear in directing and supporting the social worker and the other team members in their work with patients and families. As she travels around the state to connect with diverse staff, patients, and families, she also shares her knowledge of the organization's mission, philosophy, and operations. However, as is eloquently narrated in this case study, as frequently as the CEO goes out to teach, she also learns. Through direct field experiences with people such as Grace and her family, the CEO gathers direct information that both informs her administrative decision making and also promotes her personal understanding and growth. Administrators, managers, and supervisors who take the time and make the effort to personally connect with their staff and patients can achieve wisdom well beyond that which is found in other activities that are more removed from direct care giving. The openness to being a learner as well as a teacher is a hallmark of excellent hospice and palliative care workers, nurses, and administrators.

Grace's story resonates with me as a nurse-educator, as a former nursing administrator, and as a person with a Christian heritage. The four sets of gifts that I saw reflected in the story, and that I have discussed from my perspective, included leadership or administration; mercy; healing, helping, or service; and knowledge, teaching, or wisdom. Each spiritual tradition has unique ways of illustrating the value of caring between human beings. When people who need care and those called to provide caring are brought together, the experience provides gifts to everyone.

Provider Response
Steven M. Popkin

A social worker's care note in this patient's chart would read something like this:

> The patient's diagnosis is an inoperable brain tumor. Grace is alert, oriented, and mentally competent to handle her affairs. Grace's parents, Sarah and Joe, have lived frugally and saved for what they anticipated would be an enjoyable and easy retirement to a small farm in the north woods. Sarah has a passion for gardening while her husband, Joe, is an avid woodworker. Their grandchildren, 5-year-old Amanda and 9-month-old Todd, have come with the patient to live in the rural environment that they now call home. The estranged father of Grace's children, described as abusive, has been largely absent from the family. Efforts are being made to award custody of the children to Sarah and Joe.

There are many unknowns in the description of this family. The story is reported from Grace's point of view filtered through the narrator's poignant retelling in a way that supports Graces' perspective. In other words, the picture of an idyllic future abruptly faded when this contented couple learned that their 30-year-old daughter Grace had an inoperable brain tumor. A social worker needs to be aware of the broader issues that could affect the family's future. Did they share close family bonds in spite of the physical separation or were they far removed from each other in their daily lives? What were Amanda and Todd's relationships with their grandparents? Are these children "going home" or are they being uprooted to live with strangers? What were the children's relationships with their father? Did he abuse them? What relationships, if any, do Sarah and Joe have with the children's father? Answers to these and similar questions would help the social worker to better understand complexities in the family dynamics. Full understanding of the history and current needs of family members would allow development of appropriate recommendations to support the dying mother's wishes. The social worker must focus on Grace's desires and yet must also consider the potentially conflicting needs of the children, the grandparents, and the children's father.

There are both short- and long-term issues that must be considered in this story. Sarah and Joe are planning to gain custody of their grandchildren. Grandparents who are trying to raise young children acquire many burdens. Again, there are additional issues that must be addressed. Sarah and Joe's financial situation may not permit them to cover the cost of medical care for their uninsured daughter. In the long term, they may be unable to financially provide for their grandchildren. In a rural community such as theirs, formal community support systems may not be adequate for the grandparents. They will need to address issues such as day care, playmates, adequate schools, spiritual activities, counseling, for the grandchildren. In addition, Sarah and Joe, as older adults, may have health issues that would make it difficult for them to care for two young children. Most troubling of all, if the grandparents become ill or die, the children would again be thrown into crisis.

The physical demands of grandchild custody are coupled with great emotional challenges. Parents who lose adult children suffer immeasurable grief. Amanda and Todd may provide their grandparents with new meaning and purpose to their lives. Alternatively, the burden of responsibility might be more than this bereaved couple can handle. The children will need ongoing support through their grief. Sarah and Joe may be unable to handle the children's emotional turmoil while dealing with their own devastation.

This story illustrates some of the challenges that social workers face in attempting to balance the myriad needs of everyone in a family facing the end of life. The gift that a social worker offers is raising difficult questions with the family and helping them to

sort out ways to move forward in this most challenging of circumstances.

Life-Course Response
Celia S. Thurston and Kathleen L. Meert

In every culture a universal, but how grief is expressed varies
between and within different contexts. To add further complexity,
grief responses are usually expected to be different for survivors
of different ages. Helping children understand death and helping
them to grieve is a daunting challenge.

In a story such as Grace's, in which a young mother's life will
be lost and in which those most in position to help are also grieving,
the challenge is especially great. In the throes of a death like this
one, children's emotional and spiritual needs often take a back seat.
Adult grief is more socially recognizable and better understood.
Children are still learning how to express themselves in ways that
communicate their needs and desires. This developmental process
can make childhood grief appear insignificant in comparison to
more overt adult forms of grief. In addition, children like Amanda
and Todd may not know how to insist upon the conditions of
their wellbeing. Children have little control over their lives and
must rely upon the adults who care for them whether those adults
know how to do so or not.

Much of the work on grief and bereavement has been done
within the Western psychological framework. Well-known grief
expert Theresa Rando (1984) wrote that when it comes to helping
children learn to grieve, it is more important to understand the
patterns and complexities of childhood psychological and emotional development than it is to be familiar with the specifics of
grief theory. According to some of the classic work on children's
grief, children are disadvantaged as mourners (Jewett, 1982; Rando,
1984). The narrator of Grace's story does not explicitly develop
descriptions of the children beyond the gender and age basics;
however, we can relate elements of the story to developmental
expectations described in the literature.

Children as young as Amanda and Todd are not yet cognitively
or emotionally mature. Immaturity leaves them to face losses with
fewer coping resources than adults. Children do not yet have

sufficient experience from which to learn that the pain of loss and death will subside and life will go on. In the same way that the reactions to loss are shaped by maturation, maturation is profoundly shaped by loss. Loss can interfere with children's normal cognitive and emotional development. Amanda, at 5 years old, is most likely still listening to fairy tales and curling up on her mother's lap. In *Hansel and Gretel* (Grimm, 1857/1972) and many other fairy tales and folk tales, themes of loss and abandonment are common. Hearing folk tales can provoke anxiety and may lead children to question whether a parent might go away and leave them alone. In Amanda's case, her mother is going to go away and will not come back. Adults around her are undoubtedly talking about her mother's death and what will happen when Mommy goes away. Whether she is included in these discussions directly or indirectly, as a 5-year-old she would know that something is wrong. This experience will last a lifetime.

For an infant, such as Todd at 9 months old, life is primarily sensory rather than cognitive. He responds to touch and would know when he's being held in loving arms, especially those of his mother. Infants are also very sensitive to changes in routine and the emotional climate around them. Todd's sister at age five is most likely a concrete thinker. She would know if Mommy is present or absent, but may not yet fully understand concepts of past, present, future, life, or death. Neither child is likely to be capable of full conceptual understanding of the dramatic events that surround them. Recognition of the loss, the first step of successful mourning, may take years to develop (Rando, 1984). Articulation of the meaning of the loss of their mother at these early ages will likely be a recurring theme as they mature.

Another reason that children are disadvantaged mourners is that caregiving adults tend not to appreciate the functions and importance of "child's play." Playing out a death scene or funeral, for instance, can be easily misunderstood. Children may be encouraged to direct their play toward more positive dramas and to avoid being "morbid" or "dwelling on the sadness." From the children's perspective, however, play-acting different roles or drawing pictures of what they are experiencing and what they are trying to deal with emotionally is healthy and necessary. The expressed needs of children are often missed because they are not verbalized but rather appear camouflaged in play or changes in behavior.

Hypervigilance, increased resistance, or withdrawal can be interpreted as a child simply "being difficult." We cannot tell from the story presented how Amanda and Todd are reacting or will react in the future. But we can easily imagine that their ways of acting out their feelings might not be understood. For many grandparents like Joe and Sarah, seeing childhood grief responses can be disconcerting in the wake of their own grief, and they may not know how to interpret the behaviors.

It is expected from a child of Amanda's age that childlike communication, appropriate to her linguistic and developmental levels, might cause her to appear relatively unaffected by the loss. The literature about children's grief reveals cases in which indirect verbalized needs are discounted. For example, a 6-year-old who lost his mother might, when given a piece of buttered toast, look down at the floor and say simply, "I need more butter." What he means but cannot say is, "My mother always buttered my toast so generously. Everything I do makes me miss her so much."

Children's emotional expressions are also easily misinterpreted and underestimated. Children cannot sustain a single emotion for a long period of time but instead cycle into emotional rhythms that can appear incongruent or inappropriate. For example, a child of Amanda's age may want to sit on a lap and suck her thumb one minute and jump up to run in the sprinkler the next. An adult can wrongly assume the child is "over it" or not really grieving. Yet, adult acceptance of children's emotional expressions can have a direct effect on the children's abilities to re–express and redefine their experiences.

For Grace's children and others like them, it is critical that their issues of grief and loss be addressed in ways that are developmentally appropriate. When the issues of grief and loss are not addressed, children can assume that topics of death, dying, and loss are unmentionable. Even though it is heartbreaking to witness grief and suffering in a child, silence or denial on the part of the adults in their lives can have devastating consequences. Grief literature suggests that many adults think that children will not know the difference if their suffering is not addressed. Although it is understandable that adults might want to protect children such as Amanda and Todd from the open discussion of death and death rituals, there can be significant negative effects. Children are never really too young to experience loss in their own ways nor are they helped by adults who cannot or will not understand their grief.

REFERENCES

Donahue, M. P. (1996). *Nursing: The finest art* (2nd ed.). St. Louis, MO: Mosby.

Grimm, Brothers. (1972). Hansel and Gretel. In *The Complete Grimm's Fairy Tales*. New York: Random House. (Originally published in 1857). Retrieved January 31, 2004, from http://www.mordent.com/folktales/grimms/hng/hng.html

Holy Bible: Authorized King James Version. (1957). London: Collins Clear-Type Press.

Jewett, C. L. (1982). *Helping children cope with separation and loss*. Boston: Harvard Common Press.

National Hospice & Palliative Care Organization. (2004). *Hospice & palliative care information*. Retrieved May 18, 2004, from http://www.nhpco.org/i4a/pages/index.cfm?padeid=3281

Rando, T. A. (1984). *Grief, dying, and death: Clinical interventions for caregivers*. Champaign, IL: Research Press.

CHAPTER 6

Stories of Avery:
Living and Dying Well

Sometimes our light goes out, but is blown again into instant flame by an encounter with another human being.

—Albert Schweitzer

Avery's Story
Stephanie Myers Schim

My neighbor Avery was a "Renaissance man." Tall and redheaded with an athletic build and a warm smile, he was a wonderful neighbor. It seemed to me that there was nothing that Avery could not do or would not try. By profession he was a middle-school science teacher in the tough urban district in which he lived. He was also an old-house restoration artist. He could paint a gable, build an oak stairway, install a roof, lay bricks, rewire rooms, and install plumbing. If you needed help with a project or advice on anything from attics to zoology, Avery was your man. He was also an accomplished musician, an avid tennis player, a fisherman, a private pilot, a beekeeper, and an artist with hand-blown glass.

Avery lived with his wife Lynn in a lovingly restored 19th century house in an inner-city neighborhood. Avery and Lynn's two oldest daughters lived with their husbands in similarly restored old houses in another part of town. Their third daughter was living at home after college graduation while she decided what path her life might take next. Even with the girls grown, educated, and independent, the family remained exceptionally close to one another. They often shared meals, old-house projects, music, adventures, and most of all, laughter. Avery and his family would be described as pillars in the varied spheres of their lives—school, neighborhood, and faith communities.

As a vigorous 57-year-old, Avery had been struggling with the decision to retire from his longstanding teaching position to have more time to spend in his other diverse pursuits. Avery had a hard time making the retirement decision because he loved teaching and coaching tennis and felt truly invested in the lives of his students. In the spring of the school year he noticed some small lapses in memory which he laughingly attributed to "senior moments." Although he laughed the episodes off, it got him thinking, and he decided that the time had come to say goodbye to teaching.

As a celebration of this new phase of his life, he flew his wife and family to Florida for a vacation in June. Avery again noticed some changes in his usually sharp memory and decided to cut the vacation short by a few days and come home. He did not say anything to his family because he did not want them to worry, and had no difficulty piloting his private plane, but he was beginning to be concerned.

As a retired teacher, Avery had medical insurance. He mentioned his growing concern with memory to his wife and scheduled an appointment for a full work-up at the large medical center near their home. Avery received a physical examination, laboratory tests, x-rays, and scans. The doctor told Avery and Lynn that the diagnosis was an inoperable brain tumor. Stunned, they discussed the news with family and close friends, prayed about what to do, and then decided to get more medical advice.

They sought second and third opinions at a regional teaching hospital 50 miles away—more tests, more scans, more bad news. Lynn said that by the time the diagnosis was again confirmed, Avery's mental status had already markedly deteriorated. When the second neurologist told the couple that the tumor was growing rapidly and sitting in a part of the brain that made treatment impossible, Avery's only question was "When will I be able to fly again?" Lynn found herself in a position she could never have imagined. Her wonderful husband was rapidly losing his mind, could no longer make decisions, would soon become unable to care for himself, and would not live to enjoy the retirement they had planned.

Avery came home to die. With his prognosis of 6 months or less to live, Avery's wife found herself carefully considering what he would want her to plan for end of life. She discussed the options with her daughters and sons-in-law. She consulted with close friends and with her church community and pastors. When Avery had more lucid moments in the first few weeks, Lynn talked with him about planning, but with his very impaired short-term memory, these conversations were difficult. Physicians had mentioned hospice care at home and the family knew about hospice services, but they did not know how to get connected or whether the time was right. When a close family friend who was a physician in another town visited, the family asked about hospice. The friend picked up the phone and initiated a referral to one of the local hospice programs.

The story of the next weeks and months is a study in community. Lynn's sister, Lisa, came to visit and support the family when Avery was first undergoing the diagnostic work-ups. With the daughters' help, Lisa organized an extensive support network for the family. She began by identifying the areas that would need to be managed for the household to function. The goal was to free Lynn and the daughters from all tasks not directly related to caring for Avery and spending this precious last time with him. Lisa organized a notebook with sections labeled by time of day: morning, noon, afternoon, evening, and night. In each section, she made an annotated list of the things that must be done and those that could be done if time and energy allowed. How is the kitchen set up? Where does the garbage go? What is to be done about phone messages and visitors? Where is the grocery store? Where are the vacuum cleaner and dust mop? No detail was left to chance. Next, a few key neighbors and friends offered to make calls and line up additional volunteers. In the first few weeks, the organizers asked two people to cover each shift during the day and two at night. They paired two men on the night shift so that if Avery needed to be turned or helped to the bathroom in the night they would be there to assist. People offered to prepare and deliver every meal for the family and the helpers.

The family spent their days taking care of Avery's physical needs and keeping him as comfortable as possible. They took turns talking to him, telling family stories, and singing his favorite hymns.

Fresh flowers and family photos filled the parlor. The teapot was always on, and plates of fruit and cookies available.

The hospice program sent out a nurse and a social worker and enrolled Avery as requested. They arranged for delivery of a hospital bed when it became necessary, and an oxygen concentrator when his breathing became difficult. The sickroom was set up in a back parlor of the stately home, where pocket doors could be closed for privacy, and yet Avery was in the center of the household both physically and emotionally.

During one of my volunteer shifts, the hospice nurse visited. She spoke briefly with Lynn and then checked Avery's vital signs. With a short, "Well, it looks like he's doing fine," the nurse was gone again. I asked Lynn how the hospice service was working out, and she said that she did not want to be critical, but "there's just not much she can do." She was concerned that the physician in charge of Avery's hospice care had not yet been to visit in the 3 months since he had been enrolled. She said the hospice nurse was nice, but not very helpful. Lynn wondered aloud if the problem might be the agency's difficulty in hiring good nurses who were willing to make home visits in the inner city. I asked if she had said anything to the nurse about the family's needs, and Lynn said she did not want to make a fuss. When I asked if I might help by calling the hospice agency about her concerns, Lynn said that she did not want me "to make waves" and cause anyone trouble. Besides, she said, she had plenty of help and was surrounded by people who really did care about her, her husband, and their family.

Through the summer months and into the fall, Avery's physical and mental condition continued to decline. By August he was in bed, in a diaper, and totally dependent on care. Close and extended family, neighbors, colleagues, and friends continued to volunteer for daily support shifts and meal preparation. Friends from Avery's faith community met around his bed many evenings, playing the piano and their guitars, and singing hymns of faith and hope. Unfortunately, Avery's mellow baritone voice could no longer be raised. By late September, he had stopped eating and became ever more emaciated. Fortunately, Avery did not seem to experience much pain while dying. Even in his last months, he did not complain or appear to be in distress beyond what could be alleviated with a dose of Tylenol™.

On November 25, Avery closed his eyes and took his last quiet breath. Family members who had gathered for the traditional holiday meal surrounded him. Tears and hugs, stories and songs, joy and sorrow filled that Thanksgiving Day and the weeks that followed. Many celebrated Avery's life and gave thanks for the privilege of having known and loved him and of having been loved by him. His memorial service was an expression of community, with participants from the diverse circles of the man's extraordinary life. He had done more in 57 years than many people do in an entire lifetime. His family said that they were comforted that Avery had lived well and died well.

Community Response
Donald E. Gelfand

At one point this story is described as "a study in community." This seemingly simple term has many definitions. One approach to community is to view it as "a group of people who are socially interdependent, who participate in discussion and decision making, and who share *practices* . . . that both define the community and are nurtured by it" (Bellah, Madsen, Sullivan, Swidler, & Tipton, 1985, p. 333). This definition implies a feedback process: The actions of the group of people who form the community define its existence, and these actions in turn help to provide an impetus for its continued existence. The initial formation of community can be based on common interests and values. In many cases, community is also based on geographic proximity. The community in Avery's story appears to be based both on shared values and geographic proximity.

American families are often portrayed as disparate collections of individuals. In contrast, Avery's family can be viewed as a cohesive family—community. All of Avery's adult children are living in close proximity. The daughters are described as "grown, educated, and independent" but the interdependence of this family is striking. Avery, Lynn, and their three daughters share many activities together. As the seriousness of Avery's illness becomes clear, the family's shared practices deepen. Family members step in to nurture Avery in a new way during his last months of life.

Using an old-fashioned phrase, Avery is described as a "pillar of the community." With this pillar threatened, the community responds to the impending demise of one of its stalwarts through a remarkable model of organization. Research on caregiving clearly indicates that the primary responsibility for care of a seriously ill individual such as Avery would typically fall on the spouse. If she was unavailable or unable to care for her husband, children (primarily the daughters) would assume this burden of care. In this hierarchical model, the next level of caregiving responsibility would be other relatives (Hooyman & Kiyak, 1996).

The care provided for Avery is remarkable in that it involves multiple individuals who range from family members to members of his neighborhood and faith communities. Initially, it is Avery's sister in-law who organizes the caregiving system. With this system, she attempts to reduce the enormous burden that is often assumed by one or two individuals. She divides up daily responsibilities and parcels these out to different individuals. The division of labor in the system is, in itself, notable. More notable is the fact that Avery's neighbors and friends became key players in the caregiving process. In the most literal sense, Avery's family was his community, and his community was his family.

It is not unusual to ask neighbors or friends to provide assistance. This assistance is usually regarded as short-term and intensive: "Friends and neighbors are well-suited to provide emotional support and to perform predictable tasks, such as transportation, while families are best equipped for personal care" (Hooyman & Kiyak, 1996, p. 305).

In Avery's story, the involvement of friends and neighbors is noteworthy not only for the emotional assistance provided by these individuals but also for their willingness to undertake household tasks such as cleaning and preparing meals. Perhaps most remarkable is the willingness of neighbors to provide intimate personal care such as toileting. The assistance is extraordinary not only for its intensity but for its duration. Social support networks of family members are expected to provide long-term care, but this assistance is not usually expected from friends or neighbors. The willingness of Avery's friends and neighbors to be involved in his care for so long a period is a testament to his character and life.

The assistance offered by hospice is presented in a less flattering light. It is not clear why the hospice doctor had not visited

Avery. The hospice nurse might be competent and professional in clinical care; unfortunately, her remark about Avery's condition is realistic but uncaring. Perhaps there was a problem with the training this nurse received, or she may have been basically unsuited for the types of family situations involved in working with hospice patients. Another possibility is that the hospice nurse was overwhelmed by the presence of so much support in the home that she did not see a need for the full range of hospice services including emotional support, financial counseling, and pastoral care. Most end-of-life programs are prepared to provide a gamut of emotional and spiritual support as well as medical care.

Avery is a white 57-year-old college-educated man. The usual norm for comparable families would be for strong involvement with an interdisciplinary hospice team. The team would include social workers and volunteers who would provide counseling and emotional support. In some cultures, a strictly medical role for end-of-life providers is expected; their model is "we take care of our own," meaning everything except medication administration is the responsibility of family. As one example, Mexican families have indicated a reluctance to have a social as well as medical approach to end-of-life care used with dying family members (Gelfand, Balcazar, Parzuchowski, & Lenox, 2001). From the viewpoint of some Mexican families, it is very important that hospice care should not extend beyond the administration of medication. In Avery's story, more extensive hospice services would have been accepted if they had been offered. The reluctance of Avery's wife to request more professional assistance may have indicated that the social support of family, friends, and neighbors was filling the most important social and emotional needs.

Avery died on Thanksgiving Day, but the family did not suspend its traditional holiday arrangements. Instead, the day was devoted to giving thanks, not only for events in American history, but for everything that Avery had brought to their lives. The memorial service reflected the meaning of Avery's life for his communities. He was not a famous, rich, or powerful man in conventional terms, but he influenced his community by educating children in his work as a middle-school teacher. He influenced his family by his involvement and the relationships he fostered with them. He influenced his neighborhood by his willingness to provide assistance.

Avery's story exemplifies a *generosity of spirit* and a willingness to engage in activities that establish and maintain community. Generosity of spirit is "the ability to acknowledge an interconnectedness—one's 'debts to society' " that binds one to others whether one wants to accept it or not (Bellah, Madsen, Sullivan, et al., 1985, p. 194). It is also the ability to engage in the caring that nurtures the interconnectedness. In turn, the community responded heroically when he and his family were in need. His life and the response of the community should be celebrated. The disturbing question, however, must also be raised: Are stories such as those of Avery the exception rather than the norm in American society?

Cultural Response
Sherylyn H. Briller

For an anthropologist, Avery's story provides an opportunity to explore the end-of-life rite of passage in a contemporary urban American community. End of life is viewed as an important rite of passage in the human life-course cross-culturally (Braun, Pietsch, & Blanchette, 2000; Doorenbos, Briller, & Chapleski, 2003). Although customs related to the transition between life and death are highly variable in diverse settings, rites of passage are classically thought of as having three distinct phases: separation, liminality, and incorporation (Turner, 1969; Van Gennep, 1960).

Avery's end-of-life experience fits within this categorical scheme and can tell us about both the social space and the actors within it. The first phase, *separation*, involves a process of withdrawal from a group or status to which one previously belonged. In Avery's story, his rapid transition from a newly retired, seemingly healthy schoolteacher to a terminally ill patient with an untreatable brain tumor marks the onset of the separation phase.

The second phase is in many respects the most fascinating. This phase, *liminality*, is defined as a finite time of limbo in which people are between states of being—having left one state but not yet entered or joined the next (Turner, 1969). People in this transitional phase have ambiguous social positions; they are out of step with normal social expectations and roles.

In the past, dramatic examples from other societies were used to illustrate how liminal persons are isolated from the rest of society. For example, Van Gennep (1960), in his classic conceptualization of this transitional phase, discussed male initiation rites of Australian Aborigines. He described how boys would be removed from the wider society during these puberty rites to learn a body of knowledge known only by adult men. In that society, physical changes such as circumcision or removal of a tooth symbolized the death of the initiates' old identities and their taking on of adult values. Thus, going through physical pain was viewed as an integral part of preparing the initiates to become adult men (Elkin, 1964; Haviland, 2002). There are many examples of liminality in contemporary American society including basic training for military recruits, religious rituals such as bar mitzvah, and admission procedures in hospitals. End-of-life rituals can be viewed from the perspective of liminality.

Avery's end-of-life experience was such a time of liminality. His rapid loss of lucidity and very impaired short-term memory took him out of his important social, familial, and community roles. He was thrust abruptly into the background as a decision maker and later even as a social participant in his community. Avery's liminal status continues until he dies. On the basis of what the narrator has allowed the reader to know about Avery's personality, the reader sees clearly that this liminal state as a passive recipient of care was very much in contrast to Avery's prior social and community roles.

It is significant that rites of passage are not only experienced by individuals, but also involve groups' collective movements through these transitions. Turner (1969) wrote about a social aspect of collective liminality called *communitas*. This process involves a powerful community spirit and related feelings of intense social solidarity, equality, and togetherness. Avery's story serves as an exemplar of communitas as his family, neighbors, and members of his faith community united to provide months of difficult physical, emotional, and personal care.

With communitas, people come together and put aside their differences, including those of social status, for the duration of the liminal period. Social differences that are sharply demarcated in American society, such as occupational status, are temporarily suspended during the liminal period. Thus, it is possible to imagine that any of the men—a son-in-law, a teacher from Avery's school, a physician friend from his church, or a neighbor who was a janitor—would all equally participate in turning Avery in his bed, changing his diaper, or cleaning up vomit if he was ill during the night.

During the liminal period, social conventions of normal social life are inverted. Heterogeneous behavior becomes homogenous behavior, inequality becomes equality, social divisions become communitas, avoidance of pain and suffering becomes acceptance of pain and suffering (Turner, 1969). It is important to note that when everyday social strictures are temporarily placed on hold, people are freed to act in new and possibly highly unfamiliar ways. As Murphy (1990) eloquently described, "People relate to each other affectively and diffusively—which beneath the jargon means that they no longer hide behind narrowly defined and formal rules of conduct, but rather meet as a whole and caring people" (p. 44).

Following in this vein, liminality provides a social space for individuals to behave very differently than at other times in community life. Sankar (1999) that when someone is dying at home, basic household tasks such as cooking, grocery shopping, and laundry may be turned over to others who would not normally fill these roles. This distinction resonates with Goffman's (1959) ideas about backstage versus front stage in social contexts. In the Avery example, the reader sees members of the community cross between the functional (backstage) and the social (front stage) parts of the household.

As the narrator indicates, the family was able to function and spend "precious last time with Avery" because of the extensive support network of community members. What is unfortunate in Avery's story is that the professional caregivers were not really part of this communitas. Avery and his family could have potentially benefited from greater involvement by the professional staff. The staff could have learned much by actively attending to the ways in which this community worked together through the months of liminality at the end of Avery's life. An even richer experience for the hospice staff would have been achieved had they engaged in the communitas themselves. They did neither and a golden opportunity was missed. Communitas made this time special and extraordinary for Avery's family. Hospice staff missed the chance to experience the power of communitas. They could have participated in end-of-life care expanded beyond the realm of normal community social interaction and routine professional care. Such engagement might have swept them into new domains of working, caring, and being. The experience of communitas could have powerfully transformed both personal lives and professional practice.

All learning opportunities are not equal. Through textbook learning it is typically possible to acquire a solid background in a discipline's foundational ideas. Hands-on learning can often provide a better, more enriched human educational experience, such as is needed for those in professional caregiving roles. Yet, rarely does the chance come along to learn via a totally different realm of more intense social experience such as in communitas. Participating in such a profound social experience can lead to a great leap in both understanding and professional practice. It is critically important for an organization like hospice, which prides itself on creating innovative and humane end-of-life experiences, to recognize and then take these leaps of understanding when learning situations in life present themselves serendipitously.

The third phase, *incorporation*, occurs when a person reenters society with new social status. Avery's death can be viewed metaphorically as a process of incorporation. The Thanksgiving Day family celebration and the community memorial service demonstrate that survivors felt that Avery's spirit was "among them" although he was no longer physically present. Although Avery can not reenter the physical world, he is incorporated into his community through collective memory. For example, the storytelling at the time of his death and the days after serve to reinstate him in the social world in new ways.

Avery's death and subsequent memorial service can also be seen as a *rite of intensification*—a time that signifies a major change in the social life of the group. Rites of intensification often involve religious rituals and ceremonies that enable people to come together at a time of crisis—in this story, a great man and community leader is lost and the community must adjust to the void left by his death. Funerary rituals such as those performed by Avery's community to celebrate his life are important community markers that can set the survivors on the path to dealing with their loss and being able to achieve social reintegration. Haviland (2002) powerfully describes what can be achieved via a rite of intensification: "This unites people in a common effort so that fear and confusion yield to collective action and a degree of optimism. The balance in the relations of all concerned, which has been upset, is restored to normal, and the community's values are celebrated and affirmed" (p. 376).

The use of the concepts of communitas and rites of intensification may evoke criticism for being simplistic and for failing to reflect all of the harsh realities that are part of the difficult daily experience of providing end-of-life care. However, looking at stories such as Avery's that are outside of the regular course of events has value in expanding one's ideas of what is possible, what is practical, and what is preferable for care at the end of life. Moving beyond the familiar and opening new dialogues and new ways of thinking can spark creative new approaches to benefit patients, families, practitioners, and communities as they experience this final rite of passage.

Narrative Response
Richard Raspa

Narrative is an expressive and performative vehicle. It reveals community values, beliefs, and assumptions, and it enacts them. When we tell a story, we translate information into meaning for a community of practice. And in the telling, we constitute ourselves as members of a community—the one about which we are narrating or some other. We live our lives in communities. People become human through participation in networks of meaning-making association. In short, we enact our humanity through narrative that connects us to community.

In the act of narrating the story of Avery, the narrator makes sense of Avery's living and dying. The recounting further allows the storyteller to complete the relationship with Avery by expressing her caring for this man and acknowledging her gratitude for the relationship. Death, as 20th century American poet Wallace Stevens (1923) reminds us in *Sunday Morning*, "is the mother of beauty." Death is the indispensable event that when incorporated into a life story gives birth to our consciousness of life's beauty. Storytelling brings coherence to the pain of death and loss.

The narrator translates cold facts and data into a meaningful tale that has the power to touch people in their hearts. The translating function of narrative is intertextual. It connects the text that is being created to a canon of previous texts on the subject. This story represents Avery as a Renaissance man. In Western civilization, the Renaissance man is the cultural story of mastery achieved in multiple domains. Avery's life has been a narrative that connects isolated realms and people: art and science, tennis and music, profession and craft. Avery was a musician and fisherman, teacher and plumber, naturalist and pilot, and a keeper of bees in the middle of urban blight. He lived in the inner city—a middle-class, middle-aged Caucasian who not only restored houses, but also was committed fiercely to the restoration of human beings. He was a catalyst for architectural renewal in his neighborhood and human reclamation in his workplace. He provided help to neighbors with broken locks. He offered promise to inner-city students who came to his classes to learn science, and who came to his coaching to learn how to be connected powerfully—not to a mindless gang, but to a winning tennis team. Avery was a narrator of life's possibilities. He seemed to relish the challenge of stretching beyond the limit of ordinary expectation to sing, to make things, to teach, to fly. His was a story of lived possibilities and he created that story by participating in all the separate domains of experience. A narrator of brilliance, Avery could move people into connections with each other and with the world. He could restore things to life.

When Avery is dying, he and his community of family and friends react to death as if it were a natural and expected part of living. People come to help and there is a robust quality in their organizational flourish. "How is the kitchen set up? Where does the garbage go? What is to be done about phone messages and visitors? Where is the grocery store? . . . No detail was left to chance." They do the things that need to be done so that people can continue to live vibrant lives until the end. "The sickroom was set up in a back parlor of the stately home, where pocket doors could be closed for privacy and yet Avery was in the center of the household both physically and emotionally." The community's care for Avery is expressed in the impeccable attention to the necessities that sustain life as a human being. Maintaining biological and psychosocial necessities in both public and private spaces are conditions for human life to thrive.

The control of the household, of course, is ironic, for it measures the ultimate lack of control over the dying of Avery. But there is more here. Vibrant communities are "storied" communities. They have a repertoire of tales that translate information into a context that is meaning for a group of people who share a culture over time. Relationships within community are constituted by stories. The people who participate in Avery's dying are members of such storied communities. The narrator (one of Avery's neighbors, who declares that Avery is "a Renaissance man") shares this version of the story with others in the group of friends. It is significant that when the physician mentioned hospice-care at home, the family "did not know how to get connected or whether the time was right." The family lived vitally in communities of practice, whereas hospice was for them a de-storied institution. They did not know "how to get connected." Hospice existed for them as a faceless, cold set of procedures and rules for governing the dying and the dead. Hospice does not live as a narrative for them, and the lack of a story becomes a self-fulfilling prophecy. For hospice, Avery and his family do not seem to live as storied people either. The hospice doctor does not show up once in the 3 months that Avery is enrolled in the program. And the hospice nurse and social worker do their jobs perfunctorily and not in compliance with hospice philosophy. The hospice nurse, during one visit, briefly examines Avery and then concludes almost dismissively: "Well, it looks like he's doing fine." The response is automatic, institutional, as if the nurse is saying: "I'm just doing my job. There isn't much anybody can do here." No other interaction is reported. The hospice workers make no human connection with the family. It is story of failure.

The nurse's lack of caring is in stark contrast to the local community's caring for Avery and his family. When Avery is forced to remain in bed with a diaper and total dependence on others, volunteers participated in caring for him in shifts around the clock. They prepared meals, and even met regularly in the evening to play the piano and guitar and sing "hymns of faith and hope" to Avery. Even at the end, Avery is connected through physical care and through song and music to his many communities who accompany him on his journey to death.

It is poetic that Avery dies on Thanksgiving Day, as the family participates in the traditional American holiday, which sets aside a time for giving thanks for life. Here the narrative makes more connections. Private experience and public ceremony come together. Self and other are linked in communities of care and love. Death and life are knotted; the separation that ordinarily keeps them distinct is transcended. Avery's death is emblematic of his life, for even at the end, he is engaged in renovation and renewal. Old bonds between community members and family are pulled tighter. People give thanks at the moment of death for the exuberance that Avery brought into their worlds and for the gift of life that humans enjoy for a short while. We live our lives and live through our deaths in narrative. Narratives are the way human beings have of being human. Avery lives on in the narratives his friends and family continue to tell about this remarkable human being.

REFERENCES

Bellah, R., Madsen, R., Sullivan, W., Swidler, A., & Tipton, S. (1985). *Habits of the heart*. Berkeley: University of California Press.

Braun, K., Pietsch, J., & Blanchette, P. (Eds.). (2000). *Cultural issues in end of life decision-making*. Thousand Oaks, CA: Sage.

Doorenbos, A., Briller, S., & Chapleski, E. (2003). Weaving cultural context into an interdisciplinary end-of-life curriculum. *Educational Gerontology, 29*, 405–416.

Elkin, A. P. (1964). *The Australian Aborigines*. Garden City, NY: Doubleday/Anchor Books.

Gelfand, D., Balcazar, H., Parzuchowski, J., & Lenox. Mexicans and care for the terminally ill: Family, hospice and the church. *American Journal of Hospice and Palliative Care, 18*(6), 391–396.

Goffman, E. (1959). *The presentation of self in everyday life*. New York: Doubleday.

Haviland, W. A. (2002). *Cultural anthropology* (10th ed.). Stamford, CT: Thompson Learning.

Hooyman, N., & Kiyak, A. (1996). *Social gerontology* (4th ed.). Needham Heights, MA: Allyn & Bacon.

Murphy, R. F. (1990). *The body silent*. New York: Norton.

Sankar, A. (1999). *Dying at home: A family guide for caregiving*. Baltimore: Johns Hopkins University Press.

Stevens, W. (1923). *Sunday morning* [Poem]. Retrieved June 21, 2004, from http://www.everypoet.com/archive/poetry/Wallace_Stevens/wallace_stevens_sunday_morning.htm

Turner, V. (1969). *The ritual process: Structure and anti-structure*. Ithaca, NY: Cornell University Press.

Van Gennep, A. (1960). *The rites of passage*. Chicago: University of Chicago Press.

CHAPTER 7

Stories of Maggie: Family Dynamite

> No people are ever as divided as those of the same blood.
>
> —Mavis Gallant

Maggie's Story
Kathleen Stever

Forty-nine-year-old Maggie spoke softly, with tears streaming down her face. She had been diagnosed 18 months earlier with cancer. Three months ago she learned that despite chemotherapy her cancer had spread to her lungs, liver, and abdomen. Severe abdominal pain with uncontrolled nausea and vomiting had forced Maggie to return to the hospital only 2 days after her last discharge. Maggie had still hoped to go home and spend, "the time I have left at home with the kids."

During her current hospital stay, she was stunned to realize for the first time that she could die within weeks or months. She expressed regret that while she had been at home she had not arranged for any support for her two college-aged children and her adolescent daughter. They knew that she had cancer but did not know that the cancer had spread or that she could soon die.

Maggie had worked in a doctor's office prior to becoming ill. She was divorced and her three children lived with her. Her youngest daughter, aged 16, had been home-schooled. The two oldest children were both in college, with one living at home. Maggie's extended family included her parents, four sisters, and a boyfriend.

Her parents and sisters visited daily and spoke to her by phone several times daily. Although Maggie spoke often of her boyfriend, he was rarely at the hospital because of his work schedule. One brother-in-law, a physician, took the lead for the family in helping Maggie to weigh decisions about her care.

Maggie's private room became known for the evening parties her friends and family threw. The evening gatherings in Maggie's room began informally. Looking back, no one could remember how they started or who brought in the first of many meals that were shared in Maggie's hospital room. The meals began out of necessity. Visitors needed to eat, and Maggie longed for favorite foods such as pizza and rocky road ice cream. Over the weeks of Maggie's hospital stay, it became common for family and friends to enjoy these takeout meals with her while being kept current on each other's daily lives and spending time reminiscing. As Maggie's illness worsened, her sisters decorated her room, arranged for food to be brought in and for visitors to drop by during dinner. They were trying to make the hospital room as home-like as possible.

Maggie's 50th birthday was approaching, and her condition was beginning to rapidly change. It appeared that she would not live to celebrate her birthday. Her sisters set up several small dessert parties where they brought in Maggie's favorite sweets. Although Maggie could not eat very much, she loved watching her friends and family enjoy the special treats.

During the first week of her admission, Maggie endured multiple tests and treatments focused on relief of symptoms. Fluid was removed from her lungs to improve her shortness of breath. She received IV pain medication and also had a pain medicine patch that provided good relief. A transdermal scopolamine patch relieved her vomiting. With her symptoms under adequate control, Maggie was able to turn her attention to unfinished business.

Maggie began to talk about her hopes for the time she had left to live. She wanted to be kept comfortable and to spend time with her family. Her strong desire was to return to her own home to be with her children. She agreed to a comfort-care approach and was willing to receive hospice services in her home. In preparation for her homecoming, she began to visit the hospital gift shop, buying special gifts for her friends and family. She had each of the gifts blessed by the hospital priest.

An additional 2 weeks passed with routine testing, and then a blood clot delayed her discharge. The nursing and social work staff began to worry that Maggie's goals for the last days of her life would not be realized. She was growing weaker, becoming forgetful, and needed help with most of her activities of daily living.

Maggie's room was often full of family and friends. As her hospital stay lengthened, her children would call and reserve time alone with their mom. No other visitors or medical personnel were allowed in the room during those special visits. Her extended family was pleased with her care in the beautiful private room and worried about managing her needs at home. Maggie's sisters began to push for continued hospital care or transfer to a nursing home.

With Maggie's permission, her brother-in-law arranged for the three children to meet with her oncologist and learn the extent of her illness. Maggie's ex-husband also attended the meeting. They were stunned to learn that she might have only weeks to live. After confirming with their uncle that what they had heard was true, the children responded in a variety of ways. The younger daughter turned immediately to a local Catholic church. She had heard that there was a priest who counseled children and young adults in grief. She also arranged for a nun to visit her mother that same night. The older daughter responded by looking for ways to decrease her work and internship hours to spend more time with her mother. Maggie's son began to talk about not going away to school for the next semester but rather enrolling in a university closer to home.

The health professionals held a multidisciplinary-care conference at which they discussed Maggie's care and goals and began a coordinated effort to plan for discharge. In the midst of this planning, Maggie's mother was hospitalized, and the family began to divide their time between two hospitals. Maggie's physician met with Maggie again and outlined very clearly her current health status. Radiation and chemotherapy would not improve her condition, and they were losing the battle with her cancer. He confirmed that hospice care at home or in a nursing home would be a good choice for her. A hospice nurse came to see Maggie to talk about options for care.

Maggie continued to insist that she wanted to go home and would hire someone to be there when her children were not at home. Her extended family was in favor of a nursing home placement. They felt it would be too difficult to provide care at home and said that they were willing to pay the nursing home costs. Everyone agreed to have hospice care; they disagreed on the best setting.

Maggie's father, four sisters, and two brothers-in-law held a family meeting in Maggie's room, with a Palliative Care Nurse Practitioner (PCNP) and a social worker from the hospital staff. Maggie's children chose not to be at the meeting. The PCNP began by clarifying the purpose of the meeting. Then Maggie spoke about her need to go home and spend time with her children. Everyone in the room was in tears when she described her need to cuddle and watch TV at home again with them. Her family appeared anxious and upset when it was their turn to explain why they felt an extended care facility was the best care choice for Maggie. They worried about who would care for her when the children were at school or at work. They questioned the ability of the children to provide all of her care when they were home. The family reminded Maggie that she had wanted the children to stay in school, and they worried that full-time caregiving would make that impossible. Maggie replied, "My children told me they wanted me home." Suddenly one sister began to sob and cried out, "Maggie they can't tell you! They are scared for you to come home. They are afraid to have you die in the house. Maggie, you want the kids to stay together when you are gone. If they can't handle you being sick at home, they could move out and live with their father. Do you want that?" Maggie began to cry. "No, I don't want them to be scared, but I can't bear the thought of living in a nursing home and sharing my room. That would scare the kids too."

The social worker explained that Maggie could have a private room at the nursing home, and that the family could spend the night and continue the tradition of late-night parties in her room. Maggie would be free to come and go and could visit her own home if she desired. The room was silent as Maggie considered this information and tearfully agreed to go to a nursing home with a private room. "I want to do what is best for my kids. I don't want to add to their pain."

The family selected a nearby nursing home with a private room and unrestricted visiting hours. For the 3 weeks that Maggie lived at the nursing home her symptoms were well controlled with hospice care. Her children visited daily and members of her family took turns staying with her every night. One Friday evening, when no one from the family could be there, Maggie spent the first night alone in almost 3 months of hospital and hospice care. She died quietly in her sleep in the early morning. She was alone.

Economic Response
Allen C. Goodman

Maggie and her family were engaged in a debate that many families face when someone is dying. Many scholars talk about needing to provide a "good death" in which the patient's desires and needs are respected as paramount. However, decisions about the arrangements and setting for end-of-life care involve complex economic, as well as emotional and ethical, issues. All other things being equal, it would be preferable for Maggie to go home, maintain her function and independence, and enjoy the company of her children and other family members as long as possible. However, there are economic implications to this seemingly simple request. For Maggie, and for many others, going home requires support services, and those services come with considerable tangible and intangible costs. In economic terms, one must ask whether the benefits of increased independence and the associated quality of life are sufficient to justify the costs. Understanding the reimbursement mechanisms for hospice home care can help illuminate some of the broader social and economic issues that are in the current "where to go to die" debate. Economic analysis alone cannot provide unequivocal answers to a normative question such as this one, but it can contribute to the policy debate.

The budgetary pressure of end-of-life care in hospitals and nursing homes has promoted interest in other, less costly arrangements. The growing number of elders needing complex end-of-life care in the United States has strained existing resources. Maggie's story, however, illustrates that affordable end-of-life care is an issue across the age spectrum. Folland, Goodman, and Stano (2004) provide an extensive discussion of the economics of nonhospital-care settings. Hospice and home health programs are perceived to be cost-effective and receive billions of dollars annually from the federal government (Folland et al.). An economist would consider Maggie's story in light of current governmental hospice initiatives and a simple economic model of hospice resource costs, measured in both time and money. Maggie's story is used to provide comparisons and contrasting examples of the economic principles described below.

Medicare introduced hospice benefits in 1983, but it was the higher reimbursement rates initiated in 1989 that accelerated growth in the number of U.S. hospice programs. Higher reimbursement rates significantly increased the number of Medicare Certified Providers, improving access for Medicare beneficiaries. Hamilton (1993) estimated that every dollar increase in the daily rate would raise the probability of certification by 1.7%. In other words, once the reimbursement rate was closer to the cost of providing the care, more potential hospice service providers would become able to participate under Medicare rules. With mounting evidence that hospice programs offer financial savings, many private insurers added coverage for hospice care to their benefits. Indeed, 3,200 U.S. hospice programs served 885,000 patients in 2002 (National Hospice & Palliative Care Organization, 2004).

Hospice programs in the United States provide most of their services in patients' homes rather than in institutional settings such as hospitals and nursing homes. Most hospice programs maintain a limited number of in-patient beds for respite care and to accommodate those patients and families who cannot, or choose not, to be cared for at home. Home health care providers serve patients with acute and long-term needs, including those with disabilities, those recuperating after a hospital stay, and some people who are terminally ill but not enrolled in hospice. As of 1996 about 2.4 million home health patients were on the rolls of home care agencies at any time, and their numbers were growing rapidly. With a doubling of patients in just 4 years between 1992 and 1996, home health care became one of the fastest growing components of total health care spending. Between 1992 and 1996, Medicare spending for home health care grew from $7.7 to $18.1 billion. Medicare spending, however, fell to $7.6 billion by 1999 following the Balanced Budget Act of 1997. The economic rationale for public funding (Medicare and Medicaid) for hospice and home health care rests on the premise that it is much less expensive than either hospital or nursing home care. Even though a home health visit is unquestionably far less costly than a day spent in an institution, the effect on total health spending is not entirely clear. The principal issue is the extent to which home health services substitute for unpaid care by family and other caregivers or for institutional care. In other words, the concern centers on the possibility of shifting costs rather than overall reduction. Policy makers worry that more generous public payments for home care will substitute for previously unpaid care without significantly increasing the overall well-being of patients. For example, in Maggie's story, the argument would be that if her health insurance (or the government) would pay enough for her to receive the 24-hour skilled care that she needs at home, the family would perhaps go back to work or school and allow paid health care workers to give care that family members do not want to provide. The quality of the care might or might not be better with paid providers, but the cost of the service to taxpayers or stockholders would certainly escalate.

Pezzin, Kemper, and Reschovsky (1996) developed a conceptual approach to investigate these substitution effects. The approach begins by relating a *family's well-being*, or *utility*, to three broad categories of resources: (a) private goods that the family consumes, (b) leisure for family members, and (c) the well-being of the disabled person within the family. In Maggie's situation, the family well-being could be produced in either a hospice nursing home setting, or at her home in the community through various combinations of hospice home care formally purchased in the market and the informal care provided by family members and others. The family could use its time in three ways: (a) care for Maggie themselves, (b) work to earn income to buy market goods or home and institutional care for her, or (c) enjoy the time as leisure for themselves. The theory suggests that a family cannot obtain more of any one of these three options without giving up some of the other two. As Maggie's sister points out to her, for the children to spend significant time with her at home, they would need to give up their school activities. Maggie's family seemed prepared to give up some leisure to work to buy hospice nursing home care. Even if the hospice program costs were fully covered with nursing home care for Maggie, the family was choosing to spend their time in leisure at her bedside rather than at work as caregivers in her home. Maggie's sister says that they were not prepared to provide that type of care themselves, and they apparently expected considerable *disutility* if they allowed her to die at home.

In response to concerns that increasing funding for in-home services such as hospice would shift costs to the public sector, researchers have examined the possible effects of expanded public funding for home health care (Pezzin et al., 1996). They found that when funding levels were increased there were no reductions in the amount of informal care for married persons and only small reductions in care for unmarried persons. Thus, the benefits of expanded funding accrued mainly to the care recipients and not to the informal caregivers through more leisure time. Adequate public support for care in the home setting also affects living arrangements by increasing the probability that unmarried persons will live independently for a longer period of time. Support for greater independence at home also reduces the probability of a single person needing to live in a more costly and less desirable nursing home setting.

Economists recognize that few arrangements are free and that even the most loving and attentive treatment comes at the cost of reduced free time, reduced disposable income, and increased pain for the caregiver. Additional costs such as modification of the home setting to accommodate care, durable medical equipment, health care supplies, and out-of-pocket expenses can be calculated and are considerable. Intangible costs for caregivers in terms of personal health, emotional strain, loss of social relationships, and anticipatory grief are seldom factored into the economic equations. Even hospice care, with its many advantages, is not immune to such costs.

We do not know from Maggie's story what her financial or insurance status might have been. We do know that decisions about the setting and services for persons facing the end of life are seldom unaffected by economic considerations. Whether Maggie's care was publicly funded, paid through individual or group health insurance, or purchased directly by her family, the complex economic issues must be acknowledged. From a public policy perspective, the economics of end-of-life care options and choices are critical to families such as Maggie's.

Provider Response
Megan Gunnell

The use of music therapy as a family intervention for Maggie's case could have been a powerful way of facilitating emotional expression and opening communication channels between family members. Music, like language, is composed of tones, pitches, and rhythm. However, music does not carry the same connotations or associations that words do (Miller, 1994). Therefore, by using music as a therapeutic and nonverbal interaction between family members, one can quickly assess various aspects of the situation such as information about family roles, balance of power, triangulation, self-differentiation, or individuation.

When people are creating or listening to music together, they typically begin to engage in the experience and their focus narrows to the space of the music. They also may feel more relaxed, which mutes the inner critic that constantly censors talk therapy or other verbal interactions. An individual wholly engaged in a music exchange may become so engrossed in the experience that any other internal or external stimuli seem to disappear. Music can be a powerful therapeutic tool (Decuir, 1991).

With Maggie's story, specifically, an important motive was to protect her children from the devastation of her progressing disease and yet in doing so she may have done more harm. The children seemed unaware of the severity of Maggie's cancer. When they were informed about how much time their mother had left to live, they were shattered. A music intervention such as improvisation could have served as a catalyst for a deep and meaningful family interaction or discussion. In this type of work, each family member plays a tuned or untuned instrument and the skillful therapist supports the process on an instrument on which he or she is well versed (O'Kelly, 2002). During the improvisation, family members might have become aware of fear, anxiety, leadership, anger, sadness, anticipation, avoidance, trust, or many other various possible emotions or motivations.

Sometimes, using music as a nonverbal approach to connecting with others can, ironically, be the quickest way to a deeply meaningful conversation. A therapist might be listening and watching for adversarial or conjoint interactions, solo or duet playing, imbalances in power displayed by great variances in volume or quick shifts in playing styles, as well as any type of disconnection to the other family members playing (Miller, 1994). All of the aforementioned possibilities, if identified, could have prompted openness between Maggie and her children to freely discuss the parallels between their playing and their feelings. For example, the dramatic confrontation initiated by Maggie's sister when she speaks about the children's real feelings might have been handled more productively had they had an opportunity for music-assisted communication.

Part of the core work of dying is the completion of relationships through communication. Oftentimes when people have been wounded within families, verbal communication is inadequate, and it is socially unacceptable to express lingering resentments or other deep emotions at the time of death. Losing someone is never easy, but not having had the opportunity to say what you wanted that person to hear is even more difficult. Music improvisation can facilitate the playing out of issues such as abandonment, separation, anxiety, guilt, helplessness, denial, or rejection. The communication between Maggie and her children seemed guarded and strained. Both parties did not want to hurt or disappoint the other with their honest feelings. We do not know the extent of any lingering unresolved emotional issues between members of this family. However, families often have muted themes that go unexpressed and that compromise their ability to achieve a harmonious end for both the dying person and the survivors.

In addition to using music improvisation, song writing might also have been a very effective means of expression. A therapist can help empower patients by encouraging them to not only create song lyrics, but also to dictate musically how they would like to compose the piece in terms of tempo, style, length, instrumentation, and dynamics. Both Maggie and her children might have had an opportunity to compose songs for each other that the therapist could accompany or sing for them. Music therapy could have been a comfort to this family in that their music experiences together might have stimulated conversation that was exactly what they each wanted the other to hear. A song created in this context might well become a part of the dying person's family legacy.

Family Response
Peter Wolf

The metaphor of a swinging mobile describes the dynamics a family experiences before, during, and after the death of a family member. Just as in the mobile, when one part moves, every part is affected. Similarly, each person within the family uniquely adjusts to change; yet each person's response also affects the others in the family system. Death disrupts families and family systems. The degree of disruption depends on several factors, such as the role of the deceased in the family, power, affection, and communication patterns (Worden, 1996).

The imminent death of Maggie tipped the homeostatic balance of her family. Rather than being the family's caregiver, Maggie is now the recipient of care. This shift in roles dramatically changed the customary functioning within this family. Maggie, accustomed to being a major family decision maker, now found that her power of self-determination was greatly reduced. She no longer had the power to decide where she was to live and where she was to die.

Functioning like a mobile, the family communication patterns were thrown into disorder by Maggie's shift from central decision maker to weakened, dying patient. The current chaos of the family was evidenced in the mixed communication patterns. On the one hand, Maggie reported that her children told her that they wanted her at home. The sister, however, contradicted this idea and suggested that the children were afraid to have her home.

As a social worker, it is difficult to untangle all of the dynamics of this situation. How this incident exactly transpired is unknown. In such a fluid situation, the absence of the children from the case conference in which critical decisions were made was highly problematic and prevented the resolution of important issues.

The family appeared to face the final days of Maggie's life with unfinished business and an array of unattended emotions. The story echoes with emotions of pain, guilt, blame, and helplessness. Maggie dies in a nursing home, a place that was not her choice, and without the presence of her children. The process of dying can be seen as an event that affects both the individual and others.

Dying persons are the experts on their life (Kubler-Ross, 1997), but this perspective is not sufficient to guarantee high-quality care at the end of life. In part, high-quality care means empowering dying persons to journey the rest of their lives with the comfort of knowing their decisions are being fulfilled. To do this, we must listen to dying persons' perceptions and encourage them to tell their stories the way they want them lived. Although this approach is valid, dying also involves shifts in relationships between the individual and his or her loved ones (Wright, 2003).

It is obvious that Maggie's children are stunned by the idea that their strong, capable, hard-working mother is dying. These three children are at a vulnerable period in their lives; as teenagers and young adults, they are beginning to assert their independence. They were probably accustomed to the idea that their mother is not well, since she had been living with the cancer diagnosis for 18 months. At this point, however, their lives are threatened with further disruption. How will they be able to continue their school and social lives now that their mother is dying? Will they be able to provide her with the care she needs? Who will keep the family connected? Who will be the social and emotional anchor for the surviving young people as they experience important life transitions such as graduations, weddings, and the birth of children. On top of these questions is the added fact that their grandmother is also seriously ill and will probably not be in a position to fill any of these major social roles. For Maggie's children, the world appears to be caving in, and everything they had begun appears to be coming to a halt.

In addition, as is true of most Americans, they are probably afraid to confront the issue of dying. Never having had to watch someone die or even experiencing a death in their social circle, watching their mother die in front of them may be too much for them to face. Even though they are adults, Maggie's sisters also are not prepared, or able, to take on the responsibility of caring for her at home. The sisters make the argument that the children's reaction to Maggie's dying might be so intense that they would leave to live with their father. The magnitude of the implied threat suggests that there are additional features to the family psychodrama beyond what the narrator provides in the story. After the social worker assures them that they can visit Maggie, the family ultimately chooses a nursing home placement. This solution salves the conscience of the sisters, but it raises questions about the long-term relationships between Maggie and her family.

The end of Maggie's story is not positive: Her final wishes go unfulfilled. Some research indicates that the four most important factors at the end of life for dying persons include pain management, preparation for death (a sense of completion), decisions about treatment preferences, and being treated as a whole person (Steinhauser et al., 2000). For Maggie, only some of these factors were successfully addressed. Maggie's sense of completion and treatment as a whole person fell short, and the dominant focus of Maggie's care was adequate medication to relieve her physical pain.

One can muse upon how Maggie's final days could have been quite different had there been more extensive professional involvement and the inclusion of quality discussions with family and friends. These discussions would have focused on how Maggie could come home, spend time with her children, and die in comfortable, inviting surroundings. The discussions might have helped the family more clearly see and resolve these issues. The result would have been a different experience for Maggie and probably a more meaningful and satisfactory experience for both Maggie and her children.

REFERENCES

Decuir, A. (1991). Trends in music and family therapy. *The Arts in Psychotherapy, 18*, 195–199.

Folland, S., Goodman, A., & Stano, M. (2004). *The economics of health and health care.* Upper Saddle River, NJ: Prentice-Hall, chap. 14.

Hamilton, V. (1993). The Medicare hospice benefit: The effectiveness of price incentives in health care policy, *Rand Journal of Economics, 24*, 605–624.

Kubler-Ross, E. (1997). *On children and death.* New York: Touchstone.

Miller, E. B. (1994). Music intervention in family therapy. *Music Therapy, 12*, 39–57.

O'Kelly, J. (2002). Music therapy in palliative care: Current perspectives. *International Journal of Palliative Nursing, 8*, 130–136.

National Hospice and Palliative Care Organization. (2004). *Facts and figures.* Retrieved May 9, 2004, from http://www.nhpco.org/files/public/Facts%20Figures%2oFeb%2004.pdf

Pezzin, L., Kemper, E. P., & Reschovsky, J. (1996). Does publicly provided home care substitute for family care? *Journal of Human Resources, 31*(3), 650–676.

Steinhauser, K. E., Christakis, N. A., Clipp, E. C., McNeilly, M., McIntyre, L., & Tulsky, J. A. (2000). Factors considered important at the end of life by patients, family, physicians, and other care providers. *Journal of the American Medical Association, 284*, 2476–2482.

Worden, W. J. (1996). *Children and grief: When a parent dies.* New York: Guilford.

Wright, K. (2003). Relationships with death: The terminally ill talk about dying. *Journal of Marital and Family Therapy, 29*, 439–454.

CHAPTER 8

Stories of Malika: Defining a Person

For some life lasts a short while, but the memories it holds last forever.

—Laura Swenson

Malika's Story
Kathleen L. Meert

A 3-year-old African American girl named Malika came to the hospital with poor oral intake for the previous 2 months. She was born prematurely at 26 weeks of gestation. Complications of her prematurity included many serious issues. Malika had *bronchopulmonary dysplasia* (BPD), a chronic lung disease of premature infants. She also had *patent ductus arteriosus*, in which a blood vessel in the heart that normally closes after birth does not close properly. Another problem of premature infants that Malika experienced was *necrotizing enterocolitis with bowel perforation*. Perforation usually requires surgery to remove segments of the damaged bowel. Additionally, she had a Grade IV *intraventricular hemorrhage*, which meant that there was severe bleeding in her brain. As a result of the bleeding, Malika developed hydrocephalus and a seizure disorder. *Hydrocephalus* is a build-up of fluid in the brain that compresses normal brain tissue and can lead to death if untreated. Malika's hydrocephalus had been treated shortly after birth by the surgical placement of a ventricular-peritoneal shunt. This procedure involved putting a tube from a fluid compartment of the brain (ventricle) to the abdomen (peritoneal cavity.) Fluid in the brain could then drain through this tube under Malika's skin into the abdomen and be reabsorbed by her body. Since that time, she had had numerous episodes of shunt malfunction and infection, requiring over 50 brain operations. Because of peritoneal scarring and malabsorption of spinal fluid, the ventricular shunt had eventually been revised to drain into Malika's heart.

Much of Malika's young life had been spent in the hospital. In addition to her other complications, she was significantly delayed in all areas of development. Her physical problems, including the fluid on her brain, multiple invasive brain and abdominal surgeries, and lack of normal childhood developmental opportunities meant that Malika had many developmental delays. At about age 3 she appeared to recognize her family, but could speak only five words, had poor head and trunk control, difficulty swallowing, could not sit up or roll over without assistance, and could not sufficiently feed herself.

When Malika was again brought to the hospital, another ventricular shunt malfunction and recurrent hydrocephalus were suspected as the causes of her poor oral intake and weight loss. This time her shunt was externalized, requiring a hole to be drilled through the skull so that a tube could drain fluid from the brain into a bag outside her body. Eventually the tube was replaced with a shunt that drained fluid from her brain into the area around her lung (pleural space). She underwent six operations on her brain during this final hospital stay. She also had a feeding tube put through her abdominal wall directly into her stomach to deliver nourishment. Children born very early often receive a great amount of high-tech medical care. In Malika's story, however, her short life had already been filled with medical crises and extensive surgical interventions. Each intervention seemed to precipitate another crisis for Malika, and each procedure was complicated by postoperative pain. Multiple pain medications in varying dosages were provided; however, her pain remained difficult to control. The child was restless and cried frequently. The degree of pain and suffering worsened with each episode and finally prompted Malika's mother to agree to meet with hospice workers regarding home care after hospital discharge.

The day following the hospice meeting, Malika was found in her hospital room not breathing and without a pulse. Cardiopulmonary resuscitation was performed. She was placed on a breathing machine and transferred to the ICU. Malika was deeply comatose. Brain stem reflexes were absent except for agonal gasping respirations. The lack of brain stem reflexes indicated severe neurological damage. In this condition, Malika was not technically described as brain dead because she still had some weak respiratory effort. However, she was described by her medical team as "non-cognitive and unresponsive to external stimulation." The intensive care physician recommended that life support be withdrawn because of her hopeless prognosis. No chance for meaningful recovery was seen. The mother agreed. The breathing machine was removed, and the child died in her mother's arms.

Family Response
LaDon Harris

Hello doctors, interns, and students!

I am a single mother of a deceased 3 3/4-year-old daughter named Malika. She was born 26-weeks gestation at 2 lbs-1 ounce, and 15 inches tall. After Malika was born, I found out she had a Grade IV brain bleed bilaterally and that she had to wear oxygen. Malika's start in life was very rough. The doctors did not know whether she would live or die. Malika spent the first 2 months in the hospital until she gained enough weight for a very serious brain surgery. She had to have a ventricular peritoneal shunt placement.

About 7 days after surgery, Malika was able to go home for the first time. It felt good to be home. She seemed to enjoy it and to be looking and turning to different voices. It was great until I started noticing changes and symptoms of shunt malfunction. Her scalp was very loose and soft as a wet sponge. She stopped breathing and turned purple from head to toe. I revived her. She began crying and her normal pinkish color was back. The emergency medical technicians arrived. They told me I did a very good job, and we were off to the hospital. Then was when things started getting worse.

I was at Malika's bedside. There I was day and night never going home, praying with her father and other family members. During our stay in the hospital, chaplains knew us well. My faith in God has kept me going through this hard time. During that 3-

month stay, Malika was diagnosed with cerebral palsy, umbilical hernia, perforated ulcer, hole in her patent duct, BPD, GERD (gastroesophageal reflux disease), and a blood infection needing two blood transfusions.

During all of this, I was trying hard to get the doctors to listen. I was denied, but I was persistent; upset but never got loud and disrespectful, but very pesty. If I did not know her history and the different situations, she would have died sooner than age 3 3/4 years.

After another discharge from the hospital, we recuperated for a whole month and a half. I enrolled my daughter into two programs: the public school's Early Intervention Diagnostic Center and the Institute for Handicapped Children. Malika had physical, occupational, speech, and social therapies at three places including home. It was a rough start. She was very tight, crying, not wanting anyone besides me to touch her. As time progressed, Malika began to sit with the assistance of a feeding chair, arching her back, crying sometimes. A few months went by. Not very much progress had been made. She was examined by doctors. I was told she would not see, hear, walk, or talk. I kept praying to God and telling the doctors that was not true because she interacted with me at home.

Malika and I would sit on the living room floor, play with toys that she would maneuver well, and other things that were a challenge to her. I would read bright colorful books to her. She would take her fist and help me turn pages. I would call out the colors to her and point to the items. She caught on. I would ask her if the color she had her hand on was red. She would look back at me with this huge smile on her face and giggle with excitement, which meant "Yes." We would turn the page a few more times to something else red. I would ask if that was the color red. The same expression came upon her face but this time I heard the word "yeah" come out of her mouth. We both were so excited I began kissing and hugging her. She also said "daddy" and "ma"—this was out of the blue. I believe it came from all of the talking and explaining of everything I did to and with her.

Malika began eating pureed and soft foods. Her favorites were oatmeal—all flavors—and pudding—chocolate, lemon, and butterscotch. Yogurt was also a favorite; orange sherbet; strawberry, blueberry was a sometime flavor. Malika did not like feeding herself with her hands because she always bit her fingers. Her jaw muscles were so tight she could not move her fingers fast enough. I let her use the spoon. Food was everywhere. Eventually she would get some in her mouth. Her hand and eye coordination was off. She enjoyed trying. I would feed her first then let her take over.

I taught Malika how to untie her shoes in a sitting position. She would pull the strings a few times, and the shoes were still on. She would lean back on me and rub her feet together until the shoe came off. I would joke with her asking, "Did you take those shoes off all by yourself?" Malika would give that look and say "yeah" and start giggling. She understood a lot. Her father and I were talking about something funny and before it was complete she started laughing, and we laughed because she understood what was being said about her.

I knew my baby could do more than doctors gave her credit. Because she did not do it in their presence, it was summed up that she could not do anything. Doctors spent only a few minutes with Malika. They did not know her like I did. Even the therapists were amazed. One day at the Early Intervention Diagnostic Center, Malika was standing in a standing frame with a desktop attached. She had worked on a painting project with my assistance. Afterwards it was time to clean up. I asked Malika to wipe off the table, "Clean up the paint from the table?" She did. They were so excited. I told the teacher and therapist that she does this at home.

Outside of eating, reading, bathing, and me talking to her, the most favorite part of the evening was bedtime. I would sometimes read the Bible and get her a bottle of vanilla PediaSure™, her favorite drink. Malika would become so restless I would ask, "Are you ready for bed?" She would smile and say "Yeah." We would cuddle up, another favorite thing. We would be so busy during the day you could not help being tired and sleepy.

Well, doctors, students, and interns, mothers and fathers may not have a PhD or MD behind their names. But it does not mean that we are dumb. We have our children 24 hours a day, 7 days a week, and we know when something is wrong. Please do not feel less than a doctor when you do not know what's going on, and, in the end, what the parent is saying is true. Please do not sugar-coat any conditions or do not be without compassion. You never know, you or your children may need a doctor, a student, a nurse, or an intern to listen. I pray that God will give you patience to listen, and the wisdom to understand what our families go through and the needs of our children, not just your paychecks or degrees. There is more to medical assistance than that. I pray that God will bless you with the wisdom of life.

Sincerely Yours,
A Concerned Parent

Provider Response
Alexa Canady

This story represents one of the most difficult management problems for neurosurgeons. As the medical history points out, this child was born at 26 weeks gestation and developed most of the complications of such an early birth. The Grade IV hemorrhage, which by definition is bleeding not only into the ventricles (fluid chambers) of the brain but also into the brain, causes brain injury manifested in this 3 3/4-year-old's inability to sit, stand, or roll over. She had some cognition and recognized her family and said approximately five words. This low level of functioning occurred even with more than 50 operations culminating in the surgeon's resorting to a last-resort shunt—the shunt around the lungs that probably never worked well.

The mother comments about the difficulty getting people to listen to her and this perception is often the case. Many factors come into play, such as physician and nursing personnels' discomfort with severely impaired children, work load, and discomfort with culturally different people. As an African American surgeon, I know that minority patients, on the basis of their historical experience, are often suspicious that medical personnel do not value their children and are not giving their full effort to save them. There is also a gap between the experiences of the medical personnel and the family. In particular, more experienced medical personnel have a longitudinal sense of severely impaired children. Seasoned staff members have seen that the cute but impaired infant often becomes an older child or adolescent who is no longer cute and for whom society does not provide adequate services. This change all too often leads to destruction of the family. The fathers often exit the unpleasant situation before infancy ends, and siblings can feel resentful and ignored. Physician–parent interactions are clouded also by difficulties in understanding the true status of a child with the parents often presenting an excessively rosy picture of the child's accomplishments, some of which are random. You cannot observe a child for minutes and understand his or her abilities, and children often have more abilities than are immediately apparent because of communication difficulties. However, if you talk to the schoolteachers and therapists who are with the children for hours a day, you often find that the skills are more limited than the parents believe.

How do we manage this problem of perception? One of the problems of modern medicine is to make a family understand all of these issues on the health professionals' timetable. The families cannot. This results in decision making in the newborn period that, despite what you tell most families, selects the 1 in 1 million chance that things will work out well, causing parents to be anxious for aggressive treatment. It is interesting that just the opposite is often true in families of medical professionals. Health professionals need to recognize this dissociation of expectation and allow the family their own timetable for dealing with such a profound change in their lives. Even as we intervene and offer treatments that they are not enthusiastic about, they need to begin the education process. This education is best done during routine visits, not during crises. Physicians need to give the family a sense of the outlook and to expose them to other families with similar problems who have been dealing with their children for a longer period of time. If case management is properly done, in almost all instances physicians can help the family look beyond their protective optimism and gain a more realistic sense of the outcome. Such communication will close the gap between care providers and the family, and they will begin to feel like the physicians are with them, not against them.

In some cases, the family and the physician have genuine disagreement on the usefulness of additional intervention. There is no obligation for surgeons to offer therapy they do not feel is medically indicated and, in those rare cases, the physician should offer alternative caregivers for the family. Another step, which we have used, is to review the case with a multidisciplinary committee whose members are not involved in the care and provide an outside opinion regarding the futility of additional therapy.

In the midst of all this, it is important to remember that although for health care staff it is "just another day at work," for the family, these are the most important decisions of their lives. The journey is to help the family understand that loving and protecting their child sometimes means letting go.

Cultural Response
Sherylyn H. Briller and Allison Kabel

Malika's best interests are what everyone is passionately arguing for in this story, although from their own perspectives as a mother, as a pediatric neurosurgeon, and as the pediatrician-narrator. What is implicit rather than overtly stated here is a central issue of how to consider Malika's personhood at the time when crucial decisions about additional treatment are being made. It is not entirely surprising that core concerns about personhood were not explicitly discussed in this case as it is often taken for granted that everyone's assumptions about personhood are the same. However, it is important to recognize that *personhood*, which can be broadly defined as one's identity as a social person, is not universally constructed in the same way (Armstrong & Fitzgerald, 1996). Rather, the requirements for achieving personhood vary significantly between cultures.

In the United States, for example, cognition is highly prioritized in discussions of what it means to be a person. The ethicist Stephen Post (2000) highlights what he calls our culture's "hyper-cognitivist value system" (p. 18) in his book on ethical issues in dementia. Post discusses " . . . how our culture's criteria of rationality and productivity blind us to other ways of thinking about the meaning of our humanity and the nature of humane care" (p. 18). Consequently, he urges Western clinicians, policy makers, and social science researchers to broaden their thinking about what it means to be a person in order to move onward and create new ethics of dementia care (Post, 2000).

The connection between the ethics of dementia care and the story of Malika, a young and very ill child, demonstrates some of the fundamental issues about the status of personhood that are highly relevant across the human life course. These issues can be used to frame the heated debate over how Malika's care should proceed. Not only does our society have ideas about how personhood is generally constructed and the role of cognition in personhood, there are also ideas about what full adult personhood entails. Luborsky (1994) discusses the concept of full adult personhood in U.S. society. He emphasizes how key requirements for an unquestioned personhood in this society often include physical independence and control over bodily functions. Murphy (1987) highlights similar themes in his autobiographical book *The Body Silent*, which chronicles his gradual paralysis from a spinal tumor. He poignantly describes how his own adult social identity and personhood were repeatedly challenged during this illness experience and the onset of disability—even as he maintained his powerful and privileged role in our society as a professor at Columbia University.

The relevance of this discussion for Malika's story is that part of what remains unspoken is whether Malika could ever gain any of the aspects of full adult personhood as defined in our society. Yet, Post (2000) argues that in a broader definition of personhood part of what is important about being human includes aspects such as the ability to be in human relationships—something that Malika's mother described as sharing with her family. There are so many beautiful instances of these bonds in the mother's account of Malika's time at home: Malika responding to her family's voices, doing activities like playing and listening to books with her mother, eating her favorite foods like oatmeal, pudding, yogurt, and vanilla PediaSure™. Even as Malika became increasingly ill, she remained deeply embedded in these family relationships. It seems as though Malika's mother is trying to tell the medical staff about this very issue throughout her loving account of Malika's short life and the final comment in her letter where she says, "I pray that God will bless you with wisdom of life."

This story is complicated because it is not simply a story of the "good mother" defending Malika's personhood and the "evil" medical establishment refusing to acknowledge her personhood. The physicians' perspectives reflect issues about which they need to be professionally and ethically deeply concerned. These issues include inflicting further pain and suffering upon Malika, appropriate use of technology in prolonging her life, and who should make decisions when, as the surgeon states, "The family and the physician have genuine disagreement on the usefulness of the additional intervention."

There is an underlying tension between the family and the medical establishment's interpretations of the prognosis for a meaningful recovery. The mother interprets Malika's behavior as evidence that the child is indeed a person with a future while the surgeon fears that these behaviors are actually random gestures rather than meaningful interactions. The surgeon is also passionate about the educational need that she and her colleagues have to provide families with what she calls "a realistic sense of the outcome" and physicians' longer term perspectives from having seen such situations over time. Yet, it seemed that the mother would still ultimately question whether all of the professional clinical knowledge was meaningful without listening to parents' experiential knowledge gained from "having our children 24 hours a day, 7 days a week." She goes on to say, "Please do not feel less than a doctor when you do not know what's going on and in the end what the parent is saying is true." And the surgeon wisely points out that there are times when a multidisciplinary committee can better help to reach a negotiated solution that is, one hopes, perceived by all involved as in the best interests of the child.

Consensus was eventually achieved in this story about what would be best for Malika, but only as her medical situation rapidly deteriorated. Malika was briefly enrolled in hospice and following the withdrawal of life support died in her mother's loving arms. The decision to involve hospice at the very end of Malika's life is significant. As is true for adults, hospice care for children is often considered very late in the wake of a hopeless prognosis, after all other avenues have been exhausted.

Having seen the complexities of this story and all that went into the agonized decision making, I must underscore the uniqueness of each family's experiences. Many service providers and researchers have reported, for example, a pattern of underenrollment in hospice services within the African American community (Jackson, Schim, Seely, Grunow, & Baker, 2000; Schim, Jackson, Seely, Grunow, & Baker, 2000.) To simply rely on reported trends and conventional wisdom about African American families' low acceptance of hospice services is to forgo a more sophisticated understanding of why individual families make the particular decisions that they do.

In short, it is never in doubt that everyone in this situation wants to "do the right thing" for Malika, who has already endured so much in her short lifetime. Rather, the sticking points were: Who should make the judgments? What criteria should be used to decide? What should be the decision-making timeframe and what should be done? The mother believed it should be her right as a parent, and as the person who had the deepest relationship with Malika, to make these decisions. The physicians felt that they were bound by their professional ethics to make the best medical decision for the child and to prevent additional pain and suffering that could result from additional surgical procedures. The pediatric neurosurgeon, although she was not the treating surgeon in this story, spoke to this issue from her perspective as one who has been doing these kinds of procedures, from her long history of working in this field, and as a person with deep personal knowledge of this community.

A major issue that remained in the background was that personhood is being tacitly and variably defined by everyone involved in Malika's care. Explicit analysis of personhood issues should be part of the foreground of medical treatment and ethical decision making rather than part of the background context, as it was for Malika. The education of health care providers and others involved with families in these situations should include both the concept of personhood and its ramifications for providing health care in diverse settings.

Ethics Response
Kathleen L. Meert

Advances in medical science and technology have provided therapeutic interventions for many illnesses and conditions that would have been imminently lethal in earlier times. Although intended as tools to restore health and save lives, such interventions can at times result in the development of chronic illness and prolonged suffering. The appropriateness of interventions depends upon a careful balance of perceived benefits and potential risks or harm to individual patients. Determining this point of balance can be a difficult task for families and health professionals caring for children with severe debilitating or life-threatening illnesses. Malika's story introduces the complexities of end-of-life care and decision making for children and exemplifies the difficulty in assessing and managing pain in the neurologically compromised. It also highlights some of the issues arising from the typical late entry of children into hospice care.

End-of-life decision making is a difficult and emotion-laden process. When making end-of-life decisions with patients and their families, physicians rely on ethical principles to guide the process. In a Western society such as the United States, physicians caring for adults invoke the principle of respect for persons or autonomy (Beauchamp & Childress, 1994). *Respect for persons* acknowledges an individual's right to make health care decisions for themselves, even at the end of life. A competent adult can accept or refuse interventions recommended by a physician.

Difficulty in decision making may arise when an adult who was previously competent becomes incapacitated near the end of life. An incapacitated adult however, may have previously made personal wishes known as to what type of care he or she prefers. Prior wishes may even be formalized by some type of advance directive such as a living will or health care proxy. Advance directives help to preserve the autonomy of an incapacitated patient. If no advance directives exist, physicians rely on the principle of *substituted judgment* (Beauchamp & Childress, 1994). This concept presumes that the newly incapacitated adult did have prior wishes and that others who were in close relationship with that adult will be able to voice those wishes in the present situation. By invoking the principle of substituted judgment, it is the role of the physician to describe the patient's condition and the reasonable options for care, and it is the role of the family to provide information as to what the patient's choice would have been.

Children have not yet reached the developmental stage at which they are capable of making end of life decisions for themselves. Physicians caring for children at end of life rely on the principle of *beneficence* (Beauchamp & Childress, 1994). The goal of beneficence is not only to provide maximum benefit to the child but also to protect the child from harm. By invoking the principle of beneficence, physicians and parents are obligated to try to make decisions that are in the best interest of the child. Assessing what is in the child's best interest will necessitate assessing the child's present quality of life, his or her degree of pain and suffering, and the expectations for the child's future. For severely neurologically impaired children, assessing best interest involves assessing the child's basic human capacities, those of self-awareness and the ability to interact with others.

Deciding what is in a child's best interest at the end of life is a difficult process. Parents' perceptions of their child's basic human capacities may be vastly different from the perceptions of a physician. The perceptions of families and health professionals regarding a neurologically impaired child's developmental and cognitive abilities, quality of life, and expectations for the future are often quite disparate. When assessing these issues, families often rely on a close and nearly constant interaction with the child, the strength of relationship or degree of dependency that develops between the parents and child, as well as the hopes, dreams, and faith they hold for the child's future. Additionally, there may be conflicts between the interests of the parents and the interests of the child. Parents may demand continued therapy in attempt to maintain family integrity and avoid the pain of loss rather than allow their child to die peacefully. In spite of these conflicts, the best-interest standard requires that the interests of the child prevail.

Parents have broad authority over their child's life; however, parental authority is not absolute. Pediatricians, for example, have the responsibility to provide clearly beneficial therapy to their patients, even when parents refuse such therapy based on religious beliefs. Similarly, physicians are not obligated to provide therapies that are futile. Hospital ethics committees may be consulted. Physicians may also find it necessary to transfer the patient's care to another physician or institution. The parents may find another physician on their own or physicians and parents may continue to meet, discuss, and eventually reach consensus. Health professionals have only brief, intermittent observations of the child, but rely on their training and their own clinical experience and the experience of others who have provided care for many with conditions similar to that of their patient.

In making end-of-life decisions for children, physicians are faced with the task of explaining to parents their child's poor prognosis and the limitations of therapy. Parents are asked to assimilate this information, overcome shock and denial, and consider what their child's future will hold. Health professionals must respect parental authority; however, this respect does not relieve the health professional from the fiduciary obligation to recommend an appropriate plan of care for the terminally ill child.

Partially because of the inherent difficulties in making end-of-life decisions for children, those with chronic disabling conditions often enter the hospice system relatively late in their course of illness, if at all. There is a general reluctance to refer children for hospice evaluation and availability of pediatric hospice programs are quite limited. Unlike the elderly, children have had little time to experience life, and if restoration of health were even remotely possible, most of their life experience would be before them. Childhood death has fortunately become less frequent in industrialized countries than in earlier times. Many families have never known anyone who has lost a child and have no past experience to guide them. Many parents never really accept the fact that their child could die, even when health professionals and others have done their best to effectively communicate a realistic prognosis. An unrealistic reliance on technology often causes parents to expect that something more can always be done to save the child. Suspicions that physicians might recommend limitation of therapy because of inadequate medical insurance or inability to pay may also make parents reluctant to consider hospice care.

End-of-life decision making for children can be a highly emotional situation for parents and physicians. Both families and health professionals bring their perceptions to the table when undertaking the arduous task of end-of-life decision making for children. Discussing these perceptions openly and acknowledging the presence of multiple truths can help parents and health professionals make the best decisions for the child. A peaceful resolution requires that parents and physicians eventually reach consensus on how to proceed with the child's care.

REFERENCES

Armstrong, M. J., & Fitzgerald, M. H. (1996). Culture and disability studies: An anthropological perspective. *Rehabilitation Education, 10,* 247–304.

Beauchamp, T., & Childress, J. (1994). *Principles of biomedical ethics* (4th ed.). New York: Oxford University Press.

Jackson, F. C., Schim, S. M., Seely, S., Grunow, K., & Baker, J. (2000). Barriers to hospice care for African Americans: Problems and solutions. *Journal of Hospice and Palliative Care Nursing, 2,* 65–72.

Luborsky, M. L. (1994). The cultural adversity of physical disability: Erosion of full adult personhood. *Journal of Aging Studies, 8,* 277–280.
Murphy, R. (1990). *The body silent: The different world of the disabled.* New York: W. W. Norton.
Post, S. G. (2000). *The moral challenge of Alzheimer's disease: Ethical issues from diagnosis to dying.* Baltimore: Johns Hopkins University Press.
Schim, S. M., Jackson, F. C., Seely, S., Grunow, K., & Baker, J. (2000). Knowledge and attitudes of home care nurses toward hospice referral. *Journal of Nursing Administration, 30,* 273–277.

CHAPTER 9

Stories of Sonny:
Tattoos and Tolerance

The deepest principle in human nature is the craving to be appreciated.

—William James

Sonny's Story
Steven M. Popkin

It was late into a moonless fall evening when I received a telephone call from my office asking if I could meet with a 65-year-old gentleman named Sonny. In my job as a hospice social worker, I am often called upon to help patients and their families clarify medical, emotional, social, and spiritual realities as they face death. I was told that Sonny was on a ventilator in the ICU of a local hospital. His pulmonary specialist had written an order for a hospice consult for Sonny because of his diagnoses of terminal respiratory and renal failure and his rapidly declining condition. As I drove to the hospital to meet with Sonny and his family, I contemplated the demise of another human being, the power that nature exerts over human life, and the daunting task of trying to prepare another individual and family for the final chapter. I was not prepared for Sonny and my first experience with a terminal wean.

My first glimpse of this patient was an oblique view through the partially opened glass door-wall of his harshly lit room where he lay amidst a dismaying array of bright blue plastic ventilator tubing, flashing light-emitting diodes, audible alarms, and cascading IV lines. Vivid tattoos adorned Sonny's body from head to toe, strangely dramatic on this body that was bloated from renal failure. Enormous worn, and disfigured stuffed animals, won at the state fair, crowded the narrow bed, creating a macabre, carnival-like scene. Sonny lay unresponsive in the ICU bed as his daughter and son-in-law hovered at the bedside cherishing every movement or hint of vitality.

Sonny's medical history included coronary artery disease, congestive heart failure, hypertension, renal insufficiency, two myocardial infarcts, and a cardiac catheterization 1 year ago. He had also been recently diagnosed with lung and esophageal cancer that had spread to his bones. Six weeks prior to this admission to the hospital, Sonny had a 5-day hospitalization for a virulent respiratory infection. His current admission, now in its 12th day, began when Sonny drove himself to the hospital and walked into the ER. When his history was taken, he complained of generalized weakness, chronic diarrhea, and a nagging cough that "wouldn't go away." Sonny had a 51-year, three-pack-per-day practice of smoking unfiltered cigarettes, as well as a 30-year history of weekly binge drinking of homemade wine and "moonshine." No advance directives had been given at the time of admission to the ER or with subsequent admission to the ICU. No Patient Advocate, Guardianship, or Durable Power of Attorney for Health Care forms were ever presented.

Sonny had led a colorful life. He dropped out of high school in the 10th grade to become a merchant marine, where he began a career of dishwashing and cooking. He worked below the waterline on iron ore carriers plying the Great Lakes. According to his daughter and her husband, while Sonny was an ordinary seaman and food handler on Lake Erie, he was exposed to the art of tattooing and began to learn and practice that trade. Sonny prepared for the General Education Development (GED) test through self-study and passed it after three valiant attempts. He was a well-read man despite his limited formal education and was a self-taught minister, just like his son-in-law. Up until 10 years ago, Sonny had been employed as a short-order cook at a series of truck stops and waffle shops. By his mid-60's, Sonny's stamina had begun to ebb, he could barely see, and tremors in his hands made it impossible for him to work as a cook or tattoo artist. His application for Social Security Disability benefits had been denied several times before it was finally approved. He was then able to eke out an existence that he and his family said was like a slow death.

Sonny had only one child from his first marriage and was now divorced for the third time. Each of Sonny's former wives came to visit him while he was in the hospital, passionately expressing their devotion and sorrow that such a great man had taken ill. At one point, Sonny's daughter wryly commented on how unusual it was for Sonny to maintain relationships with his "following" of ex-wives. Sonny was described by his family members as a thoughtful, yet fiercely independent man who had little tolerance for the ignorance, opinions, or idiosyncrasies of others.

As Sonny's respiratory status deteriorated further, his physician asked him about his wishes for further treatment. Sonny emphatically declared that he "wanted to live!" When he signed a Code Status Determination form he checked "Code I: Where all medically appropriate treatment should be provided, also known as a 'Full Code.' " The other options presented on the form ran the gamut from full code all the way to "Code IV: No medical treatment will be provided except medication for comfort, also known as 'Comfort Care.' " How well Sonny understood what he was agreeing to will never be known, yet according to his physicians, his decisional capacity appeared to be intact at that time. Within minutes of signing the document to remain "Full Code," Sonny's clinical status dramatically worsened. He was intubated and put on a ventilator because of his difficulty breathing. Additionally, Sonny began receiving dialysis treatments for his failing renal function. Sonny was actively dying.

Hospital social workers met with the family and discussed a variety of care options. Usually one option would be discharge of a patient to a skilled nursing facility that provided ventilator support. In Sonny's case, nursing home placement was not an option because of his poor prognosis and rapid decline. A range of other options was discussed and each one rejected for moral, spiritual, or financial reasons. Referral to hospice for assistance with the terminal wean was the option the family tentatively accepted.

Sonny's daughter and son-in-law were at his bedside to visit when I arrived. The medical team had reported that Sonny was unresponsive to verbal stimuli and to physical pain. Family members, however, maintained that their familiar voices elicited responses from him. Although he had signed a document requesting that everything possible be done to save his life, Sonny's family was now convinced that he did not want to remain on the ventilator on the basis of the blinking of his eyelids in apparent response to their questions. This conclusion marked a turning point in the case.

Fear was evident on the faces of Sonny's daughter and son-in-law as they realized that to remove the ventilator would amount to a conscious agreement to facilitate his demise. Several times during the 10 days that he had been in the ICU, Sonny had been taken off the vent to evaluate his ability to breathe on his own. With each trial wean, he was gasping for breath within a matter of minutes or sometimes hours. These weaning attempts made the family realize what the cessation of the ventilator for the final time would be like. They also recognized that they would be the ones to make the request that would seal Sonny's destiny. They were not yet prepared to make the final decision.

Sonny's daughter and her husband could not tolerate what they perceived as the "constant pressure" to make a decision about their father. The conscious decision to "let nature take its course" was anything but natural to them. They perceived a sense of hurriedness on the part of the hospital staff, as if the ICU bed was more urgently needed for a more important patient. They believed that there was something inherently unfair in the way Sonny seemed to be a pawn in a game where the common man was being squashed by an elite establishment. The hospital staff seemed to be pushing for a decision to end Sonny's life based on their assumptions about the diminished value of his life. What Sonny wanted or did not want, in terms of his medical care, seemed to have gotten lost, and the family needed both time and support to make this momentous decision.

As the hours passed, the positions of the family and the hospital staff became more entrenched. Despite the patient's desperate state, Sonny's family would not give in to the hospital's increasing insistence that Sonny be taken off the ventilator. Charge nurses and managers, without window dressing or pretense, advised the family that they were "tying up" valuable space and resources that could be better used by patients with a greater chance of survival and recovery. The family yelled at the staff and someone pushed a nurse out of the way. Hospital staff saw Sonny's family as uncouth, discourteous, and "weird." Tempers flared and voices were raised with threats of physical violence and harsh legal action from Sonny's family. They saw themselves as being marginalized and discriminated against. The environment around Sonny became increasingly explosive.

Although Sonny's family acknowledged that there might eventually be no other alternative, they now refused to consider the terminal wean as an immediate option. Raw with rage, Sonny's daughter and son-in-law finally left the hospital to rest and regroup. Two full days later, the ICU staff nurse recontacted my hospice office, indicating that the family had now agreed to the wean and were present at bedside. With a hospice nurse, I returned to meet with the family and to obtain all the paperwork needed to admit Sonny to our hospice program. Sonny's physician, a respiratory therapist, and a chaplain were called to the bedside as is customary for a terminal wean. In this case, security guards were also called because of staff fears about Sonny's family. The presence in the tiny ICU room of uniformed security officers, the family, the hospital team, the hospice nurse and me, the stuffed animals, and the tattooed man in the bed, created a crowded carnival-like atmosphere.

With the family's consent and cooperation, Sonny was sedated, the breathing tubes removed, and the ventilator was shut down. There should have been a moment of peace and reflection as we waited for Sonny to take his last breath. But instead of peace, the scene erupted again as the hospital staff demanded that Sonny and his family move at once to a medical floor so as to vacate the much-needed ICU bed. With much effort, the explosive situation was defused, a compromise was reached, and the dying man and family made their way to a designated hospice bed on a medical floor. Exactly 23 hours after Sonny was taken off the ventilator he passed away in his daughter's arms. Sonny was and will remain a disturbing milestone in my career as a hospice social worker. Even though a decade has passed, I still recall my first terminal wean case and carry its difficult lessons with me to this day.

Cultural Response
Sherylyn H. Briller

Culture shapes all life experiences including health, illness, and the dying process. Yet, despite the central role of culture at the end of life, it is still too often ignored or minimized in discussions of how to provide high quality end-of-life care. Chrisman and Johnson (1996) provide a useful discussion on the roles that medical anthropologists play in clinical settings and how they can contribute to more positive experiences. One capacity in which such services could be more fully used is as "culture broker" in helping to deal with issues of culture clash that arise when the dying person's culture differs significantly from that of health care practitioners. The story of Sonny's death highlights how such a culture clash was a barrier to "a good death."

Sonny's death provides an opportunity to analyze how a culture clash operated "down on the ground" as Sonny, his family, and the health care team attempted to communicate about his end-of-life wishes. Several important attributes of culture have been discussed, namely that culture is learned, shared, and symbolic. Because culture is a collective entity based on common experiences and shared symbols, it is problematic when there are dramatic differences in the dying person's cultural values and those of the health care team that remain unacknowledged. Indeed, Sonny's value system, which prioritized independence, risk-taking, self-education, and nonconformity are in stark contrast with the broader cultural values of the biomedical establishment. The health care team exemplifies the cultural values of compliance with authority, risk avoidance, formal education, value on speed and efficiency, and conformity with institutional expectations.

The first evidence of culture clash appears early in the story as the narrator candidly describes his reaction to Sonny's appearance in a hospital room filled to capacity with both medical equipment and his prized possessions. The social worker is initially mesmerized by Sonny's extensive body tattoos and the large stuffed animal collection around him. The atmosphere in the room is described as "carnival-like," but to the social worker it is a macabre rather than a festive carnival mood. Yet, these stuffed animals are Sonny's cherished possessions, and his tattoos are a way of using the physical body as a form of artistic self-expression. Sonny has carried some of what is most meaningful and related to his individual identity into his hospital room literally on his back. Rather than celebrating that which is most meaningful to Sonny at the very end of his life, it seems that staff members are somewhat repulsed by his various forms of self-expression and cultural symbolism.

The second part of the culture clash relates to how Sonny's lifestyle is portrayed and judged by the staff. They find multiple aspects of Sonny's lifestyle problematic, including his "51-year three-pack-per-day practice of smoking unfiltered cigarettes, as well as a 30-year history of weekly binge drinking of homemade wine and 'moonshine.'" Anthropologists as well as others have documented similar clashes between health workers and patients over lifestyle factors such as heavy smoking and drinking that have negative effects on health outcomes. For example, one of the best ethnographic accounts to address this issue is Balshem's (1993) *Cancer in the Community: Class and Medical Authority*, which examines patient, family, community member, and health workers' explanations for high cancer rates in a Philadelphia neighborhood considered to be a "cancer cluster." Although there are some descriptions of these types of culture clashes in health care settings, fewer policy or educational pieces have been written about strategies for dealing with these issues. This deficit is particularly evident in the end-of-life literature.

The third aspect of the culture clash relates to the nature of Sonny's family network composed of kin and fictive kin (e.g., his former wives) and their interactions with the medical establishment. Although this nontraditional family group appears to get along well enough among themselves, communication between the family and the hospital staff is quite strained. Underlying issues of resource distribution and the societal value placed on Sonny's life are themes woven throughout tense discussions about how his end-of-life care should proceed. The family is angered by " ... what they perceived as the 'constant pressure' to make a decision about their father." Sonny's situation is framed by the family in the following way, "[he] seemed to be a pawn in a game where the common man was being squashed by the elite establishment." Their resentment is palpable and Sonny's son-in-law almost comes to blows with the staff over the matter. These exchanges highlight how end-of-life decision making in a U.S. hospital is most definitely foreign to Sonny and his family. They feel not only ill at ease but also marginalized and disadvantaged. Sonny's family involvement in end-of-life decision making is at the forefront of the story. The larger economic, social, and cultural factors that heavily influence how Sonny's case is discussed and managed remain troublingly in the background.

The fourth portion of the culture clash noted in the story is the fact that staff members are extremely frustrated that Sonny has not previously stated his end-of-life wishes nor completed any corresponding paperwork. Their position is that Sonny, who was already in poor health and previously hospitalized, should have prepared for the current situation and stated his wishes while able to do so. When Sonny states that he wants everything done in the height of the current crisis, it seems as if staff considers this answer to be "wrong" or inappropriate. They ask his opinion and then are the ones who are perturbed when he makes a choice for Full Code, which they see as flawed. What is disturbingly absent from the story is whether staff understood what "wanting to live" meant to Sonny and whether he knew what his life would be like on a ventilator.

All of these aspects of the culture clash contributed in large part to Sonny's care going down a path with which no one is satisfied and that does not result in good end-of-life care from anyone's perspective. Although Sonny had some voice in the initial decision making, his perspective seems barely present initially and increasingly absent as the situation rapidly spirals out of control. One ray of hope in this otherwise disheartening story is the attitude of the hospice social worker toward Sonny's death experience. The fact that the social worker still thinks about this case more than a decade later, puzzles about it, muses on it, and that it informs his current practice is a very good sign. New ways of practice can contribute to more humane and peaceful deaths in which patients' and families' real wishes are known, acknowledged, and carried out in a smooth rather than completely chaotic fashion. These kinds of death experiences would be better for patients, families, and the staff.

Sonny's story clearly illustrates the importance of understanding culture clash and its negative ramifications for quality end-of-life care. Overall, there is a need for much better in-depth education about the central role that cultural issues play in contributing to sensitive decision making that reflects the personal and cultural values of the dying person. Health care workers need to be aware of their own cultural attitudes and how these affect the communications that they have with patients and families and the way in which end-of-life care is provided. Such awareness can help to alleviate job stress and burnout by reducing the severity of culture clash experienced during the dying process.

Legal Response
George A. Cooney, Jr.

Sonny's dying is stormy and his last hours are filled with confusion for everyone around him. How could it be otherwise? The very antiestablishment attitudes and values that have brought so much character to this man's life and family have also assured his unquiet end. Those who love him do not love "the system." They appear ready to find condescension and dismissiveness in the attitudes of the hospital personnel who, in turn, are repelled and frightened by the family's refusal to play by the rules of modern-day health care delivery.

This culture clash should have set up a perfect opportunity for the law to work. Our legal system is designed to provide a social space—a courtroom or legislative chamber—where conflicting positions can be given full consideration. What the law cannot then resolve by reconciling, it resolves by deciding. The legal resolution, being authoritative, enables the parties to move past the conflict.

In this case, however, the legal system failed to provide Sonny's family and the hospital with a satisfactory answer. This failure is particularly disappointing. From the early 1990s, there has been a specific legal procedure in place for resolution of conflicts over end-of-life treatment and the authority of a surrogate to make medical decisions for an individual such as Sonny who becomes unable to make them for himself. Michigan, like many states, has a Durable Power of Attorney for Health Care law (Act 386, Public Acts of Michigan, 1998). According to that law, an individual, by formally signing a Medical Power of Attorney, can designate a surrogate decision maker. If the individual becomes unable to participate in medical treatment decisions, the surrogate has power to make decisions with the same legal force as if they had been made by the individual. Sonny had many potential surrogates within his family and "followers." He might have chosen his daughter, his son-in-law, or even one of his ex-spouses to carry out his wishes concerning medical treatment.

It is interesting to reflect that it took Michigan 15 years from the time the Durable Power of Attorney for Health Care law was first proposed in the legislature until it was finally passed. There was extensive public debate on whether the law and the recognition of an individual's rights in this regard would be the occasion of a "slippery slope" toward acceptance of abortion, rationing of health care for elders, and general disrespect for life. The law that finally passed was a compromise under which the state has functioned for more than a decade. In general, the law works well, but Sonny and his family were apparently unaware of it or chose not to exercise the options that the law provides.

Sonny might have approved of the law if he had known about it. The concept of the Medical Power of Attorney reflects the U.S. legal system's emphasis on individual rights. An individual has the sole right to control his or her own person (*Union Pacific Railway Company v. Botsford*, 1891). No one else—no health care provider, no relative—can make decisions concerning an individual's body unless the individual has appropriately delegated that decision-making authority to a surrogate. In Michigan, the courts have gone further and decided that a surrogate can make decisions that result in death only if it is clear that the individual would have made the same decision under the same circumstances (*In re Martin*, 1995).

Most people who complete a Medical Power of Attorney take the opportunity, in the same document, to spell out their wishes about end-of-life treatment. Even if an individual has not designated a surrogate, end-of-life treatment wishes may be expressed in a living will or some other document. These are usually called *advance directives*. Sometimes the wishes are a medical "laundry list" with items such as "no resuscitation if I have been in a coma for more than 3 days; no artificial or tube feeding if the coma continues for a total of 20 days." Other wishes may be in the form of a values statement, such as "If I will not be able to make a meaningful recovery, so that I can interact with other people and with my surroundings, I do not want my existence prolonged," or "I believe in miraculous recovery, and therefore I want to be given all possible treatment and care, so as to be kept alive as long as possible."

If an individual is incapable of making or communicating decisions concerning medical treatment and has neither designated a surrogate nor otherwise expressed wishes, a probate court may appoint a guardian to make decisions in the individual's best interest (Act 386, Public Acts of Michigan, 1998). If a surrogate has been appointed, and if anyone believes that the surrogate is making decisions that are not in the individual's best interest, the probate court can review the facts and can overrule the surrogate's decisions. There are thus two ways to bring end-of-life treatment issues to court for resolution.

As a practical matter, however, hospitals and health care providers faced with conflict over surrogated decisions will often not take the time nor incur the expense of going to court. They will instead attempt to establish a consensus among those family members and others who are most affected and are likely to criticize or bring legal action against the provider for treatment decisions. The attempt to establish consensus without the courts is what happened in the case of Sonny and his family once the decision was made to disregard Sonny's own decision to elect "Full Code." The collapse of that family consensus, and the efforts to reassemble it, added much misunderstanding and fear to the situation. The threats of violence and litigation that Sonny's family made and the defensive responses of hospital staff resulted in a communication breakdown. From a legal perspective, it would have been preferable had Sonny appointed a surrogate in advance. The family, working with the medical caregivers, could then have spent their time and energy helping provide Sonny with a peaceful time of dying.

Narrative Response
Richard Raspa

This case illustrates the power of our stories to shape behavior and construct reality. The stories each group tells about the other embody two social worlds: the expert society of medical professionals, and the folk culture of Sonny and his family. When we analyze from a narrative perspective, we explore how structures of meaning are produced in the interplay between different stories. The worlds in Sonny's story career off each other and distort perceptions of identity and motive so that communication is lost. Neither medical professionals nor Sonny's family have an experience of *the other*. Rather they hear only *their story* of the other. What is obscured in this language process is the failure to see the other as human. Narrative allows us to see how people invent the world for themselves in the stories they tell about their experiences.

Under the gaze of respectability and medical urgency, the professionals assess and reduce Sonny and his family to carnival figures. Carnivals are models of inversion where the social organization of a culture is capsized. Fools and clowns degrade hierarchies of power and authority in acts of revelry. The center is marginalized, and the margins are installed at the center. High and low exchange places; the abnormal becomes normative. In carnival, the world is topsy-turvy.

The narrator, a social worker, gets a partial view of Sonny's carnival world through an open door to his hospital room. As he lies there in bed, surrounded by stuffed animals, tattoos inscribed on the surface of his body, breathing with the aid of a ventilator, flashing lights around his torso, blue tubing fused to his body, Sonny appears to be some grotesque figure from a horror film, about to be experimented upon by a mad scientist. Or, perhaps, Sonny is like a man being punished by society, strapped down to undergo the death penalty in an act of retributive justice. What is present here in the hospital is sophisticated technology. What is lacking is the human touch. The narrator lets the reader know that the hospital staff is reading and reacting, maybe even snickering, at the funny "folks." Sonny and his family become objects of amusement and derision through the stories that the staff tell about his tattoos, stuffed animals, and personal history.

One way of objectifying Sonny is to interpret his life as a carnival story of marginal experiences. A school dropout who was a merchant marine, he worked as a cook and dishwasher below the waterline on commercial ships—his occupation leaving him on the boundary between surface and submarine life. He learned the craft of tattooing that marks the human body as different and exotic, further pushing Sonny to the edges of society. A self-taught preacher, he rejects official cultural institutions that legitimize occupations and social roles, isolating him further from mainstream society. Even in his intimate life, divorce does not terminate relationships with ex-spouses. In a disreputable expression of "poor taste," Sonny's former wives are all drawn together around him as if in polygamous devotion.

Of course, there are other ways of framing these stories. Medical professionals could have seen Sonny as someone who came from humble beginnings, who, full of youthful bravado, heeded the call to adventure and set out on his own in the world at age 15. He "followed his bliss" (Campbell, 1972) and embodies in his life characteristic American frontier values: self-reliance, independence, and ambition. Historically, America was settled in the tension between civilization and wilderness. The American narrative is about pioneers moving westward to the edges, the margins of society, to reinvent culture and seize the limitless possibilities promised by the American Dream.

It is, however, less complicated, and more fun, to reduce Sonny to a clown, a figure of ridiculous proportion whose family is disrupting the efficiency of care management when they protest Sonny's movement out of ICU. And, quite naturally, Sonny's family is upset when they are admonished that they are "tying up" valuable space and resources that could be better used by others. Such a story of sterile efficiency and bottom-line accountability confirms the hardness of these professionals. To the irate family, the staff have hearts of stone. "Those people" provide evidence for Sonny's family that good, sensitive people do not matter around here, that nice guys like Sonny do finish last. Ultimately, Sonny's family concludes that they are all doomed to receive abusive treatment in a place that claims to be committed to caring—the American hospital.

At the same time, from the professional viewpoint, "these people," these rustics, these clowns, would have to be upset and threaten disorder, even physical violence because they don't get what is clear as day: Sonny is dying. Nothing can save him. So what's the problem? Make the decision to wean and have done with it.

As the medical professionals invent Sonny and his family as carnival figures, the family simultaneously demonizes the professionals. There is sufficient evidence to convict from both sides. Staff blame Sonny and his family for inefficiency that will result in the failure of the hospital to provide service to others who really need treatment. Yet, from the hospital perspective, the medical professionals are acting with integrity as they allocate scarce resources to those they perceive will benefit most. They are practicing their disciplines and exercising their professional judgments in assessing Sonny a terminal patient and communicating the limits of medicine to the family. They are doing their jobs. The story reveals the irony that each side is confident that the story it tells is the correct one.

These narratives demonstrate how the objective world "out there" does not exist outside of stories. The stories each group had about the other produced pain, threats, hard feelings, and abusive communication. Narratives that configured the other as clown or demon blocked the possibility that people could be recognized and acknowledged as human beings. Unfortunately, what was lost in this case was the possibility of a good death that included a healing for the family and a joyful sense of accomplishment for the medical professionals.

REFERENCES

Balshem, M. (1993). *Cancer in the community: Class and medical authority*. Washington, DC: Smithsonian Institution Press.

Campbell, J. (1972). *The hero with a thousand faces*. Princeton, NJ: Princeton University Press, p. 118.

Chrisman, N., & Johnson, T. (1996). Clinically applied anthropology. In C. Sargent & T. Johnson (Eds.), *Medical anthropology: Contemporary theory and method* (2nd ed., pp. 88–109). Westport, CT: Prager.

In re Martin, 450 Mich 204, 538 NW 2d 399 (1995).

Public Act of Michigan, 1998, Act 386, Estates and Protected Individuals Code, effective April 1, 2000.

Union Pacific Railway Company v. Botsford, 141 US 250 (1891).

CHAPTER 10

Stories of Pearl:
Surviving End-of-Life Care

In three words I can sum up everything I've learned about life:
It goes on.

—Robert Frost

Pearl's Story
John W. Finn

Pearl was a 39-year-old African American woman. Her grandparents migrated from Alabama shortly after World War II to work in the booming industrial north. She and her sister were raised in the projects by their mother, who worked two jobs to support the family. In high school, Pearl became involved with a gang and was using drugs. Pearl's mother was very worried and confronted her. In response, Pearl moved in with her boyfriend.

Over the next 20 years, Pearl led a hard life. She was in and out of shelters, treatment programs, and hospitals. She never held a steady job and many times asked her mother and sister for money and a place to stay. Her family wanted to help Pearl but knew that whatever money they supplied went to support her drug habit. Many times Pearl's family talked to her about her lifestyle and the need to stop using drugs, but Pearl insisted that she "had things under control." Her mother said, "You don't have anything under control. You are going to get AIDS!"

On a hot day in August, 2 weeks before her 39th birthday, Pearl was brought to the ER for a suspected drug overdose. In the emergency room, she was tested for HIV and diagnosed with HIV/AIDS. When she recovered enough to be discharged, she was referred to a free clinic for follow-up care.

By the following May, Pearl was considered terminally ill. Her HIV infection had progressed to full-blown AIDS and included such complications as infections in her lungs, throat, and esophagus. She also developed very low white blood cell counts related to her progressing immunodeficiency. Then she was diagnosed with a rare type of tuberculosis that is a sure and telling sign of a failed immune system. The end of Pearl's life seemed near. She was discharged with prescriptions for antiviral and antibiotic medications.

Pearl was repeatedly admitted to the hospital with dehydration, weakness, and significant weight loss. She said she had not been able to take the medication that had been prescribed. The outpatient free clinic reported that Pearl had not come in for her follow-up appointments. Antiviral drugs and the usual antibiotics were not helpful for Pearl. HIV/AIDS treatment depends in part on rigorous follow-up with medication and nutritional support. Pearl's life continued to be chaotic, and she did not have the financial or social support needed to manage an effective treatment plan. She had been living in a homeless shelter. There continued to be a great deal of family conflict related to Pearl's behaviors. Her condition continued to worsen.

The next time she came into the ER, she had pain in both her neck and her feet and reported falling several times recently. Pearl also reported lack of appetite, constipation, loss of bladder control, a skin rash, and swollen ankles. She was described by the admitting doctors as a "very thin, frail woman who was somewhat confused" about where she was. Pearl's illness was so advanced that her prognosis was "likely less than six months" to live.

During inpatient Infectious Disease rounds an entourage of physicians-in-training, with a specialist, nurse clinician, and social worker, gathered at Pearl's bedside to discuss her case. End-of-life decisions were made in the context of teaching. The work of discussing the care options with the patient and making appropriate referrals and appointments fell to the most junior student on the team and the social worker. Pearl was still acutely ill and seemed somewhat delirious, so there was little direct conversation between Pearl and the medical team. Decisions that were made during rounds "trickled down" to the mother and sister through the medical student, nurse clinician, and social worker. They told the family that Pearl was being referred to a hospice program.

The hospice team initially arranged for hospice care in the hospital and then a 3-month trial of hospice home care. Pearl's family met with hospice staff while she was in the hospital and plans were made to take her back to her mother's home. The family had very mixed feelings about both Pearl and hospice. Pearl's sister was not accepting of the hospice philosophy of comfort care and the limits placed on CPR. There was little family acceptance or "buy-in" to the hospice practice of liberal usage of opiates for pain control. Several family members said they felt that pain medication would "feed her destructive habit" and further encourage addiction. The family was, however, pleased to learn that hospice would regularly send a nurse, home health aide, social worker, and volunteer to the home and that her medications would all be provided at no charge to the family. They also liked the fact that the infectious disease specialist who had been taking care of Pearl in the hospital would continue to manage her care at home.

At the time of Pearl's enrollment in the hospice program, patients with AIDS were supposed to be admitted to hospice only when all antiviral and prophylactic medications, such as antibiotics, had been discontinued. Hospice admission criteria were written to ensure that the patient had given up life-prolonging therapy and had made the complete turn to the acceptance of death with comfort treatments only. Although Pearl clearly met the clinical diagnostic and prognostic admission standards, she and her family had not yet given up hope for effective use of medications to treat her HIV infection. In deciding to bend the rule for Pearl, the hospice team felt that the support and structure they would provide, the access to opiates for pain control, and the family reconciliation promoted by the hospice approach might provide the stability that Pearl needed. Therefore, a creative use of the hospice benefit was seen as the only way that patient and family needs could be met. The hospice team, Pearl, and her family hoped that with added support and a stable treatment plan, Pearl would be able to comfortably come to the end of her life and achieve some peace at last.

After 3 months at home, the unlikely occurred: Pearl's illness began to respond to care. The blood and viral load indicators showed that she was getting better. Clinical findings improved to the point that Pearl was no longer eligible for the hospice benefit. Once her clinical status improved, she no longer had a prognosis of less than 6 months to live. The hospice team, working with the patient and family, had managed to stabilize her social situation, which permitted a more stable treatment program, and improved her clinical situation to the point of a dramatic change in prognosis.

Hospice staff members were highly ambivalent, having become emotionally attached to the patient. They worried that once hospice services were withdrawn, Pearl might return to her previous lifestyle. Although Pearl's sister was happy, her mother was bewildered, worried about how services would change. The hospital staff was surprised and remained skeptical about the apparent improvement in Pearl's prognosis.

After her discharge from hospice, Pearl needed to go back into the hospital for a pneumothorax (partial lung collapse) and *pneumocystis carinii* pneumonia. These are common complications with HIV/AIDS. This time, however, her immune system had recovered enough that Pearl was able to respond to antibiotic therapy. She continued the drug treatment program that she began while enrolled in hospice, and the family tensions eased over time. A follow-up telephone call 3^1/$_2$ years later revealed that Pearl continues to live her life and has established closer ties with her family. Life is not perfect for her, but life goes on.

Provider Response
Robert Zalenski

This is a surprising story. With Pearl, we see both the expected course of end of life in hospice care and an exceptional turn of events. As a physician who must deal with life–and–death decisions, rational prognostication based on clinical facts, and giving "realistic" options for care to patients and families, the story of Pearl is thought-provoking and humbling.

Pearl's HIV infection had progressed to the point where her weakened immune system allowed innocuous organisms to cause disease in her lungs, throat, and esophagus. The combination of both AIDS and the conditions in which it thrives (poverty, homelessness, and drug abuse) brought Pearl to the horizon of her mortality, and doctors forecasted that she had less than 6 months to live. Her life did not possess the kind of order needed to take many different tablets at regular times and to provide adequate nutrition and rest. Her doctors believed that death was inevitable.

The hospice team probably called a family meeting when they enrolled Pearl. These meetings are used to help the family make the transition from a curative to a palliative care focus. Three tasks essential to the journey of medical healing should be achieved in a family meeting (Brody, 2003). First, the care providers, the patient, and the family must develop a shared story of the patient's illness, treatment, and response. Second, the patient and family need to know that they are surrounded by caring individuals. Third, the patient and family must start to have a sense of empowerment, either directly or through the hospice team, that they can achieve mastery over some part of the illness. This sense of enhanced power often comes by immediately moving forward to gain control of the worst symptoms, such as pain, nausea, or breathlessness. Rapid success in symptom management then supports other efforts to improve the patient and family quality of life.

In Pearl's story, the ideal scenario proposed by Brody (2003) was not implemented quite as intended. At the family meeting, the expected trajectory of Pearl's illness was reviewed. The physician and hospice team worked with the family to help them make the transition to accepting the inevitability of Pearl's death; however, some family members were not receptive to the basic premise that Pearl was going to die. Rather than seeing themselves surrounded by caring individuals, some family members were troubled that opiates or narcotics were to be used to treat Pearl's symptoms. After all, these were the very substances which had caused so much pain and distress in their lives to date. Although Pearl and her family do not seem to have been fully empowered in the family meeting, some of their concerns were addressed. Hospice staff's promises of help from a home health aide, a social worker, and a nurse and their willingness to provide and pay for medications were ultimately enough for the family to accept the program.

Although hospice providers are charged with understanding and implementing the phases delineated by Brody (2003), Pearl's family was concerned with more fundamental issues commonly faced by families enrolling patients in hospice. Families frequently love the promise that hospice care will help the patient be comfortable, but loathe the underlying premise that active curative or restorative therapy must cease. Understandably, families are often unwilling to give up unless there is overwhelming evidence that every approach to cure or restoration has failed. Families are offered a terrible choice between comfort care only and continuation of potentially life-extending treatment. Patients and families will often refuse hospice care until the patient is perceived to be nearly dead and the inevitable outcome can no longer be denied. This limitation has been recognized as a barrier within the hospice model of end-of-life care.

From my perspective as a physician, contemporary medicine has provided an answer to this dilemma. Palliative care is receiving growing recognition as an important specialty area of practice. *Palliative care* broadens the access to comfort care to include patients at all stages of medical illness, even if concurrent disease-modifying therapies are still being used. Palliation provides physical, emotional, and spiritual comfort and healing in the face of progressive incurable illness (National Hospice & Palliative Care Organization, 2004). In cases such as Pearl's, palliative care is compatible with concurrent anti-HIV drug therapy, or with radiation or chemotherapy for cancer. Decisions are individualized and benefits and burdens are assessed. The entire team, including the patient, moves forward with a mutually agreeable plan and without specific treatment exclusions.

When the hospice program "bent the rules" and permitted Pearl access to services more like palliative care than traditional hospice, the plan was satisfactory to all concerned. The package of potentially disease-modifying therapy with expensive antivirals and antibiotics, adequate pain medication, and social support was attractive enough for Pearl and her family to accept hospice care despite their initial reservations.

Fortunately, this particular hospice was able to draw on its financial resources and its philanthropic support and to offer a comprehensive benefit package for Pearl despite her lack of insurance coverage. Unfortunately, this kind of palliative care is not funded in the United States and so is not usually provided. Interdisciplinary teams are best equipped to carry out complex care near end of life, but usually operate on a fixed per diem payment system. They cannot afford to supply relatively expensive therapies such as antiviral drugs, radiation, or blood transfusions even when such care might be helpful.

The extraordinary decision on the part of hospice in Pearl's story was to work around one of the usual stipulations for their care of a patient with AIDS. Regulations mandate discontinuation of anti-HIV therapies as an enrollment criterion. In a situation like Pearl's, regulators contend that it does not make sense to both forecast near-term mortality and continue to take futile and expensive steps to prevent death. The reasoning seems to be that if the patient is not ready to give up on curative therapy, then she is not ready for hospice. However, the additional services provided in the context of palliative care might just provide the supports needed to take medication, make lifestyle changes, and alter the grim prognosis. This scenario may be what happened for Pearl.

Another way of thinking is to consider alternative endings for the story. Despite the medical and social interventions, the outcome could easily have been Pearl's death within the predicted 6-month time period. Although current medical education does not equip many physicians to think beyond the scientific and rational aspects of clinical prognostication, Pearl's story demonstrates the importance of entertaining multiple possibilities. Physicians and other health care providers need to appreciate the extraordinary events that can occur in healing.

Although medical curricula today rarely acknowledge such "miracles," we will be better practitioners if we can expand our conceptions of what can happen in caregiving and remain open to the unexpected. Given the health care providers' training of what to expect, they agreed on which story to lay out for Pearl and her family. However, the story was wrong. This type of humbling experience is where the most profound lessons can be learned.

Economic Response
Allen C. Goodman

Economic analysis provides three levels of insight into Pearl's story. The first involves the treatment of disease and the production of health. The second is about the economic priorities placed on treatment and care in the U.S. health care system. The third involves the complex relationships of health insurance and treatment advances as health care providers look to the future of conditions such as HIV/AIDS.

First, economists tell stories about how individuals produce good health by combining nutrition and exercise, medical goods such as drugs or vaccines, and people's time. In economic language, Pearl was not purchasing "the right goods" and she was not combining them effectively with her time to produce good health. Good nutrition, for example, is one critical factor in health outcomes. In many cases, nutritional support is even more important than drug therapies for acute or chronic conditions like HIV infection. Maintenance of good nutrition can be extremely difficult for someone who is homeless and drug-addicted. In this story, Pearl apparently had access to medications that were appropriate and that have proven effective for others in the treatment of HIV/AIDS. Her lifestyle, however, including her homelessness, substance abuse, and nonadherence to drug therapies, led to an apparently critical, irreversible, and terminal condition.

An important concept in the economic analysis of a story such as Pearl's is *time*. When people cannot take care of themselves, others may provide time (and effort) to take care of them. As in Pearl's story, the time for caregiving is often a blend of donated family time and paid professional care. It is the focused expenditure of time, combined with appropriate drug therapies, adequate nutrition, and other supports that often produce better health for individuals and allow them to resume self-care. When time and care are inadequate to produce good health, family and health providers, such as hospice staff, may provide time to support achievement of a good death.

Finally, there is a large element of uncertainty in many health care treatments. Antibiotic drugs, for example, kill bacteria, but they may engender allergic reactions. Moreover, the condition itself may be viral and not susceptible to antibiotic treatment. Pearl's HIV/AIDS treatment was complex, requiring rigorous follow-up with medication and nutritional support, and she was not able or willing to comply. Yet when the hospice team "bent the rules" to offer a treatment that could only be assigned a low probability of success, the package of potentially disease-modifying therapy with expensive antivirals and antibiotics, adequate pain medication, and social support worked.

When faced with cost constraints, through insurer decisions, global budgets, capitated payments, or carve-outs, it is essential to put resources where the probability of success (and hence the probable return) is the highest. Poker players consider it to be a high risk/low payoff strategy to draw to an inside straight because of the poor odds—but the play sometimes works!

In Pearl's story, hospice care led to an improved environment and better time. Pearl appears to have learned to spend her time more efficiently to maximize production of health in multiple domains. The narrator tells us that she continued to do well after 3½ years. Pearl's treatment produced good health for her, counter to all expectations, but it would take considerably more study to determine whether the decision to offer this treatment as standard hospice care would be economically sound.

The second area for discussion regarding Pearl's story involves the economics, policies, and politics that operate in the U.S. health care system. At present, health insurers in both the public area (Medicare and Medicaid) and the private sector are often more willing to fund care provided in the highest-cost settings. If a patient such as Pearl had health insurance and was acutely ill in the hospital, health insurance would most likely pay for whatever treatment might be suggested to prolong life. Once a patient is discharged from the acute care setting, however, the cost of care largely shifts to the patient and family. In addition to being a very difficult and exacting regimen to follow, the current medications for HIV/AIDS are expensive. There are also additional costs to having a patient such as Pearl living at home again. Daily living expenses such as groceries, electricity, and phone costs increase with each additional person in a household. There are also costs associated with the loss of other customary daily activities by family caregivers, such as staying home from work, withdrawal from outside social functions, and added physical and emotional demands. Until the advent of hospice programs, families at the point where additional high-cost, high-tech medical care was futile from the standpoint of life prolongation were largely on their own.

Hospice programs have helped to shift some policies with regard to end-of-life care. After considerable debate and public pressure, insurers and those who administer the health care system determined that a more cost-effective way to deal with the terminally ill was to forgo expensive and futile treatment in favor of comfort care. A per diem system of payment has developed within which hospice programs are expected to provide all care, equipment, medications, and support needed in the last 6 months of life. Providing whatever services are needed to support the dying patient and family is often a challenge within the constraints of the low daily payment for each enrolled patient. Hospice funding is sustainable when the number of lower-need or short-term need patients offsets those with greater or longer-term needs. When a patient like Pearl benefits from hospice services to the point that she is "no longer terminal," she must be discharged from the program even though her needs for palliative care help continue.

The third area of insight suggested by Pearl's story is the unexpected effects that the advent of life-extending protease inhibitors, antivirals, and antibiotics have had on the health insurance industry. For economists, the larger story of shifts in the overall paradigm of care is important to the creation of social policy.

Over the years, there have been various attempts to address some of the issues surrounding end-of-life care for people with HIV/AIDS. One such approach was the use of viatical insurance. The term *viatical* comes from ancient Rome, where travelers embarking on a difficult journey prepared a package of supplies and money called a *viaticum*. In *viatical insurance* settlements, life insurance policy holders receive lump sums ranging between 60% and 90% of the face values of the policies during their terminal illness. The amount of the predeath benefit depends on how long they are expected to live. The shorter the time until the expected death, the larger the percentage of the policy that the broker pays to the insured. Viatical insurance is a fundamental end-of-life financial instrument. A viatical settlement can provide funds to pay for care for the dying insured in the terminal period, thus reducing the predeath economic burden on the patient and family.

In the late 1980s, viatical insurance brokers began to provide settlements to people with HIV/AIDS. At that time there was an almost certain and largely predictable probability of death from HIV/AIDS within a short time. Brokers and actuaries could calculate these probabilities and provide funds to ailing patients so the patients could have cash assets during the last few months or years.

The growing success of HIV/AIDS treatments using a potent combination of drugs called *protease inhibitors* has extended the lives of many patients. These drug therapies have been good news for AIDS patients, but bad news for many viatical insurance companies. Suppose a broker paid an AIDS patient 80% of the face value of a $100,000 policy, based on the expectation that the patient would live for no more than 2 additional years. The economic cost to the broker would be the $80,000 payment plus the lost interest amount that represents the "opportunity cost" of carrying the policy. Suppose, however, that new and improved treatment enables the insured patient to live for 4 or 5 years, or even longer. What has seemed to be a good deal for the brokers might become a money-losing proposition because they must wait longer to cash in the face values of policies that they have bought.

By the late 1990s, some viatical companies were still buying life insurance policies from AIDS patients, but these companies changed the criteria previously used to make offers to AIDS patients because it was becoming harder to predict their deaths. *Los Angeles Times* reporter Kristof (1999) observed that as AIDS became increasingly treatable, insurers expanded the viatical payment eligible pool to include late-stage cancer patients and other terminally ill individuals. This scenario has ultimately led to *senior settlements* in which healthy seniors sell their policies because potential beneficiaries have grown up, died, or no longer need financial support. With the advent of senior settlements, the viatical insurance industry roughly doubled from early 1998 to late 1999. Annual sales of such policies are now roughly $1 billion.

This analysis of changes in the insurance industry in the wake of new clinical options for HIV/AIDS patients has broad implications for the future financing of end-of-life care. From an economist's perspective, the focus is on the big picture of care financing that both precipitates and permits exceptions such as those noted in Pearl's story.

The narrator tells us that Pearl "received regular and meticulous medical attention." This would suggest that she had some form of health insurance. Given the story of Pearl's age, her life in shelters, hospitals, and at the whim of her family, it is highly unlikely that she carried life insurance, as insurers are generally reluctant to take on the risks of a person with both HIV infection and drug use habits. Had she been insured, however, her success in beating AIDS against all expectations would represent a money-losing proposition for her broker.

Many Americans with chronic and degenerative illnesses could benefit greatly from widespread access to palliative care services regardless whether they are in a hospital, a nursing home, or their own homes. HIV/AIDS is now considered a chronic disease when properly managed. HIV/AIDS patients, along with patients living with other chronic health problems, need palliative care regardless of their ongoing medical treatment or service setting. Our current system seems more willing to pay the high price of crisis support but less willing to fund health- and comfort-promoting services that would improve, and in cases like Pearl's extend, patients' lives and well-being.

Provider Response
Elizabeth E. Chapleski

Pearl's story is unique, and ironic as well. The story is an exemplar of hospice problem solving at its best. It also illustrates the kinds of family reconciliation and empowerment that are often so very critical as people face the end of a life enmeshed in their unique family and social contexts.

The idea that hospice saved her life conflicts with the goal of hospice to offer a safe and comfortable death. It has been estimated that about 12% of patients with life-limiting conditions live beyond the medically prognosticated time (Christakis, 1994). The percentage of patients discharged alive from hospice programs is estimated at 2% to 3% (J. W. Finn, personal communication, July 23, 2003). Pearl's HIV/AIDS could not be cured, but it was treated and managed so that, after 3 months she was no longer deemed imminently terminal. The hospice team is to be commended for circumventing their regulatory criteria in allowing her antiviral medications to continue as the hospice team worked with the family to stabilize Pearl's social situation.

Pearl's is a story of reconciliation in which the cycle of helplessness and family estrangement is broken. Pearl had been at odds with her family and noncompliant in every way with the prescribed medical regimen. As a homeless person and a drug addict, she lived on the margins of society, was distanced from her family, and failed to conform to normal societal expectations. When provided with instrumental help, as well as emotional support, Pearl's situation improved enough that she was doing well $3^{1}/_{2}$ years after her hospice discharge. Ironically, Pearl's life story defied normal expectations in a most positive way.

From a social work background, it is important to more closely consider how the patient-centered hospice intervention offered a sense of empowerment to both Pearl and her family. As Larson and Tobin (2000) contend, "Patient-centered medicine broadens the biomedical view to one that sees through the patient's eyes and appreciates the web of relationships and contexts within which a patient suffers" (p. 1575). With this in mind, I wonder what precipitated the family reconciliation. Was it the fact that Pearl had been declared terminally ill with only 6 months to live that spurred her mother to not give up on her? Was guilt a factor? Often cases like Pearl's are accompanied by family questions of "Could I have done something different?" In my experience, family members often wonder if the patient's condition is somehow their fault or what they might have done to avoid the present situation. The narrator of the story does not answer these questions. To really understand the dynamics of the family situation and offer appropriate guidance, these issues would need to be further assessed.

One of the fundamental objectives of hospice organizations is relationship completion at the end of life. The dying, as well as those close to them, often seek and/or grant forgiveness as death nears. However, reconciliation can take place without forgiveness and vice versa. With the social history presented in Pearl's story, it is very likely that issues such as these were in need of resolution. Perhaps it was enrolling in the hospice program that changed the context for such discussion by "bringing everyone to the table," providing the family with a forum and promising support. Truth might have been an invisible guest at that table and may have offered relief to Pearl and her family. Oftentimes, emotions such as deceit, shame, and anger accompany a personal and family battle with addiction and must be dealt with at the end of life.

One hallmark of hospice programs is the provision of individualized care that meets the needs of the dying person and their family by doing "whatever it takes." Customizing care is always a challenging enterprise, especially when the patient is a socially marginalized person such as Pearl. The hospice staff assessed Pearl's needs and then customized her care without judging her lifestyle as unworthy of special treatment. Understanding the importance of conversations at life's end about forgiveness, appreciation, love, and good-bye (Larson, 1993), hospice staff helped to create a space for Pearl and her family. The story author does not tell us if developmental growth accompanied the health stabilization and family reconciliation. We do know that the additional time offered opportunities for improved quality of life and healing of relationships. It also may have offered time for Pearl to forgive the most difficult of all persons to forgive—herself. In any case, it appears that Pearl's autonomy and choice were honored. Her family received necessary support. All were given the gift of time. That gift that can be used wisely or wasted; the choice is theirs.

REFERENCES

Brody, H. (2003). *Stories of sickness* (2nd ed.). New York: Oxford University Press.

Campbell, J. (1972). *The hero with a thousand faces.* Princeton, NJ: Princeton University Press.

Christakis, N. A. (1994). Timing of referral of terminally ill patients to an outpatient hospice. *Journal of General Internal Medicine, 9,* 314–320.

Kristof, K. M. (1999, December 9). How does a viatical settlement work? *Los Angeles Times,* C5.

Larson, D. G., & Tobin, D. R. (2000). End-of-life conversations. *Journal of the American Medical Association, 284,* 1573–1578.

Larson, D. G. (1993). Self-concealment: Implications for stress and empathy in oncology care. *Psychosocial Oncology, 11,* 1–16.

National Hospice & Palliative Care Organization. (2004). *An explanation of palliative care.* Retrieved March 8, 2003, from http://www.nhpco.org/i4a/pages/index.cfm.pageid=3657

CHAPTER 11

Stories of Henry: Family Choices and Challenges

A man's dying is more the survivors' affair than his own.

—Thomas Mann

Henry's Story
George A. Cooney, Jr.

Henry was a 62-year-old lawyer who was in a long-term committed relationship with William. Henry was a regular exerciser, and he and William shared a fitness club membership. For several weeks, Henry had been experiencing chest pains while working out on the treadmill. At William's urging, Henry had discussed the chest pains with his primary care physician and the doctor, after administering an electrocardiogram in the office, referred him to the hospital for an angioplasty. On the appointed day, Henry and William went to the hospital's heart clinic. Henry had been gathering some Internet information on angioplasty and had shared with William his concerns about the safety of the procedure. He passed a very restless night before his appointment day worrying over some of the stories he had found while surfing the Internet.

Upon arriving, Henry gave his name to the reception clerk. He was agitated and nervous. He expressed his concern to the clerk while she was taking his insurance information. He wondered aloud if the procedure was too risky. The clerk told him that angioplasty is a routine procedure and said, "Doctor X is an excellent doctor; you're in good hands." The clerk told Henry that he should take a seat in the waiting room and wait to be called for the procedure.

Although his fears were not allayed by this exchange, Henry realized that he was not likely to receive much more information from the clerk, and no other hospital employees seemed to be around to ask. Henry took his seat with William who also tried to reassure him. Henry told William, "I'd almost rather get up right now and walk out . . . take my chances and not let them do this." William replied to Henry, "Keep your eyes on the prize. You want us to be able to go to the gym without your chest hurting, right? Once they find out what's going on, and they get you on the right pills, I know they're going to tell you to get as much exercise as you can. Take some deep breaths. I'll be right out here the whole time, and in an hour we'll be on our way home with our coffees and a handful of prescription slips."

In a few minutes, Henry got up, indicating that he was going to the men's restroom down the hall. Later, when a nurse opened the waiting room door and called Henry's name, William told her that Henry had not yet returned from the restroom and remarked to the nurse that it had been a while since Henry had gone down the hall. Alarmed, the nurse ran with William to the restroom, where they found Henry on the floor in front of the sink. The nurse summoned help and started CPR. Henry was admitted to the hospital on life support.

William and Henry had been life partners for more than 20 years. William identified himself to hospital staff as Henry's closest friend when he was asked about his relationship with the patient. In response to the standard next-of-kin questions, William told them that Henry had never been married and had no children. His parents are both deceased. Henry had a sister, Suzanne, and a brother, Bart. Bart lived in a nearby suburb, and Suzanne lived on the other side of the country.

After completing the admission process, William called Bart to tell him of Henry's admission and his condition. He then tried to call Suzanne, but got her answering machine. In the past, Suzanne would not pick up the phone for William, and so he called Bart back and asked him to try and contact Suzanne.

The doctor suggested to William that because of the length of time between Henry's collapse and the start of CPR, he would be unlikely to recover consciousness. William asked if Henry was in a "persistent vegetative state" and was told that it would be difficult to pin down exactly what that term meant. According to William, while Henry had never gotten around to drawing up a Patient Advocate Designation for himself, he had always expressed to William his desire not to be kept alive artificially if there was no real possibility of a meaningful recovery.

Two days later, William and Bart met with hospital representatives to discuss the future course of Henry's treatment. Bart indicated that he had never personally discussed end-of-life wishes with Henry, but that Bart trusted William's judgment in this regard. Bart said that William had been "closer to my brother than any blood relatives." Bart added that most of his family had always treated "Uncle Henry and Uncle William" as a couple and that Henry and William had always attended family functions together, including holidays, weddings, and funerals. With a wry smile, William reminded Bart of the time one of the younger children had giggled when introducing them to a visiting neighbor child as "my Uncle Henry and Aunt William."

William and Bart agreed that since Henry's physician concurred that he was beyond meaningful recovery, life support should be discontinued. Bart and William commented, however, that Suzanne was likely to want to continue life support. She and Henry were close in age, some years younger than Bart, and had been family allies in their high school days. Later in life they became estranged, especially after Henry "came out" and began bringing William to family events. Suzanne's religious beliefs, according to Bart, allowed no room for homosexuality, and she believed her brother was condemned because of William, who "led him astray." Bart and William expected that Suzanne would also be morally offended by the proposal to end the artificial life support that was maintaining Henry's ventilation and circulation. Bart volunteered to call Suzanne and make her aware of the situation. He said he would try to bring her around to the idea that in these circumstances discontinuing life support would not only be in accordance with Henry's expressed wishes, but would be in Henry's best interests. William agreed that it would be wise to let Bart be the point of contact with Suzanne.

The night before the care-planning meeting at the hospital, Bart spoke with his lawyer, who advised that the probate court would entertain a petition for a protective order to authorize the withdrawal of life support. Bart shared this information with William and the hospital personnel at the meeting and all agreed that, while court intervention was an option, the process of bringing this problem before the court for decision would probably do irreparable damage to whatever was left of family communication.

This story illustrates the dilemma faced by the hospital in cases where a patient has not clearly designated in writing his end-of-life wishes and the identity of his chosen surrogate decision maker. The problem is by no means confined to same-sex partners or other members of nontraditional families. Had William, Henry's partner, not been part of the picture, there would still have been a dispute over appropriate care between Henry's siblings, both of which—in the law's eyes—have equal standing as family members.

Narrative Response
Richard Raspa

How real conflict feels: We feel pressure in our stomachs, our breath pushing against ribs, heat burning our throat, and sweat sliding along the skin. When we disagree deeply with someone, we are often inclined to blame the other for the problem. Accusations of malicious intent are projected. The other disappears as a human being in the world and becomes a character in our story. The other person is reduced to our invention. In moments of conflict, it is clear how we engage our lives as a story. We invent our experience in narratives. And everybody has a tale to tell.

This story is a set of interlocking narratives. The narrator is an outsider and embedded in his story of the death of Henry in the hospital are the family stories about Henry and his sister, Suzanne. The narrator is telling the story from the perspective of Henry's long-time companion, William. The previous night's Internet research on angioplasty fills Henry with apprehension. In the hospital admission process, the clerk only half-listens as she continues to fill out Henry's insurance forms. In hierarchical organizations where efficiency is a leading objective, people tend to complete the work of their job description. What falls outside the defined set of work practices is not regarded as their responsibility. Filling out forms seems to be the clerk's objective here. It is an explicit part of her job description. Compassion is vague, intangible, floating beyond institutional boundaries and goals. Compassion is what is left over after the forms are complete. It is an option, not a requisite. Henry is instructed to go to the waiting room. No one takes Henry's anxiety seriously. Even the lover, William, does not find it strange that Henry has been in the restroom for a long time.

The frame narrative expands and intersects with the family narrative about Henry's homosexuality and the different receptions Henry and his partner William received from Henry's brother Bart and sister Suzanne. Epistemological determinism operates here. In other words, everybody "already knows" how Suzanne is: They expect that she will be morally offended by their desire to end artificial life support, just as Suzanne's religious beliefs have made her intolerant of homosexuality. Suzanne "already knows" how Henry and William are—morally offensive people bent on decadence. The stories people tell about each other reinforce the original family stories about the way "those people" are. In this case, stories confine people to precincts of isolation. The dying patient Henry is estranged from Suzanne. In the hospital, the clerk is unable to comfort him, and sadly, Henry goes off to the restroom to die alone. What could have be an opportunity for healing the family conflict, even the chance to complete relationships, becomes a way to further reinforce the family's canon of stories, add to it, and keep people lingering in states of disaffection.

From the narrative of Bart and William, it is Suzanne who is the enemy. She is regarded as the cause of estrangement in the family, the one who is to blame. Her intolerant ideology has broken the family. In contrast, Suzanne's story identifies her brother Henry as the cause of the family rift. His sexual orientation is immoral and, for Suzanne, homosexuality is a sin that will result in damnation. Henry has destroyed the integrity of the traditional family with its clear and distinct gender and sexual boundaries. In this story we see how narrative can predict future action for all the characters. Each story is evidence about the way "that person" really is. Any present story is used as evidence to support previous stories and predict the way it will always be. Suzanne has evidence in her narrative to justify her assessment that Henry and William will continue to be immoral people, pollute the family, and, ulti-mately, be damned. William and Bart have evidence in their stories that Suzanne will always be a difficult obstacle to enlightened decision making. The future is assured. It will look like the past. The result is, sadly, that stories about Suzanne and stories about Henry and William abandon people to states of alienation. People are dead right about each other and, if they persist in telling the same stories, they will go to their graves in isolated states of righteousness.

Ethics Response
Donald E. Gelfand

The end-of-life model used in this book (see Figure 1.1) uses a concentric circle approach that moves from the individual through the family and to the community. In contemporary American soci-ety, there are deep questions about what is meant by the term family. This story underscores the complexity of the term. The most commonly accepted form of a family is one composed of individuals who are related by blood or marriage. However, in popular discourse, the term *family* has expanded to include many alternative forms. Families can be as varied as single parents with children, unrelated senior citizens sharing living spaces, a military unit, a company of firefighters, or a team of athletes. People in such groups describe themselves as family and fulfill common family roles for one another. Although this broad application of the term *family* may not be accepted by all social scientists, there is growing recognition that various combinations of people func-tion and define themselves as family. In recent years, increasing attention has been paid to fictive kin, individuals who fulfill im-portant family functions but are not blood or legal relations.

In the case study, Henry and William are not blood relations and do not have the benefit of any legal standing as a family. Clearly, however, the relationship between Henry and William is long-standing and equivalent to a marriage, as evidenced by the testimony of Henry's brother not only about the length of Henry and William's partnership but its intensity. Henry's sister is obvi-ously offended by her brother's open homosexuality and refuses to recognize this partnership.

Although there is the legal issue of who has the right to make decisions about Henry's health, there is also the ethical issue of what grounds are being used to make this decision. William would only have legal rights to make important decisions in U.S. states that have recognized same-sex marriages, but, from an ethical standpoint, he is the individual closest to Henry and probably most understanding of Henry's feelings and beliefs. Suzanne is presented as making decisions not based on Henry's wishes, but on her own religious beliefs and her negative feelings about homosexuality. The question then arises about the ethical and moral right of individuals to impose their religious beliefs on others, particularly at crucial points in others' lives: Is it appropriate for Suzanne to make decisions about Henry's life support based on her own religious beliefs even though they may not correspond to his beliefs?

The intense debate in the United States over this issue is not expected to abate anytime soon. The situation of Henry thus provides an important glimpse into the ethical issues that will continue to confront health care providers working with nontraditional families facing end-of-life decisions.

Information Response
Lynda M. Baker

In stressful situations, some people seek information, while others avoid it. Miller (1987) labels the former category *monitors*, that is, people who gather information to cope with stress. *Blunters* are people who do the opposite. Because information increases their anxiety, blunters prefer to avoid it. Evidence exists in this case study of both types of information-seeking behavior.

As a typical monitor, Henry seeks information from many sources. He and his physician have probably talked at some length about his chest pains and the angioplasty procedure. One can also assume that Henry has talked with William, his partner, about the procedure and his apprehension about having it done. Before his appointment, he searched the Internet to find more information about the procedure. Finally, he also sought information from the clerk at the hospital.

Henry's information-seeking behavior is typical of monitors. He is under so much stress that he is unable to discriminate among information providers. For this reason, he seeks feedback from the clerk, who is there only to obtain insurance information. Being a well-educated person, Henry has to know that the clerk is not an authority on angioplasty. Yet, talking to her about what he found on the Internet and the risks of angioplasty is done to solicit feedback from another potential information source. The clerk's remarks, albeit superficial, are nonetheless information for Henry—reassurance that he is doing the right thing and has no need to be concerned. The clerk's instructions concerning where to sit and what will happen next also provide Henry with a sense of assurance that things are proceeding normally.

Henry's sister Suzanne appears to be a blunter. Henry's homosexuality and his life with William constitute a stressful situation for Suzanne because of her religious beliefs. To alleviate the stress their relationship has caused her, Suzanne avoids her brother and his partner. She appears to immerse herself in her religion, which teaches that homosexuality is wrong. For Suzanne, then, there is no need for further information about it. By turning away from other information sources, including Henry and William, she is able to cope with the stress of their alternative lifestyle.

Henry's sudden demise creates another stressful situation for Suzanne. When she hears about his condition, she will probably, as Bart and William surmise, resist efforts to discontinue life support. Being hit with this stressor forces her to turn away from any additional information, including what she would need to make an informed decision to end artificial life support. Suzanne needs time to adjust to and assimilate the information about Henry's state. As a blunter, she will ask for information only when she can handle it. Henry might be on life support longer than Bart and William would like, but Suzanne might eventually seek the information she needs to make the decision about her brother.

REFERENCES

Miller, S. M. (1987). Monitoring and blunting: Validation of a questionnaire to assess styles of information seeking under threat. *Journal of Personality and Social Psychology, 52*(2), 345–353.

CHAPTER 12

Stories of Peter:
Trouble with God and Family

When death, the Great Reconciler has come, it is never our tenderness that we repent of, but our severity.

—George Elliot

Peter's Story
Ardith Z. Doorenbos

As a hospice nurse, I cared for Peter from the time he signed on to hospice care until his death 3 months later. Life was never easy for Peter: rewarding, but never easy. As a youth, he was "born again" into a new life with God, and Peter's work for God was demanding. As the pastor for a congregation of 500 people, Peter's days were full. Each weekday held both religious and community services. Sundays were particularly involved, with two morning services, Sunday school, and an evening service as well. Peter felt strong in knowing that he was doing God's work and that his congregation needed his guidance. His wife Anne had an equally active life, working in the parish, singing in the choir, teaching Sunday school, and raising their three sons.

Peter considered himself "truly American." For four generations, his family had been in the United States. Raised in a strong Pentecostal community, he inherited a staunch and unbendable version of the Protestant work ethic. Peter saw himself as the breadwinner, the head of the family, and the moral and spiritual guide for those he must teach and protect.

It was excruciating for Peter to learn that at only 59 years of age he had developed amyotrophic lateral sclerosis (ALS), a little-understood disease. Ninety percent of patients diagnosed with ALS die within 5 years. ALS is extremely difficult for the patient, who loses muscular, but not mental, capabilities. It is a progressive neurological disease, in which patients increasingly lose muscle control. Over time, patients are unable to focus, to walk, to talk, and, ultimately, to breathe. Through all of this, they are keenly aware of the deterioration of their physical beings. The distress of losing control of one's bodily functions is compounded by the knowledge of what one has lost and the emotional stress of imagining what lies ahead.

Peter would not last long: He did not know it, but he would have only 1 more year with his family. Peter was proud of his family, but seldom let it show. He felt that strict emotional control was an essential sign of humility befitting a Christian. He believed that only through God's grace can one enter the Kingdom of Heaven upon death, and that the body is God's temple and must not be polluted or abused. In Peter's worldview, in one moment a person can make peace with God. Peter believed he had already done that. This story is more about his struggle to make peace with his family.

According to his sons, Peter's view of the world was so rigid and stern that he had not been a very compassionate father. His sons regarded him as domineering and unsympathetic while they were growing up. As a result, all three boys had left home early. Now that their father was sick, they felt obliged to show support, but their concerns were more for their mother than their ailing father. In their estimation, Peter needed to make retribution to them and to their mother and ask for their forgiveness. Instead of bridges of healing and forgiveness being built, the chasms within the family only widened as their father's illness progressed.

When his church board made the decision to remove Peter from his pastoral duties in response to his illness, Peter's sense of loss of control became acute. With the loss of his job came a sudden and serious reduction in income. At the same time, he was swamped with medical bills for care not covered by his insurance. Peter's financial worries increased the already high level of emotional stress associated with his illness.

Eventually, Peter was referred to the hospice program. When he began hospice care, Peter was still able to feed himself. After 6 weeks he had to change his diet to include more easy-to-handle foods, then he needed liquid foods, and, finally, food supplements. As Peter's roles in his church and community ended, his ALS worsened and his physical condition declined, he said he felt as if he were disappearing.

Peter agonized over why God seemed to have turned against him. He had served his Lord so faithfully. He had devoted his whole life—his whole being—to God: Why then was God punishing him? Why did God no longer want Peter to do His bidding? Was Peter's work not good enough? How had he failed? This was the consistent theme of Peter's prayers and conversations throughout his illness. Like the biblical Job, he felt abandoned by God (Job 3–31). His congregation and his friends had turned their backs on him. As in the story of Job, he could not tell what his future held or what God's plans were for him. Peter remained very troubled by what he perceived as God's unjust treatment.

The faithful attention of his wife, Anne, remained the only stable thing in his life. Anne had always been the rock for Peter and their three sons. She had never worked outside the home, which for Peter included his "church family." It seemed to be natural, right, and God's will that Anne should care for Peter through his illness. The hospice home care team does not provide 24-hour care and Anne felt she had to deny her own needs to care for her husband properly. Peter's demands were many and seemed unreasonable to his sons. Anne worked to such an extent that one of her sons complained, "Mother, you can't let Father and his demands kill you!"

The best example of Anne's sacrifices came near the very end of Peter's life. Peter awoke many times in the night because of his ALS. Every time he needed to turn over, Anne woke up to assist him. Hospice caregivers suggested a "floating mattress" on a hospital bed to alleviate the need to turn him so often. Peter refused; he wanted to continue to sleep in his own bed with his wife. He tried various medications and interventions to help him sleep through the night but was unhappy with all of them. His attitudes were partially linked to his aversion to medication, based on his belief in the purity of the body as God's temple. The result was that Anne had to wake every time he did, to help him to turn or urinate. Peter would go back to sleep; Anne, however, could not return to sleep so easily, and her own health suffered. Peter was also able to nap during the day, whereas Anne spent the days coping with the unending chores of running a home, receiving friends and well-wishers from the church and community who came to visit, and caring for Peter by herself. His increasing needs and demands were disrupting her life and health, but her faithful care of him endured. I do not know what passed in private between Peter and Anne. I do know their sons did not feel that their father had ever tried to make peace with them and that he was taking advantage of their mother's devotion to duty.

Toward the end, Peter was waking at night and calling out for assistance from Anne every 30 to 60 minutes. The night of his death Anne got up to help him as usual. Fifteen minutes later he called out once again. Anne heard him, but was too exhausted to respond. She drifted back to sleep. She awoke 4 hours later, surprised at the length of her rest, only to discover that her husband had died. She blamed herself for not rising when he needed her that final time. A year was, in all likelihood, all Anne could have sustained this level of caregiving. Even though she did everything she could under the circumstances, I suspect that Anne will live with feelings of guilt for the rest of her life.

Everyone in the family required more assistance: Anne with accepting the limits of her ability to provide care; Peter's sons in resolving their relationships with their father; and Peter with building emotional bridges to the people closest to him.

Provider Response
Stephanie Myers Schim and Robi Thomas

The story of Peter and his family highlights the breadth of assessment provided by a professional nurse in hospice practice. The ideal nursing situation takes a holistic approach, focusing on the physical, social, emotional, and spiritual responses of human beings across the lifespan in health and illness. This holism is well demonstrated in Peter's case. The nurse's caring for the family and the community, as well as the individual patient, is apparent here. The *nursing process*, a way of approaching problem-solving through iterative cycles of assessment, planning, intervention, and evaluation, is also evident. It is from this nursing process perspective that we understand and respond to the narrative of Peter's final days.

The first phase of the nursing process is *assessment*. The hospice nurse, in all likelihood assisted by the interdisciplinary hospice team, engaged in comprehensive and ongoing assessment of the patient, family, and immediate community. First, she used her knowledge of ALS to evaluate Peter's physical condition at hospice enrollment and at each visit until he died. The nurse measured his vital signs (heart rate, breathing, blood pressure, temperature, and so forth), observed his skin condition (looking for indicators of possible breakdown), asked about his urine and bowel output, and observed his general condition. Additionally, she would have asked about and observed for signs of pain and other symptoms of physical discomfort and distress.

It is implied in the narrative that the nurse also assessed the social, emotional, and spiritual state of the patient, his wife, and sons. She observed the role relationships within the family and noted the dynamics between family members and the larger community. Family reports of their heritage, culture, and religious values provided a context within which their current social and emotional functioning were assessed. Finally, the nurse attended to the spiritual assessment that is central to the story. She had the privilege of getting to know this patient and family over a few months' time. As their rapport deepened, she was able to discuss with them the meaning of their experiences, including the painful aspects of the patient's crisis of faith.

The next phases of the nursing process are *planning* and *intervention*. These phases are implicit in this story, but one can develop a sense of some of the elements from what is written. Most important, the planning for care is usually done *with* the patient and family rather than *for* them. Ideally, the patient and family in hospice and palliative care practice are full members of the team. The nurses and other health care professionals are coaches and supporters, but the patient and family direct the care to the degree that they feel appropriate. In this story the nurse discussed options for a floating mattress, medication, and a urinary management devise (a condom catheter), to facilitate rest for the patient and his primary caregiver wife. However, the decision to use or not use these alternatives was respected and the patient was able to die in his own bed as he desired.

Other interventions that might have been part of hospice nursing care would have included teaching the extensive physical care required for the progressively immobile person (skin care, turning and positioning, transferring, toileting, and so forth), nutritional management as the ability to self-feed decreased, and management of whatever medication regimen the patient accepted.

Peter's narrative describes his aversion to taking pain medication as being related to his spiritual beliefs. The nurse may well have discussed alternatives to pharmacological pain relief such as music, prayer, meditation, relaxation techniques, massage therapy, heat or cold application, or aromatherapy. Hospice nurses are committed to the relief of suffering, yet they also recognize that for some patients suffering is a way to deal with critical faith issues. Additional interventions may have been offered. These may have included social work to help with the social and emotional issues and address the financial crisis, occupational therapy for feeding techniques, and legal help with discussion of advance directives. Referral for pastoral care seems appropriate from the narrative, but it is not clear whether such a referral was made.

Planning and intervention in this story were primarily focused on the patient and his wife. It is presumed that this emphasis was because the sons were living away from the parental home at the time of the illness. The nurse had the opportunity to do some assessment of the social, emotional, and relationship aspects of family dynamics. It is unclear to what extent planning and intervention might have been possible within the father–son relationships. Whenever possible, nurses try to be sensitive to the pre-illness family dynamics and assess for the presence of unmet emotional needs within the family. Nurses often act as facilitators for family meetings or advocates for family discussion and resolution of unfinished business. A "good death" from the narrator's perspective is one in which the family reconciles before the end, everyone is forgiven, and the patient dies at peace knowing that he is loved and has found meaning in his life. Sometimes, however, the wounds are too deep, and the time too short to achieve such closure.

Evaluation is both the final step in the nursing process and the return to the first step. The nurse constantly evaluates what is working and not working for the patient and family. On the basis of these evaluations (new assessments), the nurse develops new plans and tries new interventions. Critical to the evaluation process is the ongoing identification of patient and family goals for care at end of life. For Peter, his goal to regain some control was partially met. He was able to die in his own bed, beside his wife, and without much pain medication.

Anne's goal of fulfilling her marriage commitment "to love and to cherish 'til death us do part" was accomplished. The sons' goal for Anne, that she maintain her own health and well-being, was not fully accomplished. The sons' stated goal was to protect their mother. It may also be that an unconscious intent was to punish their father for perceived wrongs committed in their family history. Nursing experience with a wide range of families suggests that the sons may well regret not taking the opportunity to talk openly with their father and to open the door to understanding and forgiveness. However, resolution of their grief may be a life-long process that extends into and beyond the bereavement service period (Martin, 2002). The interventions of hospice include bereavement counseling, and the family could receive ongoing services to address some of their grief and guilt issues.

Spiritual Perspective
Ardith Z. Doorenbos

The religious aspects of Peter's story demand careful consideration and response. One can understand the primary tenets of Peter's religious denomination, but it would be difficult to know all of Peter's personal spiritual beliefs. Pastors such as Peter often spend a lifetime striving to ensure that the Word of God dominates and shapes their public discourse. For them, the Word is expressed in the Bible and interpreted through a legacy of denominational heritage. One might certainly assume that Peter's life of service in the pastorate resulted from a very close alignment of most of his core beliefs with those of his church.

All individuals, even pastors, need advisors and leaders. The dilemma is expressed in the folk saying, "But who shaves the barber?" Some churches provide a clear hierarchy within which parish pastors are counseled and overseen by regional leaders, such as synodical bishops, archbishops, or district superintendents. Peter appears to have been lacking an official pastoral mentor. Perhaps he saw himself as accountable first and foremost to his congregation and his God. When a pastor such as Peter undergoes a major crisis of faith, he needs a senior, more experienced counselor, who can minister to him as Peter had to others throughout his adult life. Members of the hospice team may have assumed that a religious leader like Peter needed less spiritual support, just as they might assume a pharmacist would require less advice on medication options. In fact, quite the opposite may be true. Peter could not advise himself the same way he would others, and he may have had no experience accepting the advice of others in matters of the soul.

Another troubling issue is Peter's relationship with his church. The narrator tells us that in Peter's mind the church was part of his family. To Peter, the absence of his church family from his life would be yet another example of his spiritual family shutting him out, just as his sons had. The apparent unwillingness or inability of church members to actively support Anne in her daily caregiving and ongoing household tasks is troubling. Church and community members apparently came to visit, but rather than easing Anne's burden, they seem to be adding to it. Peter's "brothers and sisters in Christ" were not evident in his life at the end, and these were additional unreconciled relationships.

From a Christian religious perspective, there are three aspects of one's life in which forgiveness and reconciliation can lead to a restoration of love, for God's plan to be fulfilled. The first of these is the individual's relationship with God. On this front, Peter experienced conflict and questioned God's love for him. The second aspect of living in need of reconciliation is one's relationships with others, especially those closest to us. The most overt troubles in Peter's situation are his strained relationships with his sons. The third aspect of reconciliation is most often overlooked. This element involves making peace with oneself and self-forgiveness. For some people (possibly including Peter), it is difficult, if not impossible, to forgive themselves until they are forgiven by others. Thus, Peter may well have felt extensive guilt, and a resulting defensiveness, about his relationship with his sons, feelings which stood in the way of his ability to reconcile with them. If a spiritual advisor could have counseled Peter to accept his shortcomings and forgive himself, as God forgave him, he might have been better able to take the initiative in reaching out to his sons in a manner to which they could respond. The sons might then have more easily accepted and rectified their own roles in the relationship and perhaps moved toward healing.

In addition to assisting Peter in achieving all three of these forms of reconciliation, a spiritual advisor could similarly have counseled Anne. The appropriate message would have been one of assurance that both God and her "good Christian husband," Peter, could and would forgive her for a moment of physical collapse. She would need to accept that forgiveness. Her beliefs could incorporate the knowledge that she could be "washed clean" of perceived or real failings and let them fall behind her as if they had not existed. All that remains in the Christian worldview is for her to forgive herself, as she was taught to forgive others.

Spiritual beliefs strongly influence not only the patient's emotional response to illness but also the physical and spiritual. The intervention of spiritual counselors or religious leaders should be seen as essential. Although hospice workers may be aware of the spiritual needs of their patients, they may be unable, for reasons of time or training, to minister directly to those needs. Even for patients such as Peter, who are presumed to have extensive expertise in religious matters, external spiritual assistance should be encouraged and facilitated to help patients and their families dealing with the crises that accompany end of life.

Narrative Perspective
Richard Raspa

This story illustrates the power of narrative to portray multiple realities. Everybody in the narrative has a story about Peter: the narrator, the wife, the sons, and Peter himself. The stories resonate with two other tales: one from the Hebrew Bible, the story of Job (Job 1–42), the other from the medieval Christian morality tradition, the story of Everyman. The interwoven narratives of Peter and his family are enriched by the religious stories, and the resulting tale presents a complex portrait of humanity suffering under unexpected affliction.

Peter's life story is the fundamentalist Christian allegory of Everyman: Human beings are fallen creatures, separated from an ideal Edenic relationship with a distant God. People must labor diligently, as directed by the Bible, in the hope of triumphing over sin. So in this knot of uncertainty, the ordinary Christian must labor in the hope that he is good enough to be saved. In this system, something gnaws at the heart: Can anyone ever be good enough? As a minister to a congregation of 500 people, Peter enacted that belief system. Every day, and thrice on Sundays, he conducted religious and community services. Peter organized his work and family life around this unyielding pattern of activity. It was his way of being good: a good minister, husband, father, Christian, and human being. For Peter, living is treacherous. The wrong choice can lead to hell. One of the ironies of his evangelical faith is the tenet that one is saved by divine grace, through belief, without regard for good works. Peter's singular focus on salvation through good works produced a joyless austerity in his life and suppressed the other theme of the Christian story: the jubilation of Christ's victory and His promise of redemption.

The consequences of this belief system are seen in the other stories. The narrator's account frames the interlinking tales of the family. Peter, according to the narrator, began to behave like Job when he discovered he was afflicted with ALS. Although the narrator observes that Peter had already made peace with God, Peter's behavior in the face of this unexpected suffering indicates otherwise. Like Job, Peter complained. Like Job, Peter wondered "Why me? What did a good person like me ever do to deserve this?" (Job 3–31). Job eventually stops complaining and comes to understand that humankind can never fully comprehend evil with our limited comprehension of the divine; the only faithful response to life is trust that God is bringing about good, albeit in a terribly painful way (Job 42: 1–3). In contrast to Job, Peter ends his days still complaining that by subjecting him to the evils of ALS, God has betrayed him.

The narrator guides our reading of the text, indicating that Peter is challenged to make peace with his family. And so we are introduced to the other stories: Anne's tale confirms the representation of Peter as the patriarch, a stern, Old Testament-like figure who insists that his family live by the Good Book. She is the faithful servant, a caretaker who puts Peter's comfort ahead of her own, and who makes sacrifices for her husband. The ideal Christian, after all, is willing to make the ultimate, Christ-like sacrifice, to lay down one's life for the sake of another. Anne's generosity provokes complaints from her children that link to their narratives of Peter.

Having left home at an early age, the sons return when they hear of Peter's illness, more to support their mother than their father. There is an unspoken question at this point in the text: Did the sons try to make peace with the father? Like Peter, the sons complain of their treatment at the hands of the father. Like Peter, they have an expectation that something is owed to them. Like Peter, they remain passive in the relationship, children who do not understand that relationships are constructs that exist between people; they are *created* by the individuals involved and, therefore, must be constantly *re*created. The sons assume, as do all the story-tellers, that it is Peter's responsibility to seek forgiveness; it is he who should apologize to the family "victims" for his unyielding and harsh behavior.

The dominant narrative is Peter's suppression, control, and need to forgive. The unspoken story embedded in the silent interstices of all these narratives is that forgiveness is everybody's responsibility. Forgiveness does not exonerate past transgressions; rather, forgiveness is an act of courage that releases both the forgiver and the forgiven from conditions of resentment. The individual who forgives is giving up his or her claim of revenge on or restitution from the forgiven. The individual who is forgiven is being told that, although transgression is unacceptable, even transgressors are fellow humans and therefore deserving of forgiveness.

Forgiveness is work that is done in the heart. It is not predicated on an expression of contrition or the offering of an apology. To forgive is not only to release the other, but also to reclaim the energy expended in sustaining hatred. Shakespeare, in *The Tempest*, encapsulates this point clearly: "The rarer action is in virtue than in vengeance" (Act 5.1.27–28). The pathos of Peter's story extends to everyone: Peter, his wife, his sons. They all are trapped, casting blame for their conditions: Peter blames God, Peter's wife blames herself, and Peter's sons blame Peter. In such a circle of accusation, individuals deplete their capacity, as the narration suggests, to "build the bridges" they need for forgiveness.

REFERENCES

Evans, G. B. (1974). *The riverside Shakespeare.* Boston: Houghton Mifflin.

Lester, G. A. (Ed.). (1984). *Three late medieval morality plays: Mankind, everyman, and mundus et infans.* New York: W. W. Norton.

Martin, S. (2002, June 17). The death of my father. *The New Yorker,* 84–87.

Shakespeare, W. (1610). *The Tempest.* In *The Riverside Shakespeare* (2nd ed., 1997). (G. B. Evans, Ed.). Boston: Houghton Mifflin.

CHAPTER 13

Stories of Jim:
Homeless and at Home

How hard to realize that every camp of men or beast
Has this glorious, starry firmament for a roof.

—John Muir

Jim's Story
Dorothy E. Deremo

Because I am the CEO of a large hospice program, the team that
took care of Jim told me his story. He was initially referred from
a large urban teaching hospital ER. Jim, a 59-year-old white man,
was a "frequent flyer" at the ER. He came in almost weekly to
dry out or, in the winter, to warm up. Jim was a homeless man
who lived in a cardboard box under a suspension bridge connecting
two major cities. There is an entire cardboard-box community of
homeless people living under the bridge.

Jim usually had one or two of his buddies with him when he
came to the ER. They were family for each other; displaced and
lonely, they clung together for support. They panhandled together,
sharing what they had, and looked out for and protected each
other. Like Jim, his buddies had been in and out of institutions
all their lives and chose the freedom of homelessness over the
depersonalization of institutions.

The ER social worker informed us that Jim was terminally
ill but refused to leave his home and "family" for a nursing home;
he was not about to go to any institution. Our hospice team signed

168

Jim into our program and made "home visits" to his cardboard box under the bridge. This was Jim's desire for how he wanted to spend his last days, and his wishes were honored.

There came a time when Jim really could not stay in his box any longer. Our staff asked him if he would be willing to go to our 20-bed suburban hospice residence. They described it as home-like. They described the residence as having "quilts and cozy bedroom furniture where even the hospital bed is made to look like one you would sleep in at home."

After describing the hospice options, the social worker asked Jim what he really wanted. Jim was becoming more uncomfortable in his box but he did not want to leave his "family." The social worker explored the notion of bringing Jim's buddies to see him at the hospice home on a daily basis. As time passed, Jim grew to like the idea and decided that perhaps moving would be the best thing to do.

When Jim was brought to the hospice home it was the first time he had slept on clean sheets in a long time. A platoon of volunteers began driving Jim's buddies to the hospice home for daily visits. Jim's friends from under the bridge did not have access to regular showers and clean clothes, so they looked very different from the other family visitors, but the facility's volunteers were gracious. Jim passed his last days cared for in a comfortable and welcoming environment, with daily visits from the people who mattered to him. Jim died in dignity and peace on a warm, sunny day, facing the hospice garden, with his "family" around him.

Policy Response

Donald E. Gelfand and Ardith Z. Doorenbos

Jim's story can be viewed as an example of the problems experienced by people who do not fit into standard categories. In addition to the fact that Jim's "family" does not fit into traditional American forms, Jim is also homeless.

Being part of a vulnerable population, such as the homeless, *necessitates* dealing with health care system gaps (Douglas, Torres, Surfus, Krinke, & Dale, 1999). In a study of health care utilization among homeless people prior to death, Hwang and colleagues (2001) found that most homeless persons were underusing health care services, even when they were clearly at high mortality risk. Only 21% of the homeless were "frequent flyers" such as Jim, with six or more visits to a health care setting before death (Hwang et al.).

Jim stays in a fixed place most of the year. He is also an extensive user of the ER. For the homeless, as for many people without health insurance or on Medicaid, the ER is the first place to turn for assistance. Both by the nature of its mission and its high costs, however, ERs are clearly not appropriate places to provide primary health care.

The usual first response by providers in a case such as Jim's might be to contact Adult Protective Services to find him "suitable" housing. Given the strapped resources of many cities, this solution might well involve a shelter. But social service workers often encounter resistance from homeless people to staying in shelters. Many homeless individuals view shelters as dangerous and unsafe, and most shelters do not allow individuals to remain inside during the daytime. For the homeless, some situations have changed for the better in recent years. Homeless individuals are no longer denied access to Supplemental Security Income despite their lack of fixed address (Social Security Administration, 2004). The homeless are becoming more integrated into our social welfare system, however slowly.

In Jim's story, instead of calling hospital social services, the ER staff referred him to hospice. Even more remarkable in the current U.S. health care system is the hospice workers' willingness to make "home visits" to Jim in the harsh physical environment under the bridge. Providing adequate care for a terminally ill individual under these conditions is obviously very difficult. The appropriate step is, then, to relocate Jim to an inpatient facility. But this is not a simple matter. Relocating an individual to an inpatient hospice has symbolic significance. First, the person must recognize that he or she is dying. Beautiful surroundings do not change this reality. Additionally, the change of setting from the cardboard community to the hospice home is a significant life transition. Jim gained a more conventional home but lost full control over his life.

For many homeless individuals, there may be additional issues. People who are homeless or housing–insecure frequently have encounters with private and governmental entities ranging from the police to social services and public health agencies. With limited resources at their disposal, these agencies are often frustrated in their efforts to advocate for the homeless. Agency efforts are sometimes thwarted by ingrained suspicion encountered among the homeless, themselves. People who are homeless frequently report feeling that social service agencies are not sensitive to their needs and set up meaningless bureaucratic hurdles before they provide assistance (Applewhite, 1997). Additionally, it is estimated that about one-third of people who are homeless have serious problems with mental illness and substance abuse that interfere with their ability to seek health care or social services (Caton et al., 2000). It is not surprising that many homeless people view health and social service workers as trying to move them off the streets and into restricted settings where they will be forced to stay against their will.

Individuals become homeless for many reasons: job loss and the subsequent inability to meet financial obligations, substance abuse, and mental health problems. Homelessness complicates end-of-life care. A stay in a hospice for individuals whose homelessness stems from substance abuse or mental health problems places additional burdens on providers, beyond the provision of appropriate care. Detoxification and psychological therapy are not services usually associated with a hospice environment.

In the past 30 years, there has been an impressive growth in the use of hospice care at end of life, and hospice care continues to be the only model of care for the dying that is recognized for reimbursement. Despite this increase, hospices currently serve primarily white middle- and upper-class communities (National Hospice & Palliative Care Organization, 2000). Documented barriers to hospice include living in lower socioeconomic urban areas, not having a safe home, and having no primary caregiver (Dahlin, 1999). These documented barriers were all elements of Jim's life.

The willingness of the hospice team to honor Jim's request about his "family" indicates the sensitivity to the need of terminally ill individuals for social support. This sensitivity, however, does not mean that the visits of homeless individuals to a hospice will automatically result in positive feelings among staff and volunteers. Education about diversity can help increase the level of sensitivity and adaptability among hospice workers, characteristics desperately needed with challenging hospice patients such as Jim

(Doorenbos & Schim, 2004). Exposure to and experience with a broad variety of cultures and individuals provide hospice workers with the experiential basis needed for them to be truly flexible. Educating staff about the need to be gracious in their welcoming of the homeless individuals required effort, but the encounters with Jim and his family provided an opportunity for hospice staff to have hands-on experience with serving a too-often stigmatized segment of the population. Hospice staff needed to understand their own personal reactions to begin to address the concerns of other patients, families, and friends who have concerns about the homeless people who became regular visitors to the hospice. Jim's hospice care provoked a reassessment of daily care policies and the deeper purpose of the work.

Providing services for a homeless, uninsured individual is to be applauded, but this story raises larger ethical and policy issues. According to Medicare regulations, hospice must ensure that services are provided in a safe and effective manner. A strict interpretation of the regulations would have excluded Jim, who had no conventional family and did not live in a "safe" home. It is a tribute to this hospice that it supported the concept of *family* as those who share the bond of kindred spirit and a commitment to care for each other through all circumstances.

Many hospices attempt to guarantee that all individuals who need care are served. The question is, however, how extensive these services can be. Medicare hospice benefits remain limited in their dollar-per-patient amounts, whereas the number of uninsured individuals continues to rise. Hospice organizations attempt to pay for services to uninsured individuals from the charitable contributions they receive. Hospice programs are also actively promoting awareness of their services among diverse populations that have not extensively used these programs. If this awareness increases the demand for hospice services, and contributions do not increase correspondingly, the resulting problem will be more demand for services than can be met. An important question must then be confronted: Is it ethical to publicize and encourage a demand for hospice services if there is no guarantee that this demand can be met? A number of answers to this question exist, including the possibility that creating more demand will force changes in the reimbursement mechanisms for services such as hospice and the possibility that these newly engaged communities will provide voluntary support equal to the increasing need. Whether these are realistic scenarios will become evident over time.

Legal Response
George A. Cooney, Jr.

In terms of the legal aspects of decision making, the handling of Jim's case by hospice appears impeccable. Jim, despite his terminal diagnosis, was mentally competent to make his own choices about care. No substituted decision making by a surrogate was needed, and the wishes of the patient were paramount. The legal requirements spelled out by Michigan's courts in *In re Rosebush* (1992) and *In re Martin* (1995), recognizing the power of a competent adult to request or refuse life-prolonging medical treatment and care, were admirably met by hospice in this narrative.

However, the situation raises some additional legal issues with implications for delivery of care in similar circumstances. One issue is the difficulty faced by health care workers who must evaluate, under field circumstances, a patient's competence to give informed consent. In Jim's story, the hospice team provided services at his home in a box under a bridge. They did not report his living conditions to city and health department authorities. This omission raises the issue of whether continuing to attend to a patient under these circumstances creates potential liability for the agency.

Although Jim remained competent to make and communicate his own decisions, dying patients do not always retain decisional capacity. In the absence of clear information about personal choices for care at the end of life, the task of obtaining consensus among next-of-kin is a challenge in the best of circumstances. It is made more difficult if the incompetent patient is outside those structures that are familiar to the people providing medical care and legal advice. Obviously, Jim's buddies are his functional family, but they have no legal status. If Jim had become incompetent, with no determinable next-of-kin, the court would have appointed a guardian to make medical decisions. Individuals in a variety of nontraditional relationships (e.g., Jim's buddies, same-sex partners, elderly couples who remain unmarried or divorce because of Social Security considerations) present problems for the legal system. The U.S. legal system was not designed to accommodate such diverse needs. In nontraditional relationships, explicit communication of preferences for care is particularly crucial if end-of-life wishes are to be honored. The possibilities inherent in a situation such as Jim's raise an important question: How can the health care legal and social service systems help persons such as Jim make their individual wishes known and knowable?

Provider Response
Megan Gunnell

The arts have been used for centuries as a means of restoring, transforming, and healing on physical, psychological, and spiritual levels. Music, art, dance, and drama are versatile and pervasive and transcend many cultural barriers. The arts have a universality that can speak to us as individuals in both familiar and primal ways. For example, along with emotional expression, music can trigger memory and stimulate associations with one's past experiences.

Music as therapy is a nonthreatening approach. The therapist uses a familiar medium that helps to relax and comfort the client. When a client feels supported and engaged in a session, the therapeutic work can seem effortless. Music therapy sessions do not focus on producing long-lasting, tangible objects. The emphasis is on the active *process* of engaging the participant in the here and now. The therapist can use music as a bridge that moves people from where they are to where they want to be. Music acts as a common denominator transcending socioeconomic status, cultural differences, values, and beliefs.

For Jim, music therapy sessions could have deepened the connection he felt with his "family," through either individual or group sessions. Because Jim's identity was greatly influenced by his communal living situation, it might have been most advantageous to offer group or "family" sessions with Jim and his friends. Ideally, a therapist could start to work with Jim and his family at his home under the bridge and continue with them at the hospice home. Many creative interventions could have been employed, such as song writing, group improvisation, drumming, and lyric analysis for life review (Bruscia, 1991). These techniques would have helped Jim to achieve goals such as increased self-expression, self-awareness, communication, and relaxation. Such therapy might also have empowered him in the realization of one of his greatest needs at end of life: maintaining a strong sense of community as a means of self-identity.

Because Jim was homeless, there were several psychosocial and emotional issues that he might have experienced. Even if music therapy services had been available, there might not have been time to develop a trusting therapeutic relationship. Some of the more complex mental health or substance abuse needs might not have been addressed. However, there is value in short-term music therapy, and for Jim, even sessions only at the very end of his life could have been meaningful.

From a therapist's perspective, the challenges in this story are many. There are simple, logistical challenges, such as how and where to work with a homeless person. Carrying an instrument, transporting session equipment such as drums or rhythm instruments for a session in the cardboard-box village under an urban bridge would have been quite a challenge. There would also be complexities in preparing and incorporating Jim's "family" into the music-therapy sessions. When the patient's background and circumstances sharply differ from the therapist's, the professional challenge is to meet persons within their own realm and design a therapeutic strategy that addresses their needs.

REFERENCES

Applewhite, S. (1997). Homeless veterans: Perspectives on social services use. *Social Work, 42,* 19–30.

Bruscia, K. E. (1991). *Case studies in music therapy.* Phoenixville, PA: Barcelona.

Caton, C. L. M., Hasin, D., Shrout, P. E., Opler, L. A., Hirshfield, S., Dominguez, B., & Felix, A. (2000). Risk factors for homelessness among indigent urban adults with no history of psychotic illness: A case-control study. *American Journal of Public Health, 90,* 258–263.

Dahlin, C. M. (1999). Access to care. *Hospice Journal, 14,* 75–84.

Doorenbos, A. Z., & Schim, S. M. (2004). Cultural competence in hospice. *American Journal of Hospice & Palliative Care, 21,* 28–32.

Douglas, R. L., Torres, R. E., Surfus, P., Krinke, B., & Dale, L. (1999). Health care needs and services utilization among sheltered and unsheltered Michigan homeless. *Journal of Health Care for the Poor and Underserved, 10,* 5–18.

Hwang, S. W., O'Connell, J. J., Lebow, J. M., Bierer, M. F., Orav, E. J., & Brennan, T. A. (2001). Health care utilization among homeless adults prior to death. *Journal of Health Care for the Poor and Underserved, 12,* 50–58.

In re Martin, 450 Mich 204, 538 NW 2d 399 (1995).
In re Rosebush, 195 Mich App 695, 491 NW 2d 633 (1992).
National Hospice & Palliative Care Organization. (2000). *NHPCO facts and figures.* Retrieved October 7, 2003, from http://www.nhpco.org
Social Security Administration. (2004). *Spotlight on homelessness.* Retrieved March 6, 2004, from http://www.ssgov/notices/supplemental-security-income/spot lights/spot-homeless.htm

CHAPTER 14

Stories of Shanti:
Culture and Karma

The body's life proceeds not lacking Work. There is a task of holiness to do.

—Bhagavad Gita Chapter III

Shanti's Story
Ardith Z. Doorenbos

When I met Shanti, she was already a very ill 64 year old woman. I was called in as an advisor, as I had worked as a nurse in India and had insight into Shanti's cultural concerns. Her breast cancer had spread to numerous other sites in her body. She was suffering with anorexia and weight loss, digestive problems, headaches, and pain in her shoulders, chest, hips, and back; she grimaced when she moved; she had shortness of breath and a persistent cough. She did not know she had cancer, or how ill she really was, nor did she want to know. "It is in the hands of the gods," she asserted. Shanti was a soft-spoken, gentle woman, and it disturbed the hospice staff to see her in constant, aching pain, yet refusing to take pain medication.

Shanti had lived in the United States for 32 years, and her family still adhered strictly to the Hindu beliefs and practices from their early lives in India. She was in an arranged marriage, and her three children, although all born in the United States, were also in successful arranged marriages. Shanti and her husband were upset because their son did not live with them because of job-related reasons. Having him live elsewhere did not fit with the close extended family pattern with which they were raised. One of their daughters did live nearby, and she provided all the personal care for Shanti during her illness. The family worshipped daily at their household shrines, visited the Hindu temple for all major Hindu festivals, and believed in reincarnation and the power of karma in their lives.

To Shanti and her husband, all that happened in this life was the result of behaviors in their past lives, and her status in the next life would be the result of her behavior in this life. This is the Hindu concept of *karma*. To Shanti, the pain and suffering she was experiencing were given to her by the gods to be endured. Relief from her pain would produce bad karma, and would have negative ramifications for her next life. Pain medication, rather than bringing relief, would prevent her soul's growth toward perfection, or *nirvana*.

The hospice staff was faced with a number of dilemmas requiring resolution. Could they admit Shanti to the hospice program without revealing the diagnosis and prognosis to her? Were they required by law or moral obligation to administer pain medication to an obviously suffering patient? How could they bring themselves to understand a patient who didn't seem to want to be helped? Could they watch her suffer each day and not be affected themselves?

The hospice staff consulted their legal and ethical experts, who determined that the patient's desire not to be informed of diagnosis or prognosis could and should be respected, both ethically and legally. Shanti was not informed of her medical situation, nor was she made aware of the end as it approached. This decision allowed hospice staff to be more comfortable in respecting the client and family wishes about not receiving information, but watching Shanti suffer was still painful for the hospice team. Shanti eventually agreed that a modicum of pain medication—only enough to allow her to retain clear thinking—would be acceptable. Her daughter, more accustomed to the blending of her Hindu beliefs with American practices, administered the medication; Shanti's husband would not.

Shanti died in relatively unrelieved pain, but the beauty of her story is that she died with a strong karma, at home, with her family around her. Following Hindu death practices, she died with her head facing north, with the water of the Ganges River sprinkled in her mouth, and a bay leaf placed on her lips. She was cremated within 24 hours as required by Hindu death rites.

Arriving at an understanding of what was important to Shanti took a great deal of time and effort on the part of hospice staff. This time and effort were well spent, for Shanti died as befitted her name. Shanti in Hindi means *at peace*.

Cultural Response
Elizabeth E. Chapleski

Shanti's story is a prime example of conflict arising from culture clash when biomedical concepts collide with cultural and religious beliefs. For Shanti's family, living within the context of a dominant culture very different from their own Hindu culture, ethical considerations are complex. American biomedical ethical principles are often viewed as incongruent, and the family feels pressured to acquiesce in the demands of the dominant culture.

Ethics deals with a systematic approach to questions of morality, providing a philosophical framework for moral decisions (Doorenbos, Briller, & Chapleski, 2003). Yet, in cases of cross-cultural interactions in the United States, whose ethics should take precedence? Clearly, some ethical principles guiding the medical system in this country are not applicable from the perspectives of other cultures. One example of this conflict is biomedicine's emphasis on autonomy and self-determination, which do not resonate for families like Shanti's who are part of more collectivist cultures that value communal decision making and believe that patients should be protected from full information about their diagnoses and prognoses.

Living in the United States and maintaining their Hindu heritage and Asian Indian culture placed Shanti's family in a difficult position when dealing with some aspects of American hospice care. It is not clear how the family came to choose hospice or what their expectations might have been when she was enrolled in the program. In Shanti's story, hospice staff made the effort to consult with a nurse experienced with Hindu beliefs and rituals who could help the staff adapt their care to better meet the family needs. The nurse consultant explained that as Hindu persons age, their quality of life is defined more by spiritual aspects than physical functioning (Kodiath & Kodiath, 1995). For 64 year old Shanti, as her physical health declined, it became increasingly important for her to focus on her spiritual journey even if it meant enduring physical pain that would seem intolerable to others.

The religious concept of karma within Hinduism is critical to understanding Shanti's story. The doctrine of karma teaches that all experience is the reward or punishment for previous actions (Bhungalia & Kemp, 2002). Karma states that health and disease are the predetermined effects of actions taken by individuals at some previous time, either in their present life or in one of their numerous past lives (Laungani, 1997). Karma gives rise to a belief that life and death are in the hands of the gods. Before the soul leaves this body, it creates for itself another. A soul continuously prepares for its next life both through, and in response to, its present circumstances, just as a person prepares for tomorrow by way of today's events and actions. At the time of death, a person who has not suffered enough in the present life will continue to suffer in the next life. Therefore, if suffering is properly endured in the current life, the reward will be less suffering in the next life. One of the important messages of Hinduism is to strive to overcome physical pain and suffering through dissociation. Instead of focusing on the pain, the focus is placed on meditation to achieve a state of peace and transcendence above physical pain. When peace is achieved through meditation, the soul is freed to return in the next life cycle in a higher incarnation. If peace is not achieved and the lesson of this life's suffering are not learned, the suffering continues in the next life cycle. It is in this sense that Hindus say that an individual creates the next life.

Within American biomedicine it is believed that severe pain inhibits a person's ability to relax and focus on achieving spiritual meaning and peace at the end of life. It is difficult for many health care providers in this country to understand why a patient would want to endure physical pain when means for its relief are readily available. Yet the power of a meditative dissociation has been demonstrated by people who walk over hot coals or rest on a bed of nails as they practice mind and spirit transcendence over the physical body. Perhaps our health care system would benefit by being more open to methods such as meditation and dissociation from pain rather than limiting care to pharmaceutical numbing of the senses. The story of Shanti and her family suggests that there is added benefit to expanding our understanding and that there are many different ways to interpret the meaning of pain and the experience of suffering.

Hospice was a good choice of care for this family because a hospital or nursing home facility would have been less likely to accommodate the observance of Hindu death rituals. Additionally, the family's cultural expectation of care for the dying at home was met. The tendency in hospice programs is to value patient control or family decisions at the end of life even when those values seem at odds with fundamental hospice values. This story underscores the necessity of tailoring hospice and other end-of-life services to meet the spiritual, religious, and cultural needs and desires of dying persons, their families, and their communities. Together, the hospice staff, the family, and Shanti found a common path that respected and honored her as a Hindu woman fulfilling her destiny in death.

Ethics Response
Donald E. Gelfand

Some questions raised by this story include whether it is ethical not to inform patients of their illness and prognosis, and whether it is ethical to not provide extensive relief from pain.

In Western medicine, physicians subscribe to the Hippocratic Oath, which stresses *nonmaleficence*, the primary principle of doing no harm. An opposing principle is that of *beneficence*, or actively doing good (Beauchamp & Childress, 1994). Distinguishing between these two seemingly clear opposites is not necessarily easy in individual cases. It can be argued that Shanti's physicians and nurses were concerned that by acquiescing in Shanti's requests they were not fulfilling their professional responsibilities to provide both adequate pain relief and a clear disclosure to Shanti about her diagnosis and prognosis. They recognized, however, that both pain control and preferences for disclosure are cultural factors.

Terminally ill individuals such as Shanti are regarded in health systems as particularly "vulnerable" and in need of special protections in matters of informed consent. Designation of such vulnerability can lead to an attitude of paternalism in which patients are viewed as less than fully capable. The U.S. Supreme Court has handed down recent decisions upholding the rights of states to ban assisted suicide. The court's rulings rested in part on the perceived vulnerability of terminally ill persons and their need to be protected from potential coercion to engage in assisted suicide. It has been argued, however, that such paternalism can quickly become a rationale for taking the rights of self-determination away from individuals. Silvers (1998) cautioned that

> . . . the history of marking marginalized groups as needing special protection is replete with instances in which to characterize a class of persons as weak is to deprive them of the power of self-determination. (p. 135)

There is concern in the medical community and among legal scholars and ethicists that the tendency to paternalism has often led to the so-called "conspiracy of silence," in which patients are not adequately informed about their diagnosis or prognosis (Katz, 1984). Physicians and other providers are sometimes afraid to talk openly about prognoses that will either reduce the patients' sense of hope or lead them to stop "fighting" against their illness (Christakis, 1999). There is fear that truth-telling about terminal prognosis can become a self-fulfilling prophecy for patients and their families; however, Western medical ethics and cultural values clearly favor telling "the whole truth and nothing but the truth." This ethical dilemma is illustrated clearly in the story of Shanti, where care providers are called upon to maintain silence about diagnosis and prognosis to honor patient and family religious beliefs.

Another ethical question faced by providers in situations such as Shanti's is whether or not to intervene aggressively to relieve pain. Data indicate that approximately 90% of all physical pain can be alleviated (Jacobs, 2003). Palliative care services are directed toward the elimination of pain using a variety of techniques and medications. Some of the medications commonly used for pain relief also diminish cognitive capacity and may render the patient unconscious as the physical processes of death proceed. Loss of cognitive capacity is considered a fair trade-off for the relief of pain and suffering because medical providers generally believe that death should not be painful or involve unnecessary suffering for patients or their families.

It is important to have a clear understanding of the concept of *suffering*. Cassell (1999) defines suffering as "a specific state of distress that occurs when the intactness or integrity of the person is threatened or disrupted" (p. 531). The following story provides another example of suffering as it relates to ethical considerations by health care providers even without the complications of cross-culture interactions:

> In recent rounds at a major medical center, a palliative care physician visited a 63-year-old woman with extensive spread of cancer. On the basis of her diagnosis, the physician was certain that the patient had only a short time left to live. The physician asked the woman about her pain, and physical assessment revealed that the patient was not experiencing physical pain. She was, however, very upset and concerned about dying. Although she was not in physical pain, she was suffering. The physician decided to reduce this woman's pain medication to a bare minimum as long as she was not experiencing severe pain. This enabled her to move forward with clear thinking to work on unresolved life and spiritual issues that would help to relieve her suffering.

Cassell (1999) suggested exploring patient suffering through questions such as "I know that you have pain, but are there things that are even worse than just the pain?" (p. 532). For Shanti, it is clear that that there were things worse than just her pain. What concerned her most was respect for her beliefs regarding the rebirth of her soul, retaining her cognitive ability to fully participate in the traditional Hindu death rites, and enduring pain and suffering according to her religious beliefs.

The ethical issues in Shanti's story are also closely related to the spirituality domain. Sulmasy (2002) defines *spirituality* as "an individual's or a group's relationship with the transcendent, however that may be construed" (p. 25). Shanti and her family have a strong relationship with the transcendent and, in this conception, strong beliefs about the administration of pain medication. In fact, the family believes that the pain is related to Shanti's karma. It is possible to argue that it would be unethical to provide pain relief to Shanti because this would violate her spiritual principles and religious practices.

Shanti's story also illustrates some important intrafamilial differences in beliefs and practices that are common within multigenerational families. It is possible that traditional Hindu spiritual beliefs are not held as strongly by Shanti's daughters as they are by Shanti and her husband. One daughter regularly administered a small dose of pain medication, but Shanti's husband never participated in giving medication. It is unclear from the narrative what this difference in the involvement of the daughter and husband in relief of Shanti's pain signifies. However, it is possible that the daughter was willing to administer this pain medication because she is less strongly adherent to Hindu beliefs, a change that some might argue is related to her degree of acculturation to Western society. Support for this argument might be seen in the fact that the couple's son and daughter live independent of the parents.

Shanti's story does not provide specifics about how certain ethical decisions, such as involvement in medication administration, were made. Shanti's husband may have wished to see his wife free from pain but not have been willing to become involved in a process that he regarded as a violation of important cultural and religious tenets. There is, however, another possible explanation. It could be that the husband did not become involved in the administration of pain relief because he regarded this caregiving as "woman's work," inappropriate work for a man to undertake.

Whatever the explanation, understanding the situation requires an approach that takes into account the complexity of large cultural issues in decision making. The story also illustrates "issues of generation or age, gender and power relationships, both within the patient's family and interactions with the health care team" (Koenig & Gates-Williams, 1995, p. 248). What this series of circumstances shows is that personal belief systems are complicated and may incorporate certain aspects and practices more strongly than others for a variety of reasons. Shanti's story illustrates the need for careful and sensitive collecting of medical and social information from the family's own perspectives to really understand individual, family, and community belief systems.

Narrative Response
Richard Raspa

Shanti's story encodes the grand narratives of East and West. In the Hindu East, living is God-centered, represented in a story in which one's life extends backward and forward at the same time. Experiences in the present are the result of behavior in past lives, and conduct in the present will determine experiences in a future reincarnation. Everything is causally connected. Everything matters here and now, forever. In contrast to the Hindu reality, the grand story of the West is person-centered. This individual life—here and now—is the one that matters. Life can be made better through technological progress. The traditions of the three great religions of the West—Judaism, Christianity, and Islam—assert a connection between time and eternity (Campbell, 1972). The linkage is linear, rather than cyclic as it is in Hinduism. After death, one's consciousness may extend into another plane, but it is this individual person—his or her soul, perhaps—that survives the body in a heavenly domain without borders, limits, extension, or time. Death signifies the end of life. In Western religious systems, there is no coming back into time. After earthly existence, there is, for some, the possibility of being with God.

Shanti's story accentuates the chasm between Hindu and non-Hindu beliefs. How to act in the face of pain and death, even the meaning of suffering, disease, and dying, are socially constructed and transmitted in stories. Shanti believes that pain medication does not bring relief but rather inhibits spiritual growth, a belief elaborated in Hindu sacred texts (Mack, 1997). There is no objective experience of pain or death. Anxiety arising from neglecting religious strictures, the narrator suggests, exceeds any bodily pain Shanti feels.

To the distress of the hospice professionals, Shanti's choice is to suffer pain without medication. It is a decision arising out of her Hindu beliefs. Pain is symbolic, the result of past actions, given by the gods to be endured, purifying the soul for the next incarnation. Shanti's choice renders American biomedical technology extraneous. In the face of her burning resolve, doctors and nurses look on helplessly as Shanti endures her metastasized cancer gnawing away at her chest, stomach, brain, shoulders, hips, and back. Shanti doesn't know—nor does she wish to know—what is happening to her body: "It is in the hands of the gods."

The narrator has to interpret for the hospice workers the idea that refraining from Western medicine in treating Shanti is not an abdication of their professional responsibility as healers. Hospice workers are coached to see that Shanti's suffering is part of a valid worldview. Shanti, too, consents to a solution that settles the conflicting claims of Hindu and biomedical practice. In her final days, she agrees that taking small doses of pain medication will not cloud her thinking. She can remain alert as the fury of pain is slightly tempered. Consciously enduring suffering is a requirement for karmic purification; consciousness gives human proportion to suffering. Despite accepting Western intervention in the form of minimal pain medication, Shanti remained conscious of her physical and spiritual self until the end. For Shanti, pain is not an experience to be manipulated by drugs, but a mode of learning and a karmic path to purification. A motif of the Western narrative, intervening and controlling natural processes, is changed here.

The narrative also speaks of how the family both retains and negotiates new variations of their traditional Hindu cultural practices. Shanti's children, although American-born, are in arranged marriages. There is a break, however, with their cultural traditions regarding living arrangements. The son is living away from his parents, a situation that causes Shanti and her husband some distress. What we are seeing echoes how the children of immigrants negotiate the claims of family customs and the often rival demands of American society. For them, being the same and being different from both other Hindus and other Americans is the normal condition of living.

In this story, the narrator serves as cultural consultant between East and West, explaining interpretative differences to Shanti and her family on the one side, and physicians and nurses on the other. She articulates the points of contention between the two cultures with respect to death and dying. In this account, the body is the site of contested meanings. In Western biomedicine, diseases are explained as biochemical, physiological phenomena. Technology can—and should—intervene and help to alter the course of corporeal processes. Although disease, in biomedical culture, is regarded as an organic breakdown which can be analyzed, treated, and, in the best of conditions, healed, there is sometimes a tendency to hold the patient responsible for the sickness. In the case of heart disease, for example, some health professionals may blame failure to practice moderation in diet or indolence in evading regular exercise as moral transgressions and the source of illness. These assessments, however, reflect the failure of the provider to communicate well rather than the moral status of the patient or the cultural imperatives of Western society. Ideally, conventional biomedicine treats diseased parts of the body as biochemical processes rather than moral failures. For the East, by contrast, disease is charged with symbolic meanings. Physical symptoms, such as pain, reflect an allegory of the soul's progress through incarnation. The body is the nexus between time and eternity. It is the site where divine power and human fallibility meet. People suffer in their bodies the consequence of moral action.

The narrator's success as a cultural advisor requires profound listening. She must listen from a place of stillness inside that is untouched by the fear and frustration around her. She must hear the stories of cultural meanings and recreate them for others—the stories of Shanti, her family, and the hospice staff. Hearing the pain and fear and helplessness is the catalyst for what the narrator describes as a dramatic transformation. There is reciprocity here. The narrator hears the stories of both Shanti and hospice staff. In turn, she retells and interprets the perspective of each side to the other.

This is a story of amazing understanding. From the narrator's perspective, everyone listens. Everyone is heard. Everyone is touched by a story and transformed. Shanti's death is beautiful, the storyteller believes, because it has integrity and wholeness. Shanti dies embracing that which graced her life with meaning. Surrounded by family, Shanti dies with her belief system intact in accordance with the prescriptions of Hindu law.

REFERENCES

Beauchamp T., & Childress, J. (1994). *Principles of bioethics* (5th ed.). New York: Oxford University Press.

Bhungalia, S., & Kemp, C. (2002). Asian Indian health beliefs and practices related to the end of life. *Journal of Hospice & Palliative Nursing, 4*, 54–57.

Campbell, J. (1972). *The hero with a thousand faces.* Princeton, NJ: Princeton University Press.

Cassell, E. (1999). Diagnosing suffering: A perspective. *Annals of Internal Medicine, 131*, 531–534.

Christakis, N. (1999). *Death foretold: Prophecy and prognosis in medical care.* Chicago: University of Chicago Press.

Doorenbos, A. Z., Briller, S. H., & Chapleski, E. E. (2003). Weaving cultural context into an interdisciplinary end-of-life curriculum. *Educational Gerontology, 29*, 1–12.

Jacobs, R. (2003). *End of life pain and symptom management: Their relevance to assisted suicide and euthanasia.* Paper presented at the NEH Summer Seminar: Ethics at the end of life. University of Utah, June 20–August 1, 2003.

Katz, J. (1984). *The silent world of doctor and patient.* New York: Macmillan.

Kodiath, M. F., & Kodiath, A. (1995). A comparative study of patients who experience chronic malignant pain in Indian and the United States. *Cancer Nursing, 18,* 189–196.

Koenig, B., & Gates-Williams, J. (1995). Understanding cultural differences in caring for dying patients. *Western Journal of Medicine, 163,* 244–249.

Laungani, P. (1997). Death in a Hindu family. In C. M. Parkes, P. Laungani, & B. Young (Eds.), *Death and bereavement across cultures* (pp. 52–72). New York: Routledge.

Mack, M. (Ed.). (1997). *Norton anthology of world masterpieces.* New York: W. W. Norton.

Silvers, A. (1998). Protecting the innocents from physician-assisted suicide. In M. Battin, R. Rhodes, & A. Silvers (Eds.), *Physician assisted suicide: Expanding the debate* (pp. 133–148). New York: Routledge.

Sulmasy, D. (2002). A biopsychosocial spiritual model for the care of patients at the end of life. *The Gerontologist, 42,* 24–33.

CHAPTER 15

Stories of Three Veterans: Spectrum of Palliation

It hath often been said, that it is not death, but dying, which is terrible.

—Henry Fielding

Three Veterans' Stories
Robert Zalenski

As a physician in the Veterans' Administration health system, I have been able to observe many cases that illustrate various aspects of care at the end of life. The stories of these three veterans exemplify the spectrum of palliative care at end of life, starting with the story of Richard, who received no palliative services during his final hospitalization. The next story is of Moses, another dying man, who received palliative care services in the last week of his life. The third case tells of George, who received integrated palliative care for several months.

RICHARD'S STORY

Richard was a 77-year-old Caucasian man who served with the 3rd Army in Europe during World War II. He had worked as a mail carrier and post office supervisor until he retired. He was now diagnosed with chronic obstructive pulmonary disease (COPD), hypertension, and congestive heart failure. Richard had experi-

189

enced worsening shortness of breath for the past 3 or 4 months, and since the beginning of the year he had lost 70 pounds. This change was very alarming to Debbie, Richard's only daughter. Always a close-knit family, after his wife's death 7 years ago, Richard and Debbie had grown even closer. Debbie had been living near her father so she could help with his daily chores and cook for him. It was important for both of them that Richard remain independent as long as possible in the home that he and his wife had shared for so many years. Although it took her time to recognize the change, when she became concerned about her father's extensive weight loss and increasing shortness of breath, she brought him to the emergency department (ED).

This was not Richard's first admission through the ED. He had been admitted to the VA hospital 3½ months before. To find the cause of Richard's symptoms, a full workup for cancer had been done. A needle biopsy of his lung, an endoscopic exam, and a sigmoidoscopy showed no signs of malignancy at that time. However, Richard was too weak to get out of bed except to go to the bathroom. He underwent an echocardiogram that showed worsening of his hypertensive heart disease. During this admission, Debbie approached her dad's physician and spoke about her concerns for her father's declining condition and her desire to not have him suffer. She asked about how to ensure that her dad might be kept comfortable. The physician talked with Debbie about advance directives and then they talked with Richard. His physician assigned to him a Do Not Resuscitate (DNR) status and eventually discharged Richard home.

When brought to the ED the next time, Richard was jaundiced, dehydrated, and had very low blood pressure. The ED physicians were unable to establish a firm diagnosis and without Richard's previous medical records they were reluctant to write another DNR order for this hospitalization.

When Richard's blood pressure stabilized, he was admitted to a medical floor. At 5 a.m. the next day, Richard's heart rate and blood pressure dropped suddenly. He was unresponsive and gasping for air. He was transferred to the medical ICU, placed on a breathing machine, and treated with medication to increase his blood pressure. With these treatments, his condition improved. Although an ultrasound of his abdomen showed multiple liver masses, there was again no confirmation of cancer. Richard's exact diagnosis remained unclear.

When Debbie arrived at the ICU, the doctor spoke with her at length and told her that there was a very poor prognosis for her father's recovery. Debbie was upset that the medical staff could not provide a clear answer about the causes of her father's rapid decline. On the basis of an uncertain diagnosis, she rejected the doctor's negative prognosis. As a result, she asked that maximal medical therapy be continued, including CPR if necessary.

By 5:00 p.m., Richard was in soft wrist restraints to prevent him from pulling out the breathing tube. Although Debbie was deeply disturbed to see her father on a respirator and in restraints, she endured watching his suffering and the continued intensive medical interventions. Early the next morning, Richard's heart stopped and a code blue was called. Resuscitation was unsuccessfully attempted for 30 minutes. The cause of death was recorded as "multiple organ dysfunction secondary to prolonged hypotension" as well as "chronic ill health with malnutrition." Debbie returned home still not knowing the underlying cause of her father's death and distraught about his suffering in the final moments.

MOSES' STORY

The emergency medicine physician took a call from the attending physician on a medical ward requesting the transfer an unstable patient from the medical ward to the ED because the ICU was full. *Reverse flow*, where a patient is taken from a hospital ward to the ED, is not standard procedure. The patient was a 54-year-old African American man, Moses, whose primary diagnosis was metastatic liver cancer.

Moses was a Vietnam-era veteran. He later held down a job as a maintenance worker for an automotive supplier. Addicted to opiates since his Vietnam days, he had subsequently traded methadone treatment for IV heroin. Moses believed that the Vietnam War had ruined his health and that exposure to Agent Orange was responsible for his liver cancer.

Moses had a large family, including two sons and two daughters, who loved him very much and who had stuck by him through his drug problems. His wife was deceased. He proudly spoke of his eight grandchildren and many nieces and nephews whom he saw each year at the family reunion in Alabama. Some years as many as 200 family members attended these weekends.

Moses had developed *hyperkalemia*, a life-threatening increase in his blood potassium level caused by kidney failure that occurred as a complication of the liver cancer. In short, he was dying. The ED doctor observed that Moses was covered in sweat, but conscious and alert. The doctor explained to Moses and his oldest son and daughter that he was very seriously ill and might die soon. When asked whether he had ever considered being on life support, Moses answered that he had thought about it. In response to specific questions, he stated that he definitely did not want to have a tube put into his lungs, be hooked up to a breathing machine, or have CPR if his heart stopped beating. He explained simply, "I don't want to die that way." His eldest son and daughter, whom he trusted with important decisions, nodded in agreement during this bedside conversation. They both had tears in their eyes.

While Moses waited in the ED for an ICU bed to become available, a palliative care consult was requested for evaluation of his condition and recommendations for appropriate care options. A second medical opinion concurred with the diagnosis of metastatic disease even though a definitive diagnosis through a tissue biopsy could not be done because of Moses' poor condition; he was simply too ill to undergo further invasive testing. Moses' son voiced concerns that previous VA doctors might have missed his father's diagnosis—otherwise, how could he have such a grave illness so suddenly? Moses' complete records were opened for his son's review. After a very frank and extended discussion, the family was finally reassured that there had been no signs or laboratory evidence prior to this admission that indicated a serious illness and that the illness really did have a sudden and unexpected onset.

A physician from the Palliative Care Service (PCS) reviewed the records and examined the patient. The PCS consulting physician confirmed that it would be appropriate to have another bedside discussion with Moses and his family to discuss whether he wished to consider comfort care options. When Moses was asked whether he was willing to talk about his illness and prognosis he said, "Yes," and indicated that he would like to again have his eldest son and daughter participate in the discussion. He said that they best understood him, his life and his values, and could best help guide him.

Moses' daughter, son, the palliative care physician, and a hospital chaplain gathered at his bedside to talk with Moses. The alternatives for intensive care or hospice care were explained. Moses thought about the choices, but shook his head saying, "I am too sick to make this decision, but I do know that I would like my son and daughter to decide." It appeared that weighing benefits and burdens of treatment options was beyond his capacity, but designating decision surrogates was not.

As the PCS physician, chaplain, and two oldest children left the bedside, approximately 25 other family members were gathered in the waiting room, anxious and anticipating news. The PCS consultant suggested to the chaplain that both he and Moses' VA attending physician present the situation, the choices, and the benefits to the eldest son and daughter with the entire group of extended family and friends present. The only available room to accommodate a group of this size near the ED was the hospital chapel. The PCS physician suggested that the meeting could begin and end with a prayer. It might just be the ideal location for such significant life decisions.

The following is an excerpt from the palliative care physician's note:

> We conducted a large family meeting in the chapel, with approximately 30 family members and friends in attendance, including his 2 grandmothers, his mother, his children, his grandchildren, nieces, nephews, and close friends of the family. The chaplain began with a prayer. Then each member of the family introduced him/herself and explained their relationship to Moses.
>
> The son and daughter designated as Moses' surrogates sat in the front row. The VA attending physician and the palliative care consultant sat in front of the entire "congregation," facing them, ready to explain and answer questions. The chaplain opened the session with an invocation of God and His healing wisdom. The two doctors explained their roles and then the whole family, one by one, stated their names and their relationships to Moses. Taking time for these introductions both informed the team about who was closest to Moses and conveyed the understanding that each family and friend's opin-

ion and presence was valued as part of the process. The attending physician, assisted by the PCS consultant, explained the diagnosis, prognosis, and the fact that we believed that Moses was dying. They described the differences between ICU and hospice care. The physicians explained that ICU care might extend his life for hours to days but would be less focused on comfort. Hospice care would provide more quality time with family and friends but possibly at the expense of fewer absolute days of survival. The ICU alternative could not promise even a single day more of life. Questions were asked and answered.

The end of the meeting was signaled by a nephew declaring, "of course, he's got to have hospice care then." This sentiment seemed to resonate with all in attendance. The eldest son and daughter who were the surrogates quickly agreed with this approach and assured the rest of the family that these wishes would be carried out. The doctors reminded the family that it was not possible to know how much longer Moses would live, and encouraged them to visit Moses while he was still in the ER. The relatives acknowledged they understood and indicated that they would be visiting. The chaplain closed the meeting with a prayer.

With the family's consensus for hospice care, Moses was first stabilized for his acute medical problem in the ED. Good palliative care does not try to shorten life, and had Moses died that night the family would have missed the opportunity for much closure. Before he was transferred from the ED, the entire family filed in respectfully, two at a time, for short visits. Each person took the opportunity for conversation and exchanges that they knew might be their last with Moses. Within just a few hours, his potassium level was normal, and he was transferred back to the medical unit instead of to an ICU bed. Moses was enrolled in hospice the next day. After 5 days under hospice care within the VA hospital and with his pain controlled, he died surrounded by his large loving family.

GEORGE'S STORY

George, a Korean War veteran, was a 73-year-old African American man with a history of hypertension and cigarette smoking. He came to the ED in early May with chest pain and shortness of breath. Diagnostic tests ruled out heart disease. A bronchoscopy revealed that his left lung contained a large tumor that obstructed the airway. A biopsy confirmed the diagnosis of small-cell carcinoma. Before his retirement, George had worked with a local construction firm. His main occupation now was the care of his wife, who had manic-depressive disease.

A schedule of chemotherapy admission that would require trips to the hospital every 28 days for 3 or 4 days at a time was planned for George. Chemotherapy began in mid-June and continued over the next 6 months. In addition to the chemotherapy, George was given several oral and inhaled medications. Although he experienced poor appetite and weight loss, George tolerated the treatments fairly well. His last chemotherapy treatment occurred in mid-November. On December 30th, a computed tomography (CT) scan of his chest showed an increase in the size of the mass in the left lung. George received another 6 weeks of chemotherapy to shrink the tumor. He was relieved to know that he had more time, because he feared that his wife would be "lost on her own" without his care and support. They had no children, and he had been acting as her sole caregiver for many years.

In late May, George came back to the ED with jaundice. Blood tests and another CT scan showed an enlarged liver with metastatic disease. When told, George shook his head, but seemed resigned to his fate, as if his failing body had already announced the news and accepted the prognosis. A palliative care specialist recommended that a family meeting be scheduled. George's sister, brother-in-law, and brother attended the meeting. His wife was too ill to come to the hospital. The mood of the group was one of openness and desire for the "straight truth" of his condition so that arrangements could be made for both George and his wife. At the meeting, George spoke directly of his cancer and his dying. He said he "had lived a long and good life" and that he had been aware from the time of his diagnosis that his life expectancy would be limited. He questioned whether treatments such as CPR or use of a breathing machine made any sense in light of his advanced cancer. He preferred to remain at home as long as possible to assist in the care of his wife. George expressed appreciation for his family, for the fact that he was not in pain, and for the life he had experienced.

George was referred to hospice home care the day after the family meeting. Within 5 days his condition worsened, he became disoriented and weak, and then he fell at home. Rather than calling 911, his family called the hospice team, and George was admitted to an inpatient hospice unit. He died 1 day later.

George received good care at the end of his life and had a good death. But this successful outcome cannot be attributed to the health care system alone. Rather, it resulted from George's own insight and willingness to accept palliative care. Terminal illness like George's cancer is best managed with a palliative or hospice-like approach based on patient comfort, preservation of dignity, honoring of preferences and goals, and support for loved ones, who will be left to grieve.

Provider Response
John W. Finn

These stories highlight the emergent role of palliative care and demonstrate different palliative care experiences at the end of life. They form a continuum, from Richard, who received no palliative care, to Moses, who received late palliative care, to George, who received comprehensive palliative care. These treatment differences occurred despite several similarities in their stories. Each man had a diagnosis or a presumptive diagnosis of cancer. Each was treated in the VA emergency care system in their terminal hospitalization. For each the ED was a less than ideal setting in which to meet end-of-life needs. Emergency departments are designed to address acute conditions and traumas with a goal of saving lives and restoring health. However, it is not uncommon, as is seen in these stories, for end-of-life care to involve both emergency and intensive medical care settings.

Richard and his daughter did not have access to a palliative care specialist. Richard was chronically ill with several conditions and likely visited the outpatient department and ER frequently. As often happens, there was a thorough medical investigation that took much time to work up his progressive symptoms, declining condition, and dramatic weight loss. Confounding the situation was a suspected but not definitively proven diagnosis of widespread malignancy. At that juncture, his daughter initiated a discussion about his condition and end-of-life wishes. He returned home for what would seem to be only a few days and then was readmitted for his last 48 to 72 hours of life. Rather than comfort measures, he received aggressive life support.

In this story, we observe a fundamental difference between physician and family perspectives on uncertainty. To a physician's eyes, the prognosis was "certain death," although the clinical diagnosis was never clear. From the family perspective, uncertainty may have driven the daughter's change of heart and her request for aggressive treatment for Richard. It is difficult for family members to understand how medical providers can be certain about impending death when they are not certain of what is wrong with the patient. Physicians need to understand that therapeutic ambivalence can result in reversal of a previous no resuscitation decision by family members. In this story, even after Richard's death, the causes listed are quite vague. An autopsy most certainly would have established a diagnosis of metastatic cancer of the liver but that information would come too late to inform decision making or care.

Moses was a younger man with a presumptive diagnosis of metastatic cancer of the liver. Once again, a biopsy failed to confirm a definitive diagnosis. In an unusual chain of events, he is sent from a medical floor to the ED because no ICU beds were available. The ED physician informed the patient directly that he "might die soon," which is remarkably honest and might even be called "assertive." Under those circumstances, the patient was able to express his preference to forego aggressive life support. A consultation with a palliative care physician was obtained, as well as a second medical opinion on the presumptive diagnosis. These consultations were made to ensure agreement that a treatable condition had not been overlooked.

As it is described in Moses' story, the family meeting was also remarkable. Once permission was obtained from the patient, the family meeting was conducted in the hospital chapel. The level of agreement among the family members is notable. Usually, consensus is the goal, not unanimity; complete agreement rarely occurs. Family members generally "agree to disagree," but settle on a plan of action with which they can all be content.

Once the hospice and palliative care decision was made, Moses was transferred to a medical floor, rather than an ICU bed, and then enrolled in the hospice program. He died within 5 days, in comfort and with minimal medical intrusiveness and maximum family support. The family was satisfied and a dying patient was cared for humanely, even if for only the last few days of life. Moses' family was extremely appreciative of the care that he and they had received. Likely, they also had a little more peace in their lives. Moses had been besieged by a terrible illness while still in the prime of life. The palliative care team felt that they had supported a good ending to Moses' life by helping to alleviate prolonged suffering and by honoring his wishes.

George was a man with limited-stage small–cell carcinoma of the lung whose disease progressed in spite of chemotherapy and radiation over the period of 1 year. This is actually quite a good clinical course for a patient with this type of malignant disease. Patients who do not respond to chemotherapy and radiation usually succumb within 3 months of diagnosis. Patients who respond with partial or complete shrinkage of their tumors live only 10 to 15 months on average (Govindan & Arquette, 2002).

George developed liver failure related to massive spread of the cancer. This prompted his trip to the ED. He was seen by a palliative care specialist, who convened a meeting with the patient and his family. The patient's honesty, mature insights, and accepting emotional state, made acceptance on the part of his family much easier. With this third story, there is a promising sense of integration of palliative care and hospice approaches within the traditional hospital ways of caring for patients with life-limiting disease. There is, however, room for improvement. Consider how the story would have been altered with even more timely hospice referral. What might have been the outcome for George and his family if he had been referred for palliative attention at the time he finished radiation therapy 3 months earlier? Or could he have had a better outcome with palliative care from the moment, 6 months earlier, that evidence appeared of an unfavorable response to chemotherapy?

At the time of Richard's death palliative care services were not readily available in the VA health system. When Moses was dying, services were just beginning to be available. George's story demonstrates a recent focus on palliative care consultation for enhancing end-of-life care within the VA system. This development is significant because the Veterans' Administration has assumed specific leadership in the field of palliative care. Recently, 6 VA medical centers have been designated to provide interdisciplinary team training in palliative care. Several have already begun subspecialty training and research programs in palliative care. Nationwide, VA medical centers are now mandated to provide palliative care consultation services using interdisciplinary teams. In the stories of Moses and George, there is little mention of other nonphysician members of palliative care teams with the exception of the chaplain in one case and the hospice staff in the other. That suggests a need for further development of palliative care at the VA medical center, which might then expand into an admitting inpatient service (palliative care beds), and outpatient services, such as a clinic for ambulatory patients, as well as interdisciplinary home visits. Early analysis suggests improved health care outcomes and better resource utilization as well as cost reduction implications (Payne, Coyne, & Smith, 2002). Once incorporated into the continuum of medical care and used in a timely manner, palliative care will likely demonstrate enhanced quality of patient care as well as more appropriate resource utilization.

Family Response
Terri Kovach

It is the patient who endures the burden of illness and oncoming death. It is the patient's family that often shares the burden of suffering. These three stories reflect some of the demands that are made of families at end of life. If uncertain about a patient's wishes, medical caregivers look to available family members for information and insight. The patient is in a vulnerable state, even if cognitively intact, and may rely on the family in a new way for advice and counsel. The involvement of family in end-of-life care in the hospital appears to mediate the use of technology and increase the likelihood of comfort care (Tschann, Kaufman, & Micco, 2003). Research on family strength outside of the end-of-life scenario suggests a number of elements that are of interest: role clarity, communication, cohesion, adaptability, and religious orientation (Krysan, Moore, & Zill, 1990). These characteristics are interrelated, and each will be examined in turn as an influence on decision making in these three stories.

Role clarity is a central element of strong families. There are different expressions of role responsibilities among these stories. One of the frequent assumptions about elderly men is that they have wives to help care for them. It is interesting that the only wife in these stories is herself the recipient of care. George's wife is mentally ill, and George insists that he would prefer to be at home rather than in the hospital, in part to maintain his role as husband and caregiver. In the absence of a wife, the caregiver role generally falls to the children, most frequently daughters. Richard's daughter accompanies her father to the hospital, describes his symptoms to hospital personnel, and at one point requests "comfort-measures only." But during Richard's final hospitalization, the daughter's dual roles as caregiver and decision maker are lost; she insists that all measures be taken to sustain his life.

Moses' role as father is quite clearly articulated, but his insistence upon family involvement has the potential to muddy the decision-making process. He had already made his wishes clear to the doctors. He did not want to be intubated or have CPR. When offered the opportunity to talk about palliative care, Moses insisted that certain members of his family be there: his daughter and one of his sons. This reflects again the caregiver role of adult children for elderly or ill parents. This is an interesting role dynamic: Moses knows what he wants, but also wants to include the family in the information process. After the first small meeting with the daughter and son present, Moses cedes the decision to his larger family and their "collective wisdom." Moses' insistence upon family presence and input reinforces his role as the father. The subsequent family meeting appears to center more on getting the family to agree to Moses' wishes than on having any genuine decision-making authority.

This large family meeting, from which Moses is absent, raises a number of ethical issues. Moses has already made his wishes clear to his hospital caregivers. He knew that he did not want resuscitation, and this had been both communicated to the team and written in a DNR order. He knew whom he wished to name as surrogates, and did so. He could not weigh the complexities of life extension in the ICU versus quality time in hospice palliative care. It was only this latter decision that he delegated, in the framework of DNR regardless (there are many DNR patients in ICU care—treatment is given to avoid cardiac arrest, but once it occurs, resuscitation is not attempted). Had the family come to the decision that they wanted more aggressive measures to be used to sustain Moses' life, it would have presented a difficult circumstance for hospital personnel, who would now be faced with a new and conflicting decision about the extent of care to be offered.

Good communication is another hallmark of strong families; clear, open, honest communication facilitates family function. At the family meeting, George spoke openly about his diagnosis and his dying. He made his wishes clear to his family and to the hospital staff about the care he wanted: He stated that he did *not* want CPR or intubation. The communication in Moses' family is inclusive. Not only does Moses want his family to know about his options, he asks that his extended family and friends be given the opportunity to talk as a group about his care. This suggests a long-held pattern of communication and openness. When given the chance to speak with him individually, family members visited with Moses in the ER as he awaited transfer.

In Richard's story, communication is confounded by the lack of a clear diagnosis. The daughter's role of caregiver and decision maker is uncertain—she must defer to her father's wishes for full resuscitation, despite his earlier wish for DNR status. Steinhauser et al. (2000) in a study of medical professionals, chaplains, hospice volunteers, patients, and recently bereaved family members, identified six components of a good death: (1) pain and symptom management, (2) clear decision making, (3) preparation for death, (4) completion, (5) contribution to others, and (6) affirmation of the whole person. The researchers suggest that patients and families fear a bad death more than the death itself. Across groups, one of the elements of a bad death was one in which treatment preferences are unclear. The uncertainty of Richard's diagnosis drives the indecision about his DNR status; this is the most frustrating component of Richard's story.

Encouragement, appreciation, and commitment are closely related and often termed *cohesion* (Krysan et al., 1990). This closeness and attachment for other family members is demonstrated in Moses' family dynamics. Family and friends are involved in his care—Moses expects them to be present at the family meeting. They participate in this cohesive family group by being present at the chapel meeting and taking advantage of the chance to speak with Moses before he dies. George's wish to remain with his family as long as he can and their homecare for him suggests family cohesiveness; he states that he appreciates his life and his family.

Adaptability can be viewed as the ability to overcome stress and crises. Adaptability is related to social connectedness, including the presence of relatives and friends in the area, and to clear roles, which help define responsibilities within a flexible structure (Krysan et al., 1990). The ability to adapt is not a static phenomenon; strategies that work well for a family with a new infant may not work well in a family with elderly parents (Olson, Russell, & Sprenkle, 1989). These three families are experiencing one of the most stressful events in the history of a family—the death of a father. George appears to have come to terms with his own dying and insists upon continuing to care for his wife as long as he is able. Once his health fails him, George is willing to accept the prognosis, accept palliative care, and remain at home with his family, who successfully care for him until just before his death.

Richard and his daughter struggle with the decisions about his care, wavering between comfort care and full resuscitative efforts over the span of 2 weeks. They face an intolerable circumstance—not knowing what is wrong. Each of these families is functioning within a framework of medical care. Richard and his daughter's inability to adapt to this new circumstance is understandable because they have few answers—or perhaps too many answers—to the question, "What's wrong with him?" The uncertainty of a clear diagnosis leaves Richard and his daughter adrift. Their efforts to understand their circumstances are foiled by each test. They are thus ill-equipped to make decisions about his care. Patients, families, and health care providers are in agreement that they want to know what to expect about their physical condition at end of life (Steinhauser et al., 2001). For some families, adapting to these circumstances with an uncertain diagnosis might prove impossible without substantial support from the medical staff.

Moses' network of friends and family came together to share the news of his illness. They banded together to form a support network while adapting to the new family understanding of his impending death. Aided by the direction of the physicians and chaplain, they share their thoughts and feelings about Moses and adapt to the new reality that Moses will not survive his illness. They collectively accept the standard of comfort and hospice care for their father and friend.

The chapel, the setting of the first meeting for Moses' family, highlights the last element of a strong family that is pertinent to these stories. Effective families often have a *religious orientation or spiritual wellness* that frames their family life. Religiousness or spirituality is not contingent upon membership in a group or attendance at services; rather, this element is viewed as a value system or underlying moral framework upon which the family rests (Krysan et al., 1990). This framework helps families make decisions, offers components of social support, and engenders a feeling of connectedness to something bigger than the individual and his or her problem. The palliative care physician's notes in this story suggest that Moses and his family have a strong spiritual foundation.

As these stories illustrate, patients do not make decisions about end-of-life care in isolation. Their families are a key element in their thinking. Families must prepare for the death of the patient as well as prepare for their own lives afterward. The elements of strong families that are used in this discussion—role clarity, communication, cohesion, adaptability, and religiousness or spirituality—formed the framework for looking at the decision-making process in these stories because family dynamics at end-of-life emerge from family dynamics across the lifespan. Family caregivers often report high levels of suffering when they observe a relative in pain, and they feel the responsibility to relieve the pain and suffering of their loved one (Ferrell & Borneman, 1999). It appears that the more involved families are in hospital care, the more receptive they may be to palliative care rather than aggressive, high-tech interventions. Families trust that medical caregivers will be able to advise them of their options, give them honest answers to their questions, and help them make decisions that will relieve the suffering of their loved ones.

Communication/Information Response
Kathleen L. Meert

Decisions made by individuals regarding their health care at end-of-life depend at least in part on what they understand of their condition and what they can reasonably expect for their future. The process of end-of-life decision making begins with receiving the bad news of having an illness that is expected to be fatal. In each of the three stories presented in this chapter the patients have chronic conditions in which there is gradual deterioration of their health over time. Each of the patients appears to have the capacity to receive information and understand and make decisions on how their care should proceed. To help patients and their families face these important decisions the bad news must first be delivered. This leads to a discussion of how, when, where, and by whom bad news should be given.

The bad news of serious and likely fatal illness should be communicated truthfully to patients and families. Truthful communication implies relaying this information in an open and forthright manner, without barriers that mislead or prevent full understanding. Before patients can begin to understand and accept their condition, they must be told what that condition is and what can be expected as a result. Truthful communication can be delivered with care and compassion and does not imply a callous recital of medical facts. Language that is used should be commensurate with the patients' and families' understanding so that they do not feel "talked down to" or that the conversation is "over their heads." If the bad news is impending death, the health professional should use the words *death* or *die* rather than assume that the listeners will draw that conclusion on their own. Care and compassion can be demonstrated by the availability, patience, and openness of the health professional to questions posed by patients and families. The health professional's posture, eye contact, affect, and tone of voice affect the patient's perception of how much the health professional cares about him or her, and whether the health professional can be trusted to provide the best care.

Silence is an important part of good communication. When giving bad news to patients and families, periods of silence may intervene. These moments of silence may be uncomfortable for the health professional; however, it is usually during these moments that patients and families are trying to assimilate information and formulate questions. Emotional outbursts are also common as patients and families learn of a serious illness. If the patients or families respond emotionally, the health provider will have to wait until they are ready and able to listen and take in more. Relying on the verbal and nonverbal cues of the patients and families is important in this process. Likewise, the health professional may display emotion when delivering bad news. As long as the health professional's focus remains on the patient, a display of emotion is usually perceived as a sign of caring.

The best time to discuss bad news with a patient and family is when the patient is relatively stable, rather than during a time of crisis. This is not possible in all situations because for some the onset of illness is abrupt, and the trajectory of illness and death is very acute. However, for those with more chronic and progressive conditions the presentation of end-of-life options and discussion of patient preferences should be undertaken before a life-threatening complication ensues. It is far easier for patients, families, and health professionals to explain, listen, question, and make plans for the patient's care when they have an adequate amount of time to do so. Decisions made during a crisis may be hasty, complicated by a lack of information and understanding, and motivated by emotional factors such as guilt or grief.

Bad news is given in a variety of places such as doctors' offices, hospital rooms, waiting rooms, and corridors. The actual location usually depends on the patient's immediate circumstances. Privacy and safety are important attributes of the location chosen for delivering bad news. Although privacy is not important to everyone, it should be available for those who need it. Because intense emotional outbursts can occur, health professionals should choose locations in which patients and families are less able to harm themselves or others and in which assistance from others can be obtained easily.

Bad news regarding a person's medical condition is usually best given by the health professional who is responsible for the patient's ongoing care. When the patient's condition is chronic, this chore is often thrust upon a health professional who has an established relationship with the patient and in whom the patient trusts. The bad news can be discussed early in the course of illness and during a relatively stable phase. Palliative care specialists have a major role in helping patients make end-of-life decisions and in providing end-of-life care. Consultation with a palliative care specialist can be extremely beneficial to a patient's wellbeing. However, the specialist's expertise does not release the health professional from responsibility of informing the patient about the condition and prognosis. Leaving this important conversation to the specialist alone can cause a patient to feel abandoned by the regular health care providers. When the patient's condition is acute, bad news must often be delivered by a health professional who has no prior relationship with the patient or family, such as an ER staff member. Even in this situation, the health professional providing the emergency care should speak with and be available to the patient and family. Leaving the bad-news-telling to someone else can engender suspicion and mistrust.

In each of the stories presented in this chapter, very little information is provided about how the bad news of terminal illness was delivered to the patients and their families. Only in the story of Moses are there references to health professionals explaining to the patient his condition and prognosis. A physician tells Moses directly, "You are very seriously ill and may die soon." This information is provided by a physician meeting Moses for the first time and in the face of an acute life-threatening complication of Moses' underlying disease. However, Moses' underlying illness is not new. If Moses' primary care physician had explored likely outcomes and treatment options with Moses earlier in the course of illness, Moses might have been spared the stress and inconvenience of a transfer from his hospital room to the ER. An earlier discussion with Moses and his family regarding the terminality of his illness might have allowed him to enter hospice care earlier, rather than in the week prior to his death.

The story of George describes a man with a progressive cancer who appears to have accepted the truth of his condition and impending death. This is evidenced by George's ability to speak directly of his cancer and his dying, his expression of gratitude for the life he has lived, and his ability to ask questions about whether CPR and the use of life support are in his best interest. How the bad news was delivered to George and whether the method of delivery influenced his ability to understand and accept his condition are unknown from the story. The only reference to a conversation between George and a health professional is the mention of a family meeting with a palliative care specialist. George has a confirmed diagnosis of malignancy, and his disease has progressed in spite of months of therapy. Earlier discussion between George and his treating physician may have led to an earlier referral to hospice care. As it was, George entered hospice care 3 months after his therapy was discontinued and only a week before he died.

The story of Richard, with its seemingly haphazard and inconsistent decisions regarding end-of-life care, is not an unusual scenario. Details of how the bad news was delivered to Richard and his daughter again are not provided. Preferences for care including the use of CPR are not discussed until Richard's daughter makes a request for an advance directive. What did Richard understand of his condition? What were his preferences? Did he agree with a DNR order? Did he request that his daughter make decisions for him? The failure of health professionals to involve Richard in the decision-making process early on when he was able, likely leads to the inconsistent decisions made for his end-of-life care. The lack of open communication from health professionals can cause patients and families to seek unrealistic outcomes. Richard suffered the major consequences of this communication failure by dying of a chronic progressive illness in an intensive care unit after unsuccessful resuscitation attempts.

In summary, the delivery of bad news is the first step in end-of-life decision making for patients and their families. In addition to the lack of detail regarding the delivery of bad news in each of these stories, there is a striking absence of recommendations by health professionals advising patients on end-of-life care. In each story, it is implied that hospice care was or would have been the best option for the patient, but in none of the stories does the health professional make that recommendation directly. A health professional's recommendations for hospice care are based in part on his or her knowledge of and experience with the patient's disease as well as their degree of certainty that the correct diagnosis has been made. For both Moses and Richard, a diagnosis of malignancy appeared most likely; however, malignancy was never confirmed in either case. Moses had become too ill to obtain a confirmatory biopsy, and Richard's several biopsy specimens failed to show malignancy. The lack of a confirmed diagnosis led to the health professional's hesitancy in recommending hospice care. Nevertheless, truthful communication with patients and families includes discussing potential uncertainties in diagnosis. Uncertainties in diagnosis make it very difficult for health professionals to make recommendations with confidence. However, uncertainties in diagnosis do not relieve the health professional from seeing the patient as a whole person, from understanding the patient's preferences for care, from presenting options, or from making recommendations based on these factors.

REFERENCES

Ferrell, B. R., & Borneman, T. (1999). Pain and suffering at the end of life for older patients and their families. *Generations, 23,* 12–17.

Govindan, R., & Arquette, M. A. (2002). *The Washington manual of oncology.* Philadelphia: Lippincott, Williams, & Wilkins.

Krysan, M., Moore, K. A., & Zill, N. (1990). *Identifying successful families: An overview of constructs and selected measures.* U.S. Department of Health and Human Services. Retrieved October 2, 2003, from http://aspe.hhs.gov/daltcp/reports/idsucfam.htm

Olson, D. H., Russell, C. S., & Sprenkle, D. H. (Eds.). (1989). *Circumplex model: Systemic assessment and treatment of families.* New York: Haworth Press.

Payne, S. K., Coyne, P., & Smith, T. J. (2002). The health economics of palliative care. *Oncology, 16,* 801–812.

Steinhauser, K. E., Christakis, N. A., Clipp, E. C., McNeilly, M., Grambow, S., Parker, J., et al. (2001). Preparing for the end of life: Preferences of patients, families, physicians, and other care providers. *Journal of Pain and Symptom Management, 22,* 727–737.

Steinhauser, K. E., Clipp, E. C., McNeilly, M., Christakis, N. A., McIntyre, L. M., & Tulsky, J. A. (2000). In search of a good death: Observations of patients, families, and providers. *Annals of Internal Medicine, 132,* 825–832.

Tschann, J. M., Kaufman, S. R., & Micco, G. P. (2003). Family involvement in end-of-life care. *Journal of the American Geriatrics Society, 51,* 835–838.

CHAPTER 16

Boundaries and Bridges

Donald E. Gelfand, Richard Raspa,
Sherylyn H. Briller, and Stephanie M. Schim

T he stories told in this book reflect the complexity of issues that surround death and dying and the depth and breadth of analysis that is required to begin to understand the end of life. In this summary chapter, we look back at our multidisciplinary discussions and what we have learned. We also propose some possible future directions in research, education, and practice. First, we revisit some of the organizing constructs, domains, and levels of the conceptual model proposed in chapter 1 (see Figure 1.1).

All end-of-life situations are framed by the stories told about them from myriad viewpoints. In the stories presented in this volume, we hear a variety of voices including those of the dying persons, family and community members, and professional caregivers. Their perspectives are often markedly different. Through narrative, the stories of the interactions between these various players, actors, and figures emerge. Whereas death is a human universal, the experience is shaped by the stories constructed about death and dying. These stories reflect the wide variety of perceptions of dying processes and the many meanings of death. The stories that begin each chapter as well as the subsequent responses are all part of the narrative process. New meaning is shaped by this ongoing and iterative process.

Narrative analysis involves paying close attention to the content, the form, and the way stories are told. Active listening to a multiplicity of voices is often required and yet does not frequently occur at the end of life. The breakdown of communication that too often happens when the listener cannot or will not hear or interpret the story as told by others can have profound consequences for the quality of dying. Sometimes the communication problems occur between members of a family as illustrated in the stories of Maggie, Henry, and Peter. At other times, the breakdown is between dying persons or families and providers as shown in the stories of Sonny, Malika, and Shanti. A more positive experience with stories and listening is seen in the story of Ron, in which the music therapist listens carefully and matches music to the family's needs. Other examples are found in the stories of Jim and Pearl, in which providers were able to listen outside of the boundaries of their experiences and find ways to change their practice to bridge significant gaps. The potential for using a narrative approach to enhance end-of-life understandings in an increasingly diverse society such as the United States is significant.

In a society in which so many different stories are told and heard about end of life, it is especially critical to consider how the construct of culture permeates the discourse. Culture, like narrative, is shown in our conceptual model as surrounding and informing all other aspects of the discussion, and this relationship was observed in both the case stories and the multidisciplinary responses. We set out to ensure that the stories presented would address a wide range of end-of-life situations and cultural contexts. Factors considered included diversity of age, ethnicity, lifestyle, family structure, socioeconomic status, and trajectory to death, among others.

Although the stories selected are not intended to be a representative collection, they offer a useful set of contrasting cases from which we may examine the rich variety of end-of-life experiences. For example, the stories of Malika and Ryan deal with death in childhood and adolescence, whereas the stories of the three veterans deal with death in later adulthood. Stories such as those of Abby and Shanti explicitly highlight ethnic traditions that guide end-of-life practices, whereas in other stories these issues remain implicit. The diversity of contemporary American family life is brought to the forefront. Many family forms are presented in the stories, including a young divorced mother (Grace) with her parents and children, a man dying surrounded by his three former wives (Sonny), and a partner in a long-term gay couple (Henry). Socioeconomic status and the attendant range of living and dying settings are reflected in the stories of Jim, homeless and living under a bridge, and of Avery, dying in his beautifully restored old home. The various patterns or trajectories to death are illustrated through stories such as those of Ryan and Henry who die unexpectedly, those of Maggie and Avery who follow a slow chronic illness pattern, and the surprising case of Pearl who defies the predicted pattern of her terminal condition. It is not possible to fully discuss all of the important factors that affect end-of-life situations. Although we place a heavy emphasis on narrative and culture as overarching constructs within which to examine the complexities of end of life, these are by no means the only fruitful pathways that might be explored.

This multidisciplinary project expanded our own disciplinary understandings of end-of-life issues. Through the collaborative process, we had the opportunity to tell our own versions of end-of-life stories, to listen to the stories of our colleagues, and to challenge and be challenged. We began with the idea that the story domains in our conceptual model were not separate and fixed, but rather intersecting and overlapping. As we moved forward together, we found that in many chapters both the stories and the responses crossed disciplinary and domain boundaries.

In some chapters, the discussion of the stories led to surprising recognition of how much we have in common in dealing with end-of-life issues. For example, in initial discussions of the story of Ron, the music therapist's intervention was interpreted from both a psychological and legal perspective wherein each contributor was commenting on how the music therapy was used to achieve a good death. Insights such as this enriched the written responses and encouraged contributors to consider ways in which stepping over traditional disciplinary boundaries could enhance their practice, education, and research. In other chapters, the discussions of the stories led to heated debate over disciplinary differences. For example, the tendency on the part of some contributors to interpret health, caring, and death in a particularly Western biomedical context was challenged relentlessly. Our awareness and sensitivity to our own cultural and disciplinary assumptions and our knowledge of the perspectives of others were greatly enhanced.

One result of our collaboration has been the confirmation that our multidisciplinary approach is a powerful way to approach the vast complexities of end of life. Another result has been our understanding that the next step for our partnership is further movement toward the integration of knowledge and the development of trust across traditional academic and service silos. As we move forward, we continue striving to develop our partnerships and collaborations to achieve an interdisciplinary integrated perspective that is consistent with our project's name and purpose.

Multidisciplinary conversations are essential to research, education, and practice. In working with the stories in this book, it became evident that there are many changes needed in end-of-life care. In the following paragraphs we identify some of the more urgent areas for change. Recommendations are numbered for ease of reference; numbering does not imply importance or urgency.

Research

Research on end-of-life related topics is increasingly emphasized in a variety of disciplines. A few significant directions for multidisciplinary research that are suggested by the end-of-life stories and multidisciplinary responses are presented here for consideration.

Research is needed to provide better understanding of personal, family, and community preferences with regard to end-of-life care. Particular emphasis should be placed on cultural, religious/spiritual, and other factors that influence choice, decision making, and communication of decisions.

Throughout this book, we have seen that culture and narrative are central to the dying experience. However, there is currently inadequate research exploring the ways in which these constructs profoundly influence every aspect of end of life. Understanding the context of preferences is crucial to the provision of information and treatment. Recommended research areas follow.

1. *Research on family, friend, and community responses to loss with attention to effectiveness of various forms of grief and bereavement support.* Even if individuals die alone, the impact of their death can be widespread. Some persons, such as Ryan's parents, are able to find meaning in a death by becoming involved in community activities. In other cases, family members and friends may not find adequate resolution to their loss on their own. Because deaths occur at various moments in the life course, continuing research attention to ways in which people incorporate these losses into their life experiences is necessary.

2. *Research on diverse and emerging concepts of family and how these varied family forms interact with lay and professional caregivers at end of life.* The story of Henry illustrates one of the challenges faced as health care and society expand recognition of diverse family forms. In Henry's case, as in the case of Sonny and his three ex-wives at the bedside, staff are presented with different "family" participants in health decision making than they may be accustomed to recognizing in these situations. Avery and Jim's stories highlight in very different ways the need for better understanding of how to support family and community members who take on traditional family roles.

3. *Research on process and outcomes of alternative and complementary therapies in terminal illness, including modalities such as music therapy, aromatherapy, and massage, as well as uses of theater and the visual arts.* Given the very diverse circumstances of dying presented in these stories, it is apparent that there needs to be an equally diverse range of care options available to dying persons and their significant others. Alternative and complementary therapies are gaining wider recognition within the Western biomedical community. Various interventions, using a wide range of therapies, should be further examined to assess how they can be used most effectively to address diverse needs at end of life. Broadening knowledge about these alternative therapies as well as cultural and narrative competence at end of life and how they can be used together is an exciting proposition.

4. *Research on processes and outcomes of a wide range of palliative care options from both patient and provider perspectives.* Palliative care has been shown to improve the quality of life of dying persons and their families. However, there are significant gaps in the present knowledge of aspects such as the economic implications of palliative care interventions. More work is also needed to define ways to improve the match between the specific needs of individuals and the palliative modalities provided. Palliative care has largely been limited to hospice programs and primarily has focused on cancer patients. Additional research on palliative interventions with people with heart disease, AIDS, pulmonary diseases, diabetes, and other life-threatening conditions needs to be conducted. Research on the impact of expanding palliative care approaches across non-

hospice settings and the relationship of such expansion on patient and family outcomes is important.

Education

Education in end of life is becoming more common within a variety of academic and health care practice disciplines. The recommendations presented in this section include education for professionals, students, and the general public.

1. *Educate health care professionals and students in the health care professions regarding cultural and narrative competence.* This process includes education about narrative theory, particularly how central storytelling and listening are in everyday life and health care interactions. Education should also include experiences with diverse clients and populations, knowledge development regarding inter- and intra-group variations, and sensitivity to individual perspectives. Education should provide specific practice skills that are necessary to support the provision of care that meets client, family, and community needs in different contexts.

   Health care providers are not often educated regarding cultural and narrative concepts. Such education must go beyond cookbook descriptions of ethnic group variations, values, and norms. Knowledge of group patterns is important, but individual assessment and intervention is key. Understanding the cultural and narrative traditions of the health care professions is critical, as is insight into personal values, beliefs, and stories that providers bring to their practice.

2. *Educate health care professionals and students in the health care professions toward skilled communication with patients and families on end-of-life issues such as prognosis, care and setting options, methods for palliation, and expectations.* The development of *narrative competence* would greatly enhance provider communication at end of life. Narrative competence is the recognition of patterns of meaning embedded in the stories told, empathic response to the stories, and collaboration with the storyteller in creating new stories of what is possible. Education and opportunities to practice active listening to narratives (patient and provider stories) should be a central element of provider education as well as interpretation skills.

3. *Educate academic and practice professionals in multidisciplinary groups whenever possible, including collaborative classroom work, group projects, and clinical rotations.* Specialized programs on end of life are being developed in law, medicine, nursing and social-work schools. Education limited to disciplinary approaches hampers the ability of practitioners to treat patients from a holistic perspective. It is possible to draw on the field of gerontology for exemplars of such interdisciplinary education. In addition to interdisciplinary end-of-life courses, students from different professional disciplines need to be encouraged to interact in a variety of clinical practice settings.

4. *Provide in-service education for current health care practitioners and interaction opportunities for academics to connect to practice in end-of-life care.* Specific end-of-life education is a relatively new area. Including end of life as an important topic for in-service education will augment knowledge for a variety of practitioners. End-of-life in-service training will also help the dissemination of new knowledge and approaches in the field. Interaction between academic and service professionals, as demonstrated in the Wayne State University End-of-Life Interdisciplinary Project (WSU–EOLIP), has enormous potential to enrich the discourse and practice in both academic and service sectors.

5. *Provide a variety of public forums and other mechanisms for open discussion of end-of-life issues, including alternatives for care and care settings, legal issues, health economics, and public policy regarding death and dying at local, state, and national levels.* Many of the problems shown in the stories stem from a lack of discussion and planning on the part of individuals, families, and health care providers or organizations about the uncomfortable but important issues related to end of life. In death-averse societies, talk about dying is often postponed or avoided until a crisis occurs. There are currently few opportunities for community discussion on the larger public issues surrounding end of life. Public debate is enriched by the broad diversity of contemporary American society, but such diversity complicates policy discussions. Local dialogue could productively occur in the context of various religious and spiritual communities, neighborhood centers, schools, and civic organizations. In professional realms, better visioning/planning or discussion for

how health care professionals will provide high quality end-of-life care should occur on a more regular basis.

Practice

Practice in the health care professions is expanding to include more attention to issues of death and dying, but changes are still required at all levels. A few significant directions for multidisciplinary practice are suggested in this section. Much of the rationale for these recommendations has already been established as practice is closely integrated with research and education.

1. *Health care organizations need to support cultural and narrative competence among providers at all levels of health care, including both professional practitioners and support staff.* Support for cultural and narrative competence can be demonstrated through in-service education, professional conferences, competency testing, and patient or provider observation and evaluation. Collaboration with colleagues in the academic disciplines could enhance organizational efforts toward the desired competencies.

2. *Establish multidisciplinary palliative care consulting teams in health care systems to increase patient and colleague access to excellence in palliative approaches and integration of treatment and palliation across the life span.* In addition to the need for more research and education on palliative care, many hospitals and health systems have not yet incorporated palliative care practice. Multidisciplinary palliative care teams have been shown to be effective in symptom control and treatment of advanced disease based on client prognosis and family desires. New models of palliative care need to be explored and supported across the full spectrum of health settings. As palliative care teams expand, many of the elements of hospice care will become available in other settings such as inpatient and outpatient facilities, long-term care, and home care.

3. *Provide coordinated community referral for end-of-life services and support systems. Also encourage community assessment of existing and desired services to identify gaps and implement programs to address specific unmet needs.* The notable expansion of information in recent years through innovations such as the Internet

has created a challenge for providers and the public in filtering good from bad information. Individuals and families facing the end of life need access to reliable and valid information sources and assistance with interpreting the vast amount of information available. Information resources may include specific Web sites, books, pamphlets, and groups that provide support for dying persons and their families. Information specialists and librarians could collaborate with public health nurses and health educators to assist communities in identifying existing resources, assessing specific community needs, and filling resource gaps.

4. *Encourage creative approaches to meeting unique patient, family, and survivor needs within the constraints and limitations of traditional Western biomedical health care systems.* Cultural and narrative competence require that health care system stories become more flexible. Organizational stories, in the form of rules, regulations, and policies, often create barriers for appropriate adaptation of care. Physical facilities also limit interactions that could help dying persons and their family and friends. An example of this is seen in the story of Maggie, in which the evening parties that were so important needed to be confined to her small hospital room. Abby's traditional Ojibwa death rituals that were carried out in a nursing home setting were very meaningful to her daughter Mary and other members of the family and quite moving to the staff as well. The story of Grace illustrates yet another creative approach. The type of letter-writing and videotaping used in the story of Grace, along with activities such as journaling, reminiscencing, and oral history, provide possibilities to capture personal life stories, transform them, and transmit them as legacy.

5. *Practice actively hearing and understanding the rich and diverse stories that people tell in their living and dying and appreciate the gifts that participation with others as dying people, family members, friends, and colleagues provide.*

Springer Series on Death and Suicide

Robert Kastenbaum, PhD, Series Editor